Mary Bell Macdonald.

Stockinish,

Harris.

16. 9. 51

BRICKS *and* FLOWERS

ROUGHFIELD

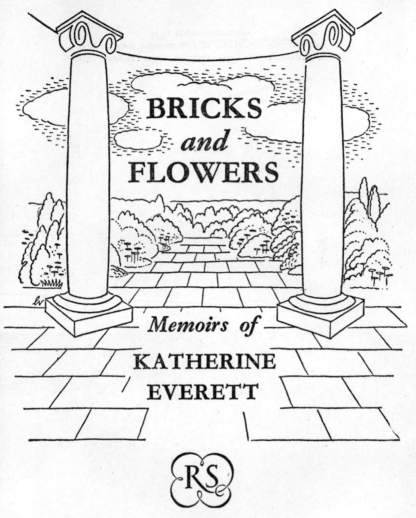

BRICKS *and* FLOWERS

Memoirs of

KATHERINE EVERETT

THE REPRINT SOCIETY LONDON

FIRST PUBLISHED 1949
THIS EDITION PUBLISHED BY THE REPRINT SOCIETY LTD.
BY ARRANGEMENT WITH CONSTABLE AND COMPANY LTD.
1951

PRINTED IN GREAT BRITAIN BY RICHARD CLAY AND COMPANY, LTD.,
BUNGAY, SUFFOLK

CONTENTS

ILLUSTRATIONS

The author is indebted to the Earl of Powis for permission to reproduce the Herbert family group, the original of which is in his
possession; and to Earl Ferrers and to *Country Life* for permission
to reproduce the photograph of Staunton Harold. The photographs of Roughfield were taken by Vera and Humphrey Joel.

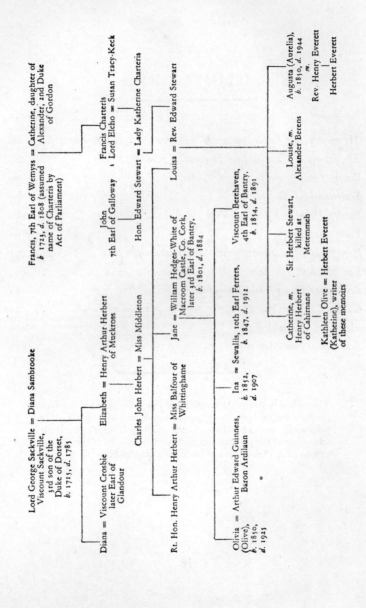

Francis, 7th Earl of Wemyss = Catherine, daughter of
b 1723, d. 1808 (assumed   Alexander, 2nd Duke
name of Charteris by   of Gordon
Act of Parliament)

Lord George Sackville = Diana Sambrooke
Viscount Sackville,
3rd son of the
Duke of Dorset,
b. 1715, d. 1785

Francis Charteris
Lord Elcho = Susan Tracy-Keck

John
7th Earl of Galloway

Hon. Edward Stewart = Lady Katherine Charteris

Diana = Viscount Crosbie
b. 1810,   later Earl of
d. 1925   Glandour

Elizabeth = Henry Arthur Herbert
of Mucktross

Charles John Herbert = Miss Middleton

Louisa = Rev. Edward Stewart

Rt. Hon. Henry Arthur Herbert = Miss Balfour of
Whittinghame

Jane = William Hedges-White of
Macroom Castle, Co. Cork,
later 3rd Earl of Bantry,
b. 1801, d. 1884

Viscount Berehaven,
4th Earl of Bantry,
b. 1814, d. 1891

Louise, m.
Alexander Berens

Augusta (Aurelia),
b. 1810, d. 1944
m.
Rev. Henry Everett

Herbert Everett

Olivia = Arthur Edward Guinness,
(Olive),   Baron Ardilaun
b. 1810,
d. 1925

Ina = Sewallis, 10th Earl Ferrers,
b. 1852,   b. 1847, d. 1912
d. 1907

Catherine, m.
Henry Herbert
of Cahirnane

Sir Herbert Stewart,
killed at
Metemmeh

Kathleen Olive = Herbert Everett
(Katherine), writer
of these memoirs

Chapter One

MY FAMILY

TWO brothers, members of the Pembroke family, whose ancestors had been involved in the Wars of the Roses, fighting on the Yorkist side, came to Ireland in 1656 and were given land around and far beyond the shores of the Lakes of Killarney. These brothers were our ancestors, one Herbert having the great estate of Muckross, and the other the smaller property of Curren and Cahirnane, the latter being my home. Our own rent-roll was not large, and from the time of my birth in 1872 was declining, but my father, like most Irish landlords, was determined to maintain appearances, and to do so we kept carriages and horses, boats and boatmen, gardeners, gamekeepers, farm labourers and a great many servants. No money was spent on amusements : books were not bought, holidays were not taken, and our clothes were made at home of harsh Kerry frieze, woven of the wool shorn off our own sheep into a material which we hated, for it tickled, and looked like dirty porridge.

We thought our family important, and this idea was based partly on what we had to write out and learn of the section in " Landed Gentry " devoted to our family, which began, " The name of Herbert (her Bert, illustrious Lord) stands so prominent in the records of British history and has been ennobled at various times ". We thought that our name, meaning illustrious Lord, was a wonderful idea, and this was justified by the many stories we were told of the grandeur of Muckross in the day of our great-uncle, Henry Arthur Herbert, who had married a Miss Balfour and had also imported from Scotland as well as his bride all the heads of departments of his household and estate. He built a large house in the Scottish baronial style and a church in the village; was Member of Parliament and Lord Lieutenant for County Kerry and Chief Secretary for Ireland in 1857.

In 1861 Queen Victoria stayed at Muckross House, and I have a long letter written by Henry Arthur's daughter Ella to her aunt, Jane Bantry, her father's sister, describing the visit and saying what a wonderful success it all was. She gives an hour-to-hour account of their doings, and describes a drive, the royal family being in a carriage with four horses and outriders and a mounted bodyguard, other carriages following and, last of all, a rabble, some on side-cars, some on foot, but all shrieking and cheering. On another day they went on the lake, and Ella notes how splendid the barge looked when the eight rowers held their oars straight up in the air as the Queen stepped in, adding that they were the finest men in the countryside and wore white duck trousers and dark blue jerseys, while the wivern—the family crest—flashed in gold on their oars and looked so well embroidered in scarlet on their sleeves. The barge went off first, and was followed by a number of fine boats, but Ella regrets that a lot of rough people came too, in anything that could float, and made a great noise.

The event—a water hunt—planned for that day was a failure. All the previous night men, boys, and dogs had been on the Eagle's Nest mountain watching a magnificent stag which, when the barge was sighted, they were to drive to the shore of the lake and force to take to the water. The boats were to follow to whichever island he landed on, and there the poor creature would be killed and the horns presented to the Queen. The stag, however, did not play his intended part, for he dashed past his guards and streaked off to the Macgillicuddy Reeks, a wild range of mountains some fifteen miles away, and was not seen again.

" We waited for such a long time," Ella writes, " and were so disappointed, but the Queen admired the view."

Not a word is said about the personality of any of the guests, nor is any hint given of their reaction to the Irish welcome they had received : that the Queen admired the view is stated over and over again, but no other remark is quoted.

Reading about this visit while suffering from present-day difficulties, it seems to have been a remarkable effort for a private family to have made, for in those days the help of a catering firm was probably not called in. For the royal parents and their four children the billiard-room was made into a dining-room, so that they could have their meals alone at their pleasure; and there was a Lady Churchill, a Miss Wortley, and a General Grey in attendance, who, together with a governess and a tutor, were served in another room, while the housekeeper gave up her domain to an unspecified number of maids and valets. Ella adds, " Of course the Guard of Honour were given refreshments every day downstairs ". She had previously noted that this Guard consisted of about a hundred splendidly mounted men, but nothing is said of their own staff who coped with it all. She ends her letter by saying how delighted she is with the Queen's parting gift to her, which she describes as " a very large round gold brooch with a branch of holly on it, the berries being made of coral and the leaves of a bright green enamel ".

Some twenty years later Muckross House was closed and trustees were appointed to take charge of the estate and to attempt to pay off the debts, but their efforts failed. All sorts of theories were held to explain such a complete financial collapse from real wealth in so short a time, some people saying it was all owing to borrowing money from money-lenders, and others that there had always been too much reckless spending; a kinder view was that it was due to the great reduction in rents.   My father believed that the crowning disaster was the last owner's idea that he could make money and thus save the place, his first scheme being to turn the many birch-trees that grew on his mountains into cotton reels, with which the world could be supplied.   He was advised to start in a small way, but he would have nothing to do with what he called a " hole-and-corner business ", and meant to do it in a big way.   He went to America, where he bought materials for a private railway, a steamer, and also a good deal of machinery, borrowing money to pay for it all; but everything went wrong : the mountain was too steep for the railway, the lake too deep and the river too shallow for the transport he had planned. No reels were made, and his gear was taken by creditors and sold for scrap.

Unfortunately, he still thought in millions, and decided that there was copper on his property, which he would start mining.   A great deal of money was borrowed for this venture, but nothing came of it except a sheet of blue-green water where the limestone rock had been cut away, and which became known as " the Copper Folly ".

My father kept Cahirnane going for many years after Muckross had foundered, but of the thousands of acres once owned by the Herberts in County Kerry, not a single one is held in their name to-day.

Chapter Two

OUR HOME

THE nursery was in an attic of our large house, and we spent many hours looking out of its window, where so often the view of lake and mountains was hidden by rain. The rainfall at Killarney is the second highest in the British Isles, and a gloomy explanation of this was given us by Archdeacon Wynne, vicar of our church, who kept weather records and who told us that the Atlantic lies west of Ireland and the prevailing winds blowing across it gather moisture which forms clouds; these are then blown over the low coastlands till they strike the Killarney mountains, where they break and are dissolved and rain pours down upon us. While one mass is being emptied, the wind has been gathering more from the sea, so it seldom stops raining here. The air was damp and heavy, and there was a dreamlike, brooding calm about the landscape, with its lush, almost tropical growth and immense trees. The wood-pigeons' mournful note, heard so often from the shelter of the woods, seemed to express the spirit of the scene. Raging storms could shatter this calm, but when the wind had passed, and the rain fell gently and steadily once more, the land resumed its depressing, brooding air.

As a child I was vaguely conscious of a sadness in our surroundings, but the earliest emotion that I can remember was fear, and that fear was focused on my mother. I was not alone in this; for my father—a grey-headed, white-bearded giant—was afraid of her, too. We sometimes watched him standing outside the glass lobby doors which protected her rooms, waiting for a moment when she would go into a dressing-room where she kept medicines, and, having seen her shadow pass, he would hurry into her bedroom to wind the clock. He had a passion for clocks, but he would resist the lure of any clock if she reappeared too quickly.

She was an unhappy woman; often ill and always neurotic, she suffered from headaches and, because she was unable to bear pain, doctors gave her morphia injections, or she would sometimes give them to herself. She never attacked us physically, but I think we might have accepted that sort of treatment better than the intangible sense of her suppressed fury. I find it difficult to explain why she dominated and terrified everyone in the house, down to the humblest servant; possibly her mind was unhinged, and this, together with her religion, made her spirit into a battlefield which everyone sensed but could not understand. She had been urged by her family to marry my father, her parents clearly having been glad that she should marry any-one, even a man more than twice her age, who seemed to be rich and had a large property in another island. On her marriage she was transported to a gloomy house in Ireland, accompanied by a husband with whom she had not a thought or taste in common, whose main interests were hunting and looking after his estate, and who kept out of her way as much as possible.

Having no country interests, she was irritated at seeing lavish expenditure on things for which she cared nothing, while she had very little money; but perhaps her greatest trial was being deprived of the religious ritual she loved. She disliked the local church, with its Low Church services, yet this was the only one she could attend. Often she slept badly, and would wander about at night carrying a bedroom candlestick and talking to herself, dressed in a grey dressing-gown, her prematurely grey hair, which matched her light-coloured eyes, hanging loosely round her white face. I would sometimes wake to find her stooping over my bed, and would lie petrified, hardly breathing, and though I

pretended to be asleep until she went away, I would hear her
as she moved about the room muttering to herself about her
sorrows or saying verses from the Penitential Psalms.

Years later I asked one of her sisters, to whom I had
become attached, why she, who was so kind, had done
nothing to help us when we were children.

" We were so thankful, my dear, to get rid of your
mother," she had explained, " that we all decided to have
nothing to do with her or her vipers."

Poor, helpless little vipers !

As a very young child, my German nurse, Maria, gave me
affection, and I was devoted to her. She would take me
into her bed and tell me stories of her home in a forest and
of her family; sometimes she described the horrors and the
sufferings of the 1870–71 war, and I felt the deepest pity and
admiration for the noble German soldiers when they were
wounded and suffered from the brutal treatment wreaked
on them by the cruel French ! Every story ended in a
talk on religion of the emotional, evangelical, sentimental
type. I suppose she was a Lutheran; she certainly inspired
me with unquestioning faith, and I longed to be in the
Heaven we sang hymns about, where all was tenderness and
love. We seem to have done a lot of weeping together,
which culminated in the awful night when Maria told me
she was going away because she was dismissed. I felt
abandoned, my world shattered, and I thought my beloved
nurse was wronged. I believed I had cried all night in her
arms—probably actually for about half-an-hour—while
she kept begging me to bring my sorrows to Jesus, who
would understand and comfort me, for He loved children.

After Maria left I was put in the care of German
governesses, and we had a series of these unhappy women
who complained of " Heimweh ", " Herzschmerz ", and
" Sehnsucht ". I can still picture their shadowy figures
sighing beside the schoolroom fire, while the gentle rain,

which seemed ceaseless, raised the level of the lake and river, seen from the misted windows. They taught us about events and periods immeasurably remote from our own, and our confused minds swung from the progression of the Heilige Grail and descriptions of the Nibelungen Lieder, to the Heptarchy and off again to Greek mythology with its many strange relationships, headed by Jove, which my perplexed mind thought was another name for Jehovah and whom I pictured as being exactly like my father. Then there might come a session with the Merovingian kings, and another day we might discuss the Ptolemies or the possible origin of the Sphinx, all this being imparted eagerly in German to rather listless pupils.

My mother had definite views about our education, which did not accord with those held by any of our governesses, except perhaps on the importance of foreign languages; these my mother thought essential, believing that they would act as a deterrent to our acquiring the native brogue, of which she had a horror. She held, I think rightly, that any deviation from correct English was wrong and a loss of caste. We were forbidden to use any nicknames, or to overwork any one word or misapply a word. I remember when I must have been very young, sitting at luncheon and seeing a jam roll pudding brought in, oozing rich jam, and saying in my usual frightened whisper, " Oh, what a lovely pudding ! "

Instantly my mother's pale eyes were fixed on me with what we used to call her gimlet look as she announced, " If you think it ' lovely ' you can look at it and not eat it," and for the rest of the meal I sat looking at my empty plate, struggling to hold back my tears while listening to my mother making that unattractive smacking sound so many Victorians made when eating something they liked. But I do not call food beautiful or lovely now.

Another of my mother's educational ideas was that we

should understand the Peerage, the order of precedence, and how to address each degree in speaking and writing. She questioned us on this subject herself.

" What is a Marquess's wife called ? " she asked me.

" A Marquesette," I answered firmly. The glint in her eye shook my assurance.

" And how do you address his second son ? " she continued.

" Sir Christian—Sir Christian name," I faltered, but I knew I was lost.

" Go away, stupid, ignorant child. You are almost unteachable, if not *non compos*. Write the question and the correct answer twenty times and bring the paper to me before you go to bed."

Indifferent to the English Peerage, we took to chanting triumphantly, " We are illustrious lords," in reference to the derivation of our name.

On one occasion our mother, hearing us do this, interposed, " I don't think you have much to be proud of on that score; all that the Herberts have ever done that I can see is to dissipate their fortunes. Through me," she continued, " you have distinguished ancestors; my father was descended from many great Scottish families and some great English ones; indeed, my two brothers were educated as King's scholars at Winchester without cost to their parents, for they could trace their descent directly back to the Plantagenets." (Many years later I learnt that there were so many others with such claims that my uncles were the last boys to benefit from this privilege.)

My mother went on to explain that even the Sackville link with the Herberts came to us through her. She went on to say, " Lord George Sackville's unfortunate daughter had miserable health and spirits after her marriage, partly owing no doubt to this wretched climate. I have been told she used to walk about old Muckross house at night, wailing and wringing her hands, with her head tied up in red flannel. What a different fate from Lady Glandour's, her beautiful sister ! "

It was not snobbishness on my mother's part to value her ancestry so highly; it was the fashion of her day. Indeed, for long after that time profound interest in genealogies continued, more especially in Ireland. At any social occasion you might hear a remark such as, " Wasn't the wife of Maurice O'Meara of Ballyduff the daughter of Tom Cassidy of Castle Cassidy ? and that would make her our cousin to Sir Timothy . . .", etc., and the topic would be followed up in all its ramifications with the eagerness of hounds on a hot scent.

Even the servants were interested in such discussions. One day when I was a child we were in the pantry watching the butler cleaning plate, and he said something about a tenant not having paid his rent, and then added, " There was some as thought as how the master should have married a fortune, but for all he chose breeding, for it was well known of the mistress that her blood was so blue a silver spoon would stand up in it." At the time I believed that this referred to a physical fact, which I thought added to my mother's alarming qualities. Another educational idea of my mother's was that we should understand Bradshaw and learn to make our way by its guidance from any given point in the British Isles to any other. I have instinctively fought shy of railway guides since those days.

When we were older she made us write letters, some for use and some for practice. A letter in the third person to a Duchess was of the latter kind; while those describing the character of a cook or governess were for use and had to be correctly expressed, spelt, and written before they were passed for signature and posting. Another exercise was to read a leading article from *The Times* at speed and then to write out a précis of every salient point in a compressed form, omitting all platitudes; which was good training, for I now read leading articles and skip the many platitudes automatically. Another effect of this training was perhaps not so happy, for it tended to produce a rather telegraphic way of expressing things, avoiding trimmings and losing the grace and ease of pleasant writing. But every medal has its reverse side, and the exercise sharpened our wits.

From a very early age we were made to play whist for money. I was supposed to be delicate, and this annoyed my mother, who I think felt it was poaching on her special preserve, so at seven or eight years old I was sent to the south of France, where an ex-governess ran a boarding house. I can remember the basement and a wistaria which was of enormous size and incredible loveliness. Between tea and dinner-time I was allowed to go to the drawing-room, where the guests, who all seemed old, sat knitting or talking or occasionally playing cards.

One evening a white-haired General exclaimed : " Anyone like a rubber ? " and two old ladies responded. " Who'll make a fourth ? " he asked.

" I will," I said, not at all nervous, for no general was as alarming as my mother.

" What ? " he said, staring down at me. " Have you learned to play ? "

" Oh yes, long ago; we have to play for money to make us attend."

" And for what stakes do you play, child ? "

" Ha'penny a hundred, and it sometimes takes all our moth money—we catch clothes moths at twilight and stick them on gummy paper and get wages, two moths a farthing."

We played, and at the end of the game the General, who had been my partner, gave me our joint winnings and said, " That's for playing up well," adding, " Upon my word, I should as soon have expected a white rabbit to sit up and say it played whist; and she attends too, which is more than can be said for some people," he added, looking round the room.

I suppose it was the unexpected riches, the praise, and being compared to a white rabbit that have left that scene etched on my mind.

The lesson with my mother that we dreaded most was scripture, for it was very different from the teachings of Maria, who had inspired me with real unquestioning faith which my mother destroyed, although her own belief in the Anglo-Catholic movement was ardent. Our daily lesson was based on a book of questions and answers on the doctrines of the Church, the compiler of which must have had a sadistic temperament, for the questions would start with apparent simplicity and then double back, contradicting all you thought you had understood. They seemed devised and planned to trip the pupil, and in this they succeeded all too well with me. The intricacies of the Real Presence, Transubstantiation, the Virgin Birth and the Trinity reduced my childish mind to such entanglements and confusion that my mother seemed really convinced of my hopeless imbecility, and I can still remember muttering over those incomprehensible answers before going into her presence with the feeling that I really was imbecile or at least *non compos*, which I thought was a sort of half-way state.

Once I found a satisfactory answer to a long, involved question : it simply said, " That is a mystery," and I felt I had found a raft in that stormy sea. I applied this same answer to other questions, where indeed it might well have fitted, but my mother was not one to be taken in with this expedient, and I was forbidden ever to give that answer again, was ordered to write out and learn two pages from the hateful book, and, what was worse, to return to be examined on what I had written.

We did not see much of my father, but he was always kind

to us, and if we were alone with him at luncheon he would be cheerful, telling us where he had been riding and talking about our ponies. When my mother was well enough to come down we were all more silent. She would sit at one end of the table with her special diet of chicken or game, jellies and creams, while we had mutton—fresh mutton, salt mutton, roast or boiled mutton, for we killed our own sheep—this meat usually being followed by a milk pudding.

In Victorian days many parents shouted at their children in a way that is never heard to-day, and my father had this habit, a favourite trick of his being to let us go up the back stairs to the schoolroom at the top of the house after we had been to his office on the ground floor, and then bellow without ceasing till we had rushed down again, when he would whisper, " Shut the door." There was no anger in this manœuvre, as there often was when dealing with my brother, for he and my father did not get on. Sometimes at luncheon my mother would comment on some practical thing my brother had done very badly. We knew this meant trouble, and before long my father would be shouting at him while he sat slouched in his chair till, unable to bear it any longer, my brother would leave the room, clutching his glass of wine, and my mother would say the noise had given her a headache.

I hated these scenes, and a kind old servant, trying to comfort me after one of them, explained, " Don't be fretting about the master roaring; sure, he's like the thunder, making a grand noise and no harm in it. Now, the mistress is like the lightning : one look and it would near kill you."

Such was the atmosphere of our home. It is easy to condemn my mother as an odious woman, for she had a difficult character, but her lot as a young bride would have tried any girl of her temperament, and it helped to make her the self-centred invalid she became. Ireland in the 1860's, when she married, was a century behind England in

[23]

amenities, and life was lived almost as in feudal times. My father had his own interests and cared nothing for social life, of which there was little enough; she was intellectual, and there was no one with whom she could exchange ideas. The climate was enervating and depressing, and the old Cahirnane House, where she started her married life, was devoid of the most elementary comforts, the only sanitation when she first arrived being a series of erections like sentry boxes.

"It really was horrible," she said when describing the place to me years afterwards. "There wasn't a tap or a closet in the house, and I had to make my way out past all those great wet laurels to huts—eight of them, beginning with a giant-sized one down to one for a dwarf or an infant. I wanted, of course, to slip out unseen, but an old man—Patrick Doran was his name, though everyone called him Patsy the Bucket—would be at my side directly I appeared, with an old carriage umbrella as large as a tent, and would insist on coming with me and choosing which booth I should occupy. 'The middle one, I should say, my lady—that's three up from this end—would just suit your ladyship, and they are all fine and clean,' he would point out. It was no use my telling him quite stiffly, 'You can go now, Doran', for he would only answer, 'Faith, I wouldn't do that and be leaving yourself to go back in the rain; I'll be waiting for you.'

"It was all odious, and I made your father see how much I disliked it, and everything else about the place." She paused a moment, and added, "The first present he gave me after our marriage was a w.c. from Cork, which he had fitted up in time for Christmas."

Chapter Three

RETAINERS

IN spite of the stress and strain, our home life was not without its compensations during my childhood. All the servants, both indoors and outdoors, were our friends. Kind, fat Hannah, a housemaid, was always ready to tell us stories, our favourite being how she missed her chance of going to America.

" Wasn't I the big fool," she would say, " with me uncle over beyond sending me the fare and I going down to Cork with me shawl on me head and me bundle in me hand and come ten miles in the ass cart to the quay, that when I saw the great ship six feet from the side and the black water below I let out a screech. ' I'll never lep it,' says I, ' and what's more I won't try,' and it was a stout lump of a girl I was then and not so nimble, so back home I went on the ass cart, and that's how I come to be here and not over in America. It was the Will of God, no doubt."

There was old Ann, the cook, angelic to us and brutal to her kitchenmaids whom she selected herself from among the daughters of lodge-keepers, gardeners, or tenants. She worked them hard and would teach them nothing, often locking herself into the larder when preparing anything special, which she would even cover with her apron while carrying it to the oven, for fear they should pick up a hint. She would make them scrub and scour and clean and peel potatoes, and would beat them over the head with a wooden spoon, but if a protesting mother came to see her, Ann would be all honey.

" Ah, then, Mrs. Sullivan, I'm glad to see you," she would say. " Sit down while I make you a cup of tea. And is it about Bridgy you'd have a chat ? The girl is raw, yes, very raw, but isn't she the fortunate one to be getting the best of training and the good food and the warm bed."

"Well, indeed, you're right," the confused mother would agree and add, "But for all she says you beat her."

"Well, before God, that's a great lie; if I'd give her a tap so she wouldn't be idling the day away that's no less than my duty to try to put a shape to her." Then, turning the subject with a most satisfied air, Ann would enquire, "Is your tea to your liking, mam? Just say the word and I'll make you more."

The muddled and mollified mother would respond, "You're too good and the tea is grand, and strong enough for a mouse to pass over it." And she would settle down to enjoy Ann's genial company and the warmth of the great stove.

We enjoyed it, too, for our schoolroom fare was austere, and very different would be those unauthorized titbits pressed upon us by Ann.

"Here, love, would you taste a bit of the meringue I am after making for the mistress and wait till I get the whipped cream to it, 'twill do you good," or, "I have a nice wine jelly that I put in the little shape, along with a bit of the marzipany cake so you might fancy it."

We always did, but if, however, we said anything about the weeping kitchenmaid, Ann would retort, "Take no notice, she's just trash and I'll be shut of her, forbye she's leaving on Saturday and I have a decent girl coming."

They were never, however, considered decent when *in situ.*

Sometimes I would slip into the servants' hall at their dinner-time, which was later than ours, and would sit on the butler's knee when I was very small, and he'd say, "Have a sup of tea, little love," and give me some out of his saucer.

Ann never came to any meal, and when we asked why

there would be smiles and evasion, and much later I realized that Ann liked her private nip of whisky, interspersed with bouts of hard drinking, in spite of which she remained with us for thirty years. Treatment was always the same, and when I was older I was often the intermediary, going down to the kitchen and taking her aside to say :

" Dear Ann, you have been very bad again and now you must see the Friar; he's been sent for and he is coming this morning."

Ann would be offended, tossing her head, on which she wore a large white turban, and saying, " No manner of need to trouble the Holy Brother; tell him I'm busy about my work."

In due course the Friar would come, sandals, brown habit and cord complete, and would be alone with Ann for about half-an-hour, after which reformation was assured and lasted from three to six months; but we never knew how he dealt with her.

Outside there was plenty to interest us : the stables were full of horses, ponies, and dogs and, presiding magnificently over it all, Delany the coachman, who had ten children and, in addition to his grooms, taught relays of his little boys to attend him. I can see him standing with a small boy on either side, each holding a top boot and, as soon as he had inserted his feet in them, dropping on their knees and polishing vigorously.

We named all the babies born on the place, and Delany's last being twins, we called them Daniel Deronda and Decimus, thinking how splendid they would sound if they became doctors and were knighted, but unfortunately Mrs. Delany added Patrick to Decimus and they degenerated into Patsy and Danny, after which we felt that future grandeur was improbable.

The coach-house and stables were new, but the dairy was in a very old, stone-built barn, divided into three parts, in one of which stood an enormous churn—a vast barrel with a handle at either end which two men would turn for hours. The old woman called Mary the Dairy would come in from time to time and call upon Heaven to know why the butter was delaying, muttering incantations and prayers in Irish, and we would beg her to tell us what she was saying.

" Just calling on God and the Devil to hasten up, for I have it all to wash and stamp for the house."

" And a bit for yourself," one of the men would add, for, like others on the place, Mary did her illicit trading.

Large pans of milk stood in the centre of the barn, there were no windows anywhere, the rough stone walls hung with cobwebs, and Mary would slide a dirty finger over the cream to taste how ripe it was for skimming. The butter she made was excellent. What we enjoyed most was her bedroom in the third partition, also stone-walled and cobwebby and quite dark, unless the half-door was open, when we could see all the walls, which were filled with hooks and brackets on which hung or stood stuffed hens, ducks, geese, turkeys, and guinea-fowl. She would tell us the names and cause of death of them all. She had stuffed them herself. Some were rather moulty and the shapes were odd, but to be so honoured they had to have met an abnormal end.

She slept in a wide, deep bunk fixed to the wall and apparently full of rags, but not alone, for whichever of her flock needed nursing shared it with her : sometimes it would be a turkey with the pip or a wounded duck, but more frequently a neglected new-born family.

" Don't you sometimes kick them ? " we would ask when a dozen ducklings were disclosed at the bottom of her lair.

" Why would I, and they so light and small they can slop through my toes and I not know it ? "

And well they might, for Mary stood in her short ragged petticoat with bare feet and splayed-out toes in wet or cold, and we never saw her otherwise on weekdays; but on

MY MOTHER
AND FATHER

(*left*) MYSELF (aged 12)

MY GREAT-GRANDMOTHER
(Lady Katherine Stewart)

THE FAMILY OF CHARLES JOHN HERBERT OF MUCKROSS AND HIS WIFE LOUISA
ANN MIDDLETON, DAUGHTER OF NATHANIEL MIDDLETON OF BRADFORD PEVERELL

(*Left to right*) Charles (killed by a cricket ball at Eton); Emily; Maria; Jane;
Louisa, *m.* the Rev. Edward Stewart (my grandmother); Henry Arthur Herbert

BANTRY HOUSE

STAUNTON HAROLD

The following inscription is carved over the door of the church: " In the year 1653 When all things Sacred were throughout ye nation Either demolished or profaned Sr Robert Shirley, Barronet, Founded this church; Whose singular praise it is to have done ye best things in ye worst times And hoped them in the most calamitous. The righteous shall be had in everlasting remembrance."

Sundays the old and dirty figure was transformed. In a large wooden chest she kept the outfit : a white goffered cap, a black cloth cloak of superfine quality, very full and reaching down to the ground, with a hood at the back, and a large, box-like pair of boots which she would sling by their laces over her arm.

" When do you put them on ? " we would ask.

" On the chapel steps, and a cruel sore hardship it is on my feet; but isn't it well known you can't get to Heaven but through Purgatory ? "

" Do tell us what else you have in your chest," we would beg.

" My shroud; and it's of the very best, as it should be against the awful judgment day," she would answer as she crossed herself, but she never showed it to us.

We often went to the walled garden which was half a mile from the house and looked through a little barred and locked gate to the lower garden, which was sheltered and full of flowers and scented with a verbena at the entrance and bounded on one side by a high rock from which tumbled white and yellow roses. I always pictured the Garden of Eden as being exactly like it. Here we would shriek and yell till Tom, the half-wit son of the gardener, would come shambling and frolicking down to let us in. He had a face like a baboon, entirely surrounded with grey whiskers, and, though of limited mind, he had his gifts, one being spinning half a plate on his thumb, which turned right back, making a large earth-stained platform for his half-plate to whirl round on.

If we went into the beehive-like cottage in the middle garden, his father, who looked the younger of the two, might be sitting over the turf fire, where an earthenware teapot always stood in the ashes. Tom, who was the house-keeper, emptied the teapot on Mondays and put in the first two teaspoons of tea, a poor brew, but by adding two teaspoons each succeeding day, by Sunday it was half full of tea-leaves and of potent strength.

We had endless jokes with Tom, and would ask him when he was going to get married. He would grin widely and say maybe next fair day he would find himself a fine fat woman to bed down with, upon which his father would order him out to work and tell us to get out too. Then we would follow him to the upper garden, where sometimes he would handle bees to amuse us. Lifting up a straw skep while we ran shrieking to a safe distance, he would throw handfuls of bees into the air, indifferent to the wide halo of angry bees around him.

Our greatest treat was to get Tom to stand on his head, but this required preparation : first he would scoop out a hollow in the earth, then fold his battered hat into it and lower his head, rolling it round and round till he was satisfied, while his straggling grey hair mingled with his whiskers. He was double-jointed, and would spread his hands on either side with an Anglo-Saxon look of angularity, and after staying in this doubled-up position for a tense moment, his thin legs, crowned with enormous boots, would shoot into the air and immediately start dancing a jig in time to melodious whistling, coming from Tom's grey, tangled head. We would roll on the ground with ecstatic laughter as the upside-down boots kicked out and pattered with ever more complex steps and the whistling grew faster and faster. The more we laughed the more pleased he was, and when exhausted he would sit down and tell us how much they laughed at the fairs he went to, it being evident that he felt this to be the best kind of applause.

From the garden we might go on to the lake-shore to see the salmon haul—a most scriptural scene. Four fishermen went out in a heavy boat and threw out the net, and on returning walked slowly, bent forward, with the rope over their shoulders, drawing it in. Hauling was best towards evening, when the lake would be flushed with sunset colours and would send gentle ripples towards the shore, and tiny waves would break on the edge over short, tufted grass or little pockets of pebbles and sand.   Gradually the net would draw closer as the fishermen, silhouetted against the shining scene, dragged its weight in, until at the last they turned to face the water, pulling the net hand over hand, watching intently in complete silence up to the last breathless moment when suddenly would come a silver flash and where all had been quiet all was excitement.   Three leaping fish were on land, entangled in the net, their lovely life ended by thuds from a horrible stick ironically called " the doctor ". Laughter and betting on the weights, settled by the stillar, would follow, and one of the men would start running for the house with a salmon neatly looped by his gills and tail, and we would follow him, after a last look at the mountains and their reflections in the lake, broken by the dark figure standing in the boat and casting out the net once more.

The man with our fish would be well ahead of us and going in great haste, as my father held the theory that a salmon, to be worth eating, must be in the pot within twenty minutes of being alive in the lake.   He thought a rod-caught fish inferior, the struggle before the end making the curd less fine and creamy; what he would have thought of the degenerates who can eat it out of a tin I cannot imagine.

We would walk home past the mouth of the river, the sedge-grass, reeds, and wind-bent trees aglow with evening light, and watch for the flight of duck or see high up in the darkening sky the wedge-shaped pattern of wild geese before we passed into the deep shadow of the lime avenue, at the end of which we could see our house—our rather ugly house.

Chapter Four

ESCAPE

CONSIDERED from our present-day standards it is difficult to estimate whether my parents' taste was inherently bad or whether it was merely representative of the vandalism of their times, but certainly all they did was unfortunate, and neither of them on the score of æsthetics questioned whether they were acting rightly.

They had pulled down the old family house, one of the few remaining Queen Anne buildings in Ireland. Some years later Lady Kenmare told me she had tried to persuade my father to spare this charming period building, which for a comparatively small expenditure could have been modernized, and if necessary added to, but I fear that, owing to prejudice between our respective families and suspicion as to the motive for this advice, my father's determination to destroy this gracious home was only hardened. He replaced it with a vast cube of grey cement which turned almost black in the constant rain, and around windows and the hall door adorned it with Bath stone which grew a moss-green mould. In character it was rather like the houses built by the local authorities (called the Congested District Board) all over Ireland, but these were small square boxes, while ours was a very large one.

The interior of the house had some dignity as regards the principal rooms, for the architect had observed the Georgian rule of two cubes, and they were large ones, but others were a single square or some even half a square, and were like high cells. The wood-work was all varnished pitch pine, and glazed red and green tiles were laid round the hall stove.

My father devoted enormous energy to destroying the

charming surroundings of the old house; blasting away rocks on which grew ancient yews, he made straight terraces with rigid, steep, cement steps where once peacocks walked the wandering paths between yew hedges, and he did away with the topiary work, some of which represented the peacocks in formal green. He was happy in destroying it all and pleased with his own creation, but Nemesis overtook him, for he spent so much on his building that he carried a burden of debt for the rest of his life, which became more harassing every year. He would sit alone in the large, bleak dining-room with an oil lamp giving too poor a light to read by, and brood over his financial worries, a glass of whisky and cold water by his side, from which I hope he got a little comfort. He was getting too old to hunt, and indeed could no longer afford to do so, and the lands he had loved and ridden over so often had become a burden.

He was a good and generous landlord, and his tenants were attached to him, but they belonged to the Land League, under whose edict they had to withhold their rents; he was so kindly that he could not bring himself to dismiss any of his employees when they and their fathers before them had worked on the place for so many years. I think he felt helpless to cope with his difficulties, and no whisky-and-water could relieve him from the constant fear that his bank would demand the reduction of his overdraft.

He had great energy and liked practical work. The grounds around the house had outcrops of rock everywhere, and my father decided to remove them—an absurd effort and quite useless, but blasting became a sport we all enjoyed. The selected limestone would have a deep hole bored in it and then be filled with gunpowder nearly to the top, the final inch being packed tight with sacking and a short twisted end left hanging out. I can see my father's immense figure dominating the group of workmen as he superintended the carrying out of this primitive process, while behind him

B

dogs barked and we jumped about, wild with excitement. Every now and then he would shout, " Get out of the way and take the dogs," but we never went till everyone was ordered to a safe distance, except the man who was left to put a match to the end of sacking. Directly this was done my father's loud voice would urge him to run, which he was already doing, while we waited breathlessly for the explosion.

If it was successful, the roar would be resounding and lumps of stone would be flung into the air; if a failure, only a dribble of small bits would be ejected on to the ground. Either way the process would start over again, while men were sent to gather the pieces scattered on the field, which would be used for mending the walls which during the famine years had been built all round our place, or for adding to the pig-sties. My father could always find some use for them.

I, too, liked making things and would collect bits of wood and broken mirror for dolls' furniture, and I wanted to make pictures of the sky and lakes and mountains, but my earliest effort became a tragedy because it meant so much to me and I had dwelt so long on thinking how to do it. One evening I had seen a sunset over the lake, which made a glittering golden path across the water—the rest of the water, the mountains, and the islands remaining a dusky blue with deeper shadows, which made the golden path more wonderful. All this I had seen out of the nursery window and, seeing it, felt it to be so breath-takingly beautiful that I must make a picture of it, this seeming all the more essential because it had all faded and gone while I watched, though I was still quite clear about what it had looked like. I had no doubts of being able to do it, but I felt my paints were inadequate. I had a small box of water-colours, hard little cakes; and, of yellow, only ochre and a little gamboge, neither of which, I felt sure, would look right for the golden path, but I remembered where I had seen something like it : the bright tinfoil on a shirt-button card under the buttons, which I could get from the workroom. The blue was also a difficulty, for I had used all my cobalt, and I felt prussian blue might be wrong for the soft colour of the mountains, so I decided to do it on a sheet of the blue office paper, and for days I lived in the dream of my wonderful picture. I snipped out fish-like shapes from the tinfoil and tried to gum them on, and I painted the mountains, but the rather glossy paper rose in blisters with little streams of paint running from them; the gum went everywhere, and the gold fish shapes became unmanageable, some of them sticking in the mountains and some getting upside down, and all got dirty and despair filled my heart, for in place of my vision I had made a disgusting, frightful mess.

I have made many failures since those days in trying to realize something in my mind, but I have never suffered such distress as over that first nursery effort.

When I was much older I enjoyed drawing and painting and became a good copyist, even my mother considering me to be an artist, and when I was nineteen I had my first view of real art and also of a way opening out to me for a permanent escape from my home. We had gone to English health resorts and abroad from time to time with my mother, and difficult pilgrimages these journeys were, but the real beginning of a new life happened in a most un-expected way.

We had neighbours, Lord and Lady Kenmare, always referred to by my parents with an oblique note of dislike. They were far richer and more important than we were, and they, too, had built a house, a very different one from ours, which my father used to refer to as " that institution " or that " town-hall full of a lot of foreign stuff ", though perhaps envy and jealousy had something to do with this prejudice. There had also been prolonged feuds with intermittent lawsuits between the families, disputes about properties and boundaries, with the permanent basic contention about the possession of various portions of the bottom of the lake, since we had one shore and they another, and our family usually seemed to have been on the losing side. With the ownership of the much-contested bottom of the lake went that of the islands, little rocks a few feet out of the water, with fern-fringed edges reflected so gently that one would not have thought such pretty, peaceful places could have stirred so much embittered feeling—which feeling, incidentally, when discussed in the Chancery Courts with every available appeal applied for by the loser, was very costly.

It was to the head of this rival family that I owed my escape from home. At that time my mother had become increasingly unbalanced and was constantly under the influence of morphia; she had relays of maids and nurses who never stayed long. I think our kindly old doctor must have told Lady Kenmare something about us and our difficulties, for she came to call—a thing she had not done for years, and on a day when my mother was well enough to be downstairs lying on the drawing-room sofa while I read to her. Lady Kenmare, who had been a daughter of Lord Charles Thynne, was splendid-looking, white-haired, very upright, and wore beautiful pearls.

" I have come to ask you a favour," she said, after the first greetings had been gone through. " Will you let your girl come and stay with me ? I hear she is so clever at drawing and needlework, and I have started a school of crafts for the boys and girls of the town, and she could help me so much with it."

I could hardly believe it when my mother meekly agreed. Perhaps she was flattered, and Lady Kenmare, with her beauty, rank, charm, and dignity, was a person people did agree with.

It was like being whirled away to another planet to find myself in that lovely setting. The house stood on a hill, and the gardens fell away towards the park and lake and mountains—gardens of which I was subsequently reminded in Italy, for there were fine wrought-iron gates, carved well-heads, vistas with statuary in the distance, fountains, and lead vases; but there were far more flowers than you would ever find in any Italian garden. Lady Kenmare was a pioneer in this as in other things and an early follower of Mr. Robinson's revolutionary ideas, but she combined them with a well-thought-out architectural setting.

The treatment of the large rooms was equally impressive, for each contained a collection of antique furniture, both English and foreign. The windows had brocaded curtains, Persian carpets were spread on the parquet floors, and the dining-room walls looked rich and glowing, being hung with Cordova leather. The contrast with my home was painful, for my poor father, frightened at the cost of his building, which had been far more than he had meant to spend, had cried a sudden halt over furnishing, so that some of the high plate-glass windows had no curtains, but only striped linen blinds and pitch-pine varnished shutters which closed with an iron bar across them, and much of the house had an unfinished, bleak look. Here everything was luxurious and lovely.

Lady Kenmare took me to see the school of crafts she had started and we saw the Carrickmacross and Limerick lace the girls were working at. They were all doing shamrock leaves, while the boys, who were learning wood-carving, had patterns of intertwined snakes.

"You must go to the convent where they teach needlework," my hostess told me, "and learn the limitations imposed by this sort of lace, and then you will have a good chance of improving it."

I spent several mornings with cheerful nuns who kissed

me on both cheeks and showed me what they were doing. The library provided me with illustrated books, from which I set to work to make designs for the needlework and the wood-carving. We were planning a four-poster bed which the boys were to carve and for which the girls were to make the hangings of white silk embroidered in gold and silver thread from an old Spanish pattern I had copied. Lady Kenmare would come to the library where I worked and would say, " Clever child ! that is just what I wanted." It was wonderful to be praised and encouraged, and an antidote to the *non compos* treatment. Then she would add, " You must study art, as you are so interested in it," and as I could not explain how hopeless the idea was with my home background, I only said, " I haven't any money."

" Well, you must earn some," she said, and secured me an order to copy miniatures, from which more orders followed.

My visit was prolonged, and as week followed week I gradually began to feel that I could not go home again to face the aimless life, my mother's terrifying anger and clouded mind, and my father's unhappy melancholy. The more I thought of it the more sure I felt that I must escape somehow, yet I couldn't stay with Lady Kenmare indefinitely, and anyhow she was soon going to London.

On a visit to my mother she told me she had heard from Ina Ferrers. " Poor thing ! " she said, " she is always so ill—that cold climate doesn't suit her, and she is so much shut up she even thinks of getting a companion."

Ina Ferrers was my mother's first cousin, as a glance at the family tree will show. She married Lord Ferrers, who owned Staunton Harold, a large house in Leicestershire.

Hearing about this letter from my mother, I decided to write to my cousin saying that if she would let me come as a companion I would do all I possibly could for her, read to her, or do anything she wished. The answer came on very thick paper with a coronet and a quantity of information about posts and stations engraved on it, and the first sentence dashed my hopes, for it began :

" No, I have given up all idea of having a companion, and I don't care either for being read to."

But it then went on to suggest a long visit.

I went to see my mother, agonized as to whether she would let me go. She seemed indifferent, and I found in subsequent years that once away I hardly existed for her; I suppose this came from the self-centredness natural to the neurasthenic. Her mind seemed incapable of taking an interest in anyone or anything that did not affect her own comfort and, as the inevitable result of such a point of view, she was a lonely, unhappy woman.

Chapter Five

STAUNTON HAROLD

ON a cold winter morning I was driven up in a carriage and pair to an enormous square brick house standing on rising ground and with a church on the other side of an immense circle of gravel. I was nervous. The footman rang the bell, and the door was opened by another footman with a powdered head and white silk stockings, and on his arm a silver horseshoe, which I was told later was in memory of the escape of Mary Queen of Scots from Chartley Castle, another Ferrers property, when she rode away on a horse shod with horseshoes mounted on three stilts to disguise the manner of her going. A butler in black stood on the other side of the door. I felt very insignificant.

When I got into the stone-flagged hall I was immediately met by the glass-eyed stare of an enormous bull, far more startling than the footman, although I had never before seen anyone dressed as gorgeously as he. The stuffed bull had wide horns and stood on a wooden platform, a perfect toy for giant children, but they would have had to be twenty feet high to have played with him. He was a specimen from the herd, descendants of Roman cattle who roamed the park at Chartley Castle.

I seemed to walk for a very long way in charge of a house-keeper wearing the traditional black silk dress with a gold chain round her neck and tucked into her belt. She took me up a wide staircase, down a long passage, round the corner, down another long passage, at last opening a door into a bedroom. Everything in this house seemed to be on outsize lines, and this room was too.

The housekeeper stood for a moment at the door and then said : " Her ladyship doesn't come down before tea-time, and his lordship is out for luncheon, which will be served at two; I will send the maid with hot water and she can unpack for you if you give her the keys. And would you take a glass of wine and some biscuits ? "

" No, thank you," I answered, afterwards regretting this, for I was very hungry; " and I should rather unpack by myself, please."

I felt I would prefer to see to my own modest possessions. Left alone, I looked round my room, and the most cheerful thing I could see in it was the large coal fire. The writing-table was wonderfully equipped with everything one could possibly use, even to sheets of various stamps. The walls were very high and papered in dull olive green, which the expanse of carpet matched, and all the furniture was large. The marble-topped washing-stand had a double set of jugs and basins on it. Three high sash windows looked over fields and some groups of bare, wind-bent trees which cut off the distance, and a grey sky hung over this neutral-coloured land.

I unpacked, feeling that no matter how I arranged them my things made very little impression on the huge wardrobe, chest of drawers, and dressing-table, and after fidgeting about for what seemed a long time I opened my door and, finding all dead still and quiet, I decided to take a look round. I went down the long passage, but did not venture to open any of the many doors, found the staircase, and looked at the stags' horns that bristled from the stone walls, and when I reached the hall I saw it was bigger than I had realized, even the stuffed bull looking quite modest in the distance. Here, too, it was completely quiet except for my own footsteps, which seemed to echo on the stone floor, so I tried to see how far I could get by walking only on the many animal skins spread about, but when I nearly fell over a tiger's head on one of them I quickly went across to examine the bull. Its glass eyes stared into mine and seemed to say, " What are you doing here ? " so emphatically that I ran back up the stairs and down the long passages to my room.

A gong boomed through the house, and in the hall I found one of the gorgeous footmen waiting to show me the way. The dining-room, as I had expected, was a vast room with a round table in the middle and only one place laid at it, but covered with silver, fruit, and flowers. Realizing that three men were waiting on me, I was paralysed, and hardly knew what I ate, and I suppose I was tired and overwrought, for suddenly the orchids, the grapes, and the peaches seemed floating in a mist. I blew my nose. I refused a wine, only to be offered another kind and then another. That afternoon I went to sleep on the sofa in my room.

Tea was in the Long Room downstairs and not in the drawing-room, which was on the first floor. When my cousin Ina came in I was there alone, and I thought her quite lovely—tall, and very fair, and wearing a smoke-blue velvet dress. She was kind, welcoming, and charming, and said :

" I am so sorry Ferrers had to be out for your first day, poor little neglected Irish cousin—ah, here he comes."

And a thin man arrived who, taking no notice of me, went eagerly up to Ina saying, " How are you, my darling ? "

" Fairly well," she answered, and was it my imagination that made me think she shrank away from him ?

At that moment a procession arrived, consisting of the butler and three powdered footmen, one of whom put out a tea-table, while another laid a fine lace cloth on it, and a third put a silver tray with teapot and kettle on it. The ritual was perfect, one man replacing another automatically, while canary-coloured china appeared and a quantity of varied foods—rich cakes and plain cakes, scones and biscuits, thin bread and butter, white and brown—and when all was completed the butler announced : " Tea is served, my lady "—a fact we could scarcely have failed to know. This statement was the only active assistance he had given to the performance, and then the procession withdrew.

Meanwhile I had been looking round the room. It was indeed a long room, all white and gold, with three cut-glass chandeliers hanging from the high ceiling. All down the length of the room were groups of palm-trees and flowering white lilac-trees in pots, flanked by primula and orchids.

So began my visit, which lasted through a long, cold winter, during which I grew very fond of Ina and got to know her as well as anyone could in those sad years of her life.

One evening when we were alone she asked me, " Can you remember Bantry ? You used all to come there at Christmas, driving over the mountains from Killarney with relays of horses till my father got too old to have parties."

" I never went there after I was five, but I remember the great terrace with all the steps and statues."

" That was at the back of the house, and the front looked over the bay—that lovely bay."

Her eyes seemed misted for a moment and she said no more.

Another time she talked of her home and said, " I loved it as I never can love any other place, and after my sisters had married and my father had died I lived there for ten years with my brother, and I do not think there ever was a happier partnership. We left each other perfectly free to go or come and to do exactly as we liked, and as we knew everyone and entertained a great deal in an easy and informal way, people liked coming to Bantry."

" May I tell you something ? " I interrupted. " Just before I left Ireland I met a Major Hewson who talked of you, saying you were the most enchanting person he had ever known and that every man in County Cork laid his heart at your feet, and that you were kind, but kept everyone at a friendly distance."

She made no comment, but went on to tell me, " I was alone near Avignon, one of the quiet little French places I liked, when I heard quite by chance that my brother Berehaven was married. It was a cruel shock, coming like that and so unexpectedly, and I made a great mistake by writing a hasty, ill-considered letter of reproach about his marriage and his choosing a Roman Catholic to be his wife, and so I closed Bantry to myself for ever."

" So then you married Ferrers ? " I said, after a long pause.

" Yes; he had been devoted to me for many years."

Ina was always loyal to her husband and never criticized him, but years later her sister, Olive Ardilaun, when talking to me said she thought it had been a disastrous marriage.

" You see," she had said, " Ina had been mistress of Bantry for so long; her brother Berehaven was younger than she was, and she did anything she liked and entertained all sorts of people. With her unusual charm and considerable beauty, many men were in love with her, and she should have chosen an easy-going Irishman instead of Ferrers, who was possessive and never let her go anywhere without him, enforcing upon her the kind of life he approved of, which was dull and socially very formal. She realized almost at once that she could never escape, and that feeling and the climate shattered her health."

I settled down at Staunton Harold, becoming indifferent to the presence of servants and accustomed to the ritual of meals, even the dinner, which was the most elaborate of them all, with its many courses and champagne every night.

The strangest ritual was the Sunday morning performance. I was told to be ready in the hall at five minutes to eleven, where I found two processions drawn up on either side of the stuffed bull, one headed by the housekeeper, with all the maids behind her, dressed in black with little black bonnets, and on the other side the butler and the menservants, no longer in their eighteenth-century dress, but all in dark suits. I stayed at the back of the hall, while a bell was ringing from the church across the gravel and everyone stood quite still. Then Ferrers came, looking slighter than ever, and wearing a tail coat and carrying a top hat. Deviating for the bull, he walked between the ranks of servants to the hall door, which at that moment was opened by an elderly man carrying a black velvet cushion on which was a large key, who came in and stood behind Ferrers. The housekeeper darted towards me whispering, " Walk beside his lordship and stay with him," and then she led the maids to the church, followed by the men, and lastly by Ferrers, who put on his top hat as he crossed the gravel.

The church seemed fairly full, the women sitting on one side and the men on the other. Inside we paused for a moment while the man with the cushion locked the door and led us to the front pew, placing the key on a shelf in front of us, and as soon as this was done the bell stopped and an old clergyman came in and read the service in a slow, droning voice. It seemed dull till Ferrers whispered to me, " Stand up," while everyone else was kneeling, and I heard the slow voice add to the prayers for the Royal Family, " And for Sewallis Edward, Earl Ferrers, Ina Maude, Countess Ferrers, the Lady Augusta Palmer, the Earl's sister, and Katherine Herbert, the Countess's cousin." I felt horribly self-conscious, and when the prayer was over subsided on to my footstool uncertain if I was going to laugh or cry.

Everyone left the church before we did and then the door was locked and the key returned to its caretaker.

Later I asked Ina what happened to the clergyman.

" He's locked in the church, but we feed him—if you look out of the window you will see his luncheon going in. Also," she added with a smile, " what the French call a *chaise percée*, and at three he takes a children's service, and the evening service at four, after which he is let out. Ferrers doesn't like him, for he neglects the people and doesn't trouble if anyone is ill, but although it's our private chapel and not under the Bishop's jurisdiction, we can't get rid of him, as he won't resign."

I did look out of the window, and saw a procession going to the church, headed by the man with the key, followed by objects held on poles. It looked like an old illustration of the Ark of the Covenant.

The days took on a regular routine for me. I painted in the morning, having asked Ina if I might copy the Romney in the big upstairs drawing-room and she having answered after a moment's pause, " I really think you might if you don't move it, for you couldn't do it any harm, and Ferrers never goes in there."

This delighted me, and I said, " I must get a canvas and some paints."

" I wish I could do more to amuse you, but order the

side-car and drive into the town—that might amuse you," she added.

I was familiar with Irish side-cars, which were always shabby and you lolled across the seat and rested your elbow in the middle and had jokes with the driver while the horse got along with a sort of smooth run, the whole affair being casual and easy-going; but here, standing on the immense sweep of gravel, was such a side-car as I had never seen. It gleamed with yellow varnish, and the seats were covered with crimson velvet. On the driving-seat, sitting stiffly upright, was a coachman in cockaded top hat, white breeches, and polished high boots, and between the shafts was a very large, handsome black horse with silver-mounted harness. I got on the side seat feeling that lolling was not possible, but when the high-stepping horse started and we rocked away down the avenue I nearly fell off. The cold was piercing, and jokes with the coachman were unthinkable.

Later when Ida asked me how I had enjoyed my drive I answered that I thought these Midlands too cold for a side-car, but that I had never seen such a smart one.

" Of course not; it's a complete misfit here, as I am." Then, as if correcting herself, " Ferrers most kindly had it built for me, thinking I would like an Irish vehicle; but I am caged, if only by this climate."

Although she suffered from bronchitis and threatened lung trouble and constant asthma, which strained her heart, she was unfailingly kind and never complained. She asked the estate nurse to show me anything that might interest me on the place, and the latter, who had a pony cart and a stout pony, took me first to see the gardens, where we found the head gardener in a very heated orchid house. Then the nurse went off on her round, while the gardener showed me these astonishing flowers, after which we went through the vineries, a melon house, a carnation house, and a mixed greenhouse, gay with primulas and cyclamens. He also showed me a perfectly appointed potting-shed and a tool-shed where the tools were all clean and polished, and then pointed out the bothy.

" How many men have you ? " I asked.

" Eight men and six boys. I like to start them young and take them right through from plain weeding and digging to pruning, budding, grafting, and propagating, and then through the glass work, and I make them study, too, and master names ; then when they know their job it's a satisfaction to find them a good place."

" Just when they are trained and useful ? "

" Yes, certainly. His lordship and his father before him always held it our duty to train and then place our people, and I feel the same; coming from here they mostly have good prospects. One boy of mine is well up at Kew, while another is head at the Duke of D . . .'s."

We then went into his attractive house overlooking the garden to see his prizes. The walls of the sitting-room were hung with framed certificates, first prize here and first prize there; on the mantelpiece and chiffonier were silver cups of all sizes, all with inscriptions of past successes, and his pride and pleasure in them were very attractive. All the time he talked of " my orchids " or " my grapes ", and I felt when I left him that he was a completely happy man.

One afternoon the elderly agent took me out to see the Home Farm, the prosperous look and perfect order of which made it unlike any farm I had ever seen. " The finest shorthorn herd in the country," he stated as he took me through the sweet, clean cow-house. "All bred here, for his lordship's father was a real farmer and did everything regardless of cost, but on good common-sense lines. He would try experiments; whether it was cows, pigs, fowl, or wheat, we must improve them, and it was the same with the land, for which he bought new machinery and used mole-drains on the hillside and drained marsh lands."

I was shown the stables, with heavy, hairy-hoofed horses, calves, and pigs all housed so well, and I thought how much better their buildings were than the cabins people lived in at home. It all seemed on such lavish lines, and I asked the agent, " But does this pay ? "

" Ah, young lady, it would take me too long to make you understand that. If you mean could a working farmer do it as we do, he couldn't, for he has to take the short view and can't afford risks. But it pays a fine dividend in other ways than making money, for every tenant on this estate and many an outsider have benefited by what we have done. It is people who have the will and the means who have raised the level of British farming. We show our beasts, we publish our milk results from good breeding, and our blood has spread far and wide. We lend our machines to our tenants and buy good seed in bulk and sell it to them in small lots for no more than they would pay for poorer quality. Some years we make a loss, and others not, but we keep accounts. Everything that goes to the house is charged at market rates, and at the Estate Office the accounts are analysed, and by doing this over a number of years we know what outlay has paid and what has made a loss. Suppose we give five hundred pounds for a bull ; it may take several years to see if it has paid us in the quality of the calves we got by him—but there, I shouldn't be talking to you of such things."

His interest seemed so profound that I felt he might go on indefinitely, and it was time to get home for tea.

Another day I went with the nurse to see the head game-keeper on his large settlement with hundreds of coops in a field, long rows of kennels, and a substantial house.

" The spring's the time to see the place," said the keeper when he met us ; " then maybe I shall have a thousand chicks running round."

" Chickens ? "

" Young pheasants, miss; and a hundred hens to mother them."

I was taken into the house, where there were antlers on the walls and stuffed birds in glass cases and many photographs of shooting groups.

" That was the best day we ever had," he said, pointing to a group surveying dead birds. " And it was published, too."

He showed me the same picture in *The Field*. There were photographs of dogs pointing, dogs retrieving, and men firing. After talking of good seasons and wet seasons, of good shots and outstandingly good shots, he finally announced, " There's not many can beat us in the way of sport, for his lordship gives me a free hand, and I can show as pretty a day's sport as you'd find anywhere."

As we went out he pointed to an unpleasant sight, though it seemed to gratify him : on a long wire hung bedraggled feathered corpses of magpies and hawks, and the skins of stoats and weasels were nailed on boards.

"Vermin," he said with scorn; "that's the place for them."

The nurse, a cheerful, talkative woman, told me of her work as we drove home.

" You see, I nurse them all, from the babies to the older people, when they need it. You should ask her ladyship to let you go through the house with Mrs. Mellish, the housekeeper."

This I did, and I was shown the kitchens, the stillroom, the pantry, and the strong-room, and the locked door of the muniment room, the laundry, the linen room, and the sewing room, and everywhere I saw young women at work wearing gay print dresses and pretty mob caps.

" I take a great interest in my girls," the housekeeper told me. " When they apply for a vacant place I let them take it, but I watch them, and if I see they are not getting on well, I advise them to change when they get the chance to another department, better fitted to their taste. If we don't promote them here when they are trained we find them good places, but most of them get married after they have been with us a few years, and they make good wives, for they know how their homes and children should be kept. When they marry from here his lordship gives them two leather-covered armchairs. It was his father who started that, for the old gentleman used to say, ' Make them comfortable after the day's work and there is more chance they will agree '. Her ladyship gives a nice china breakfast and tea service."

My days settled into fairly regular ways, painting in the mornings and after luncheon going for walks, often visiting the gardens, where the head gardener always welcomed me and was always interesting. Tea in the long room was followed by Ferrers telling us how well or how badly he had played golf. He had a private course and kept a professional, and he would describe his fortune at every hole, and then produce several little books bound in red leather and look up what he had done on the same day twenty years ago, then do the same for ten years ago. I would be embroidering a bedspread and scarcely listening to reading out of so many putting strokes, so many drives, and sometimes the measurement of these drives, and Ina, lying on the sofa knitting some white garment, would patiently assent with sympathy or commendation as a pause demanded, but it was an automatic response.

This quiet, regular life would go on for weeks, and then there would be a shooting party.

"No one to amuse you, dear, I'm afraid," Ina said. " They are all elderly and Ferrers' contemporaries, but you can go out with the guns if you like."

They were elderly : Lord and Lady this, Mr. and Mrs. that. I joined them for the first day's shooting, which was all taken very seriously, Ferrers, his keepers and beaters having everything planned to the last minutia. These stout men in their tweeds and heavy boots were expert shots. Each guest was given a particular stand, with an attendant behind to load his guns, the wood was encircled, and we could hear the cries of the beaters and the crack of their sticks on the undergrowth, then a shout of " Mark ! " and the whirr of wings above us. Guns would be flung up, each barrel fired, and the gun changed with swift precision of movement. Few birds got away; most of them would be one moment living things, flashing across the sky, and the next falling, fluttering masses of feathers, which would hit the earth with a dull thud. There were so many of them that the guns would get hot and the air vibrate with the sound of firing, but it would be over quickly, and men and dogs would collect the birds before a move was made to another stand and quick death repeated.

The shooting was carefully timed and planned to meet the luncheon brake. Trestle tables would be put out in some sheltered spot and an excellent hot meal served, but not lingered over, for the days were short and there was more killing to be done. The shooting would end again on a pre-arranged spot, where the hundreds of birds were laid out for inspection and the total given, which total would be posted that night to the sporting papers.

The evening was soporific.

I went out each day, for in spite of the horrible side of it there was excitement and interest in watching an exhibition of brilliant skill, but I broke down and left them on the rabbit-shooting day.

The kind of rabbit-shooting which meant walking several miles or scrambling up a mountain-side to get half a dozen, which would be thought quite good, was familiar to me : rabbits turned out by half-trained dogs and often escaping into the thick cover I was accustomed to seeing. With this idea, I wondered at these people condescending to rabbits, but was told it takes more judgment and quicker shooting than any rocketing pheasant, and you mustn't poach the next man's ground.

The guns were standing at intervals at the side of a wide grass ride, and an army of beaters was in the wood behind us with the dogs, the rabbits having been previously driven into it for days and their holes stopped. They broke cover in hundreds, and attempted to cross the ride in a flash, but most were killed, a few were wounded, and a very occasional one escaped. At the height of the shooting nothing could be done about the writhing, wounded creatures trying to drag themselves to safety, and it was so horrible that I left and made my way home. No doubt it was over quickly, for soon the fusillade stopped, and before long I heard it begin further off.

At night we sat in the big drawing-room upstairs, never used except for parties. It was interesting in this house to see the evidence of the taste of various generations. The old gentleman who had valued comfort had furnished the bedrooms with sound, ugly mid-Victorian furniture, no doubt discarding pieces we should value to-day, and the tiger skins in the hall and other sporting trophies had been sent home by his uncles, who had held positions in India. His great-grandfather, who had furnished this splendid room, had been a man of taste who had travelled and had bought pictures and furniture and the carved Italian mantel-piece. There were Italian primitives and Dutch interiors. The furniture was mellow and beautiful, little having been added since his day, and even the curtains of Genoese velvet and the Aubusson carpet were as he had left them; the room being so little used and so well cared for, they looked as if time had hardly touched them.

Here the women of our party would be knitting or doing cross stitch. They admired my bedspread, and when I told them I was doing it for an order, I was at once given orders to do two more.

" Show them your copy of the Romney," Ina said.

I brought it from the corner of the room, framed in an old swept frame I had found in an antique shop, and at that moment the men came in and Ferrers, seeing me steadying the picture on the floor, said, " When did you take that down ? "

I realized from his voice that he was angry.

Ina interposed quickly, " The picture hasn't been touched; that's her copy."

" Shows how good it is, for the owner to mistake it for the original," one of the men said with a loud laugh.

" Is it for sale, too ? " a woman asked, and the man who had laughed said :

" If it is I'm a buyer. I always liked that little lady."

" Copies of my pictures are not for sale."

There was an uncomfortable moment after Ferrers' statement till Ina started talking about the day's sport and I went away, taking my copy to my room.

I was in bed and nearly asleep when Ina came in carrying a candle and looking startlingly pale and tired, with dark shadows under her eyes. I sat up and held her hand.

" Have you been worried about the Romney ? " I asked.

" Ferrers was vexed, and he has asked me to make you promise never to part with it."

She stopped and kissed me, saying, " Dear child, you are in no way to blame. Good night."

I never saw her again, and I have still got that copy.

The next morning I heard she was ill. She became worse, doctors arrived and nurses were sent for, and I thought perhaps I ought to go away, so I said something of the kind to Ferrers.

" It would be best as soon as you can arrange to do so," he told me.

I clearly had to, though I longed to see Ina once more. She died some years afterwards, and during those last years Ferrers allowed no visitors, wanting to be everything to her himself. I heard that after her death he was utterly desolate, but he never relaxed in doing what he believed to be his duty, and continued his county work, keeping everything going on the place right up to his own death.

I think I understand why Ferrers did not let Ina go abroad : he could not let her go alone—he could not have endured that—and he would not leave his post.

Our life in that great house was dull and may have been a little absurd, with its pomp and formality, but there was a fine side to the tradition that was unbroken for generations— a tradition of mutual obligations and service recognized by all, from the owner down to the humblest dependant. There existed a bond of pride and love of the place among them all, pride perhaps more actively felt by the employees in their various departments than by the owner, and everyone was assured of comfort and security.

Such places have almost ceased to exist in England, yet I can think of no group of human beings in any present-day setting to compare with this estate, where, as in many others, the mutual feeling was so kindly and where there existed an almost communal enjoyment of the expenditure of wealth.

Chapter Six

INTRODUCTION TO AURELIA

WHILE I was staying with my cousin Ina she had given me an immensely long letter, written on many unnumbered loose sheets in large, untidy writing.

" I wish, dear, you would answer this for me. Aurelia

is as much your relation as mine, and I think she must be mad, for she keeps writing to me for money, though I never met her. First it was for temperance meetings, and I sent her something, which I am sure was a mistake, for she has kept on ever since asking for subscriptions for all sorts of things—a soldiers' home, or a drunken artist she says she is reforming. I wrote and told her quite firmly I was not going to send money for any cause and asked her not to write again, but now I get this letter wanting money for a new drum for the Salvation Army, and I can't quite make out whether she means to play it herself, as she refers to ' my band '. Will you put her off firmly and make her understand I do not wish to have any more letters from her ? "

I wrote to this effect, and had an even longer letter in reply, asking me to beg the Ferrers to finance a shop she wanted to start, and assuring me that if they would invest one thousand pounds in it they would get back two in no time.

There were several additions to the letter after her signature, and one of them said, " I wish you would come and stay with me; you could help me in so many ways."

The letter came from a rectory in the South of England.

When Ina fell ill I decided to go there, having no other alternative except to go home.

There was no one to meet me at the station, so I took a cab, and when I arrived at the rectory—a large red-brick building—there was no answer on ringing the bell, so the cabman put my luggage in the porch and I was left alone. The porch itself was rather surprising, for on its walls were paintings of lions and tigers in a verdigris-green jungle which was peeling in spots, as the plaster had not taken kindly to oil paint. Having taken in this decoration I rang again, but getting no response I went into the hall and sat down to wait, trying not to feel depressed.

The silence was suddenly broken by someone coughing, and as the sound came from close to me, I knocked at the nearest door and was told to come in.

An elderly clergyman writing at a desk looked up and said in a kindly voice, " Well, my dear, what can I do for you ? "

" I have come to stay. Aunt Aurelia invited me—I am Katherine Herbert."

" Ah yes," he answered vaguely, and I felt sure he had never heard of me. " I hope you will have a pleasant time. My dear wife is not always punctual, but she will be delighted to see you."

And with that he dipped his pen in the inkpot and I felt dismissed.

Sitting alone in the hall once more, I observed my surroundings. It was an untidy place, and there was a great deal of furniture in it, and on the wall an enormous picture of lions, from which it appeared that someone must have a perfect passion for these ferocious beasts, and I felt far from sure that I was going to have a pleasant time. Then I heard steps on the gravel and a girl came in, followed by a curate.

" Do you know when Mrs. Everett will be in ? " I asked anxiously.

" No, no one could tell you that," the girl answered, and the curate interposed :

" But perhaps I can help you or take a message ? "

Again I explained why I was there.

" We'll see that your luggage is taken up to your room— Aurelia has probably forgotten that you were coming," said the girl.

" How dreadful ! " I exclaimed. " Ought I to stay ? "

" Don't worry, she will be very pleased to see you. And now let us introduce ourselves. My name is Louie Green, and my guardians placed me here as a paying guest because a rectory sounded so suitable, and he "—indicating the curate—" is called Marmaduke Percival du Cane. With such a name he had to go into the Church," she added, laughing. " He is no relation of mine, but nice to tease, and is supposed to be useful to the rector."

A strange-looking man with goggling eyes carried up my trunk and shambled off.

" Who was that ? " I asked Louie.

" A sort of artist."

" Does he live here ? "

" Only after he has got very drunk, and then Aurelia collects him and does some praying over him. This time she kept him so long on his knees that he got desperate and drank methylated spirits. You should have seen his eyes roll when Aurelia said she would put a light to his mouth and he would blow up, and he believed it because he was still queer from the effects, but he is better now."

" Did he paint all the lions and tigers ? "

" Oh no, they were done by another artist she helps."

" Are there no servants ? " I asked, looking round the room, in which the bed was not made up.

" There is one called Lizzie, who is always here, and she is a perfect marvel. She would have had it all nice for you if Aurelia had remembered to tell her you were coming. Then there are all sorts of strays who come in to help— people in trouble or out of work or gypsies or girls from a home."

Tea was a depressing meal, for I was nervous, the curate silent, and Louie making rather foolish conversation; but when Aurelia came in the atmosphere changed, for she was so full of vitality, and pleased to see me. Though making no apologies for having forgotten I was coming, she welcomed me warmly, as I saw later she welcomed anybody who turned up. She was about forty, very fat, though all her movements were vigorous; her cheeks were bright pink and her eyes very blue, and she was untidily dressed and wore men's boots.

All I tell of Aurelia I feel sure will be thought exaggerated and improbable, yet whatever I write of her I shall still feel that " the half was not told ". People have said, " She was so like my Aunt Julia or exactly like Mrs. So-and-so." She may have been from one facet, but no one has been completely like her, or so I believe. She had imperturbable sweet temper, was always in good spirits, kind to everyone when she realized kindness was needed, and quite indifferent to and unconscious of discomfort—her own or anyone else's. People have thought her untruthful and dishonest, but I don't think she had any idea she ever failed in either of these ways, for she always acted on impulse, and at the moment believed what she said to be true. In years to come, if I left my purse where she happened to see it she might take something out of it, as likely as not to give to someone else, and if reproached would answer vaguely, " You oughtn't to mind helping people." Indeed, when she had anything to give to others she was splendidly generous. Her self-confidence was unlimited, especially in her business and organizing capacity, which an unbroken series of failures never shook, and she had a delightful voice and great personal charm.

On this, my first contact with her, I was both attracted and puzzled as she chattered away telling stories it was hard to believe, and then produced a letter, telling us with gusts of laughter, " I got this from the old P.G.'s upstairs. They have paid up and are going to-morrow, and will then hand me the key of their room, which they have never allowed anyone into." And with more gurgles of amusement she added, " I am to send their letters to the dead-letter office."

She began to invent absurd theories about them, suggesting that they might have kept a sweet-shop, and when they had made a lot of money sold the shop and worked off their ill-feelings by putting poison in the last of their sweets and posting parcels of them from some strange town to everyone they disliked. Then they changed their name and had hidden in her rectory.

" They are more likely leaving because they haven't had enough to eat," Louie put in pertly.

" But there's always enough to eat," Aurelia answered vaguely.

" But not perhaps what they expected for all you are charging them."

" No. I am sure they are hiding from some crime."

And she started on a fresh theory.

The morning after I arrived Aurelia put us—Louie, the curate, and me—to address envelopes from a long list of names and to put a lithographed letter into each envelope. I read the letter, which was an impassioned appeal for subscriptions for a Soldiers' Home, badly expressed, but vivid with sentimental descriptions of homeless soldiers being saved from drink and disgrace by the beautiful and prayerful atmosphere of this place, where excellent lemonade was provided.

We worked away all the morning, and Aurelia was delighted when we gave her a packet of ninety-four letters, all stamped and ready for the post.

" Guess how much these will bring in," she asked gaily.

" Perhaps fifty pounds."

" More like hundreds of pounds, I hope," she answered. " And I am sure they will, for I have prayed hard about them. By the way, I asked two officers I met to come in for tennis this afternoon."

The two young officers arrived, perfectly turned out, their white trousers spotless, and carrying rackets and shoes. Aurelia received them with her natural cordiality, and we all went down the garden, which was beautifully kept by the Rector and his man, whereas the tennis lawn, in which he took no interest, was neglected, the grass uncut, no net, and, of course, no marking. Our visitors looked blank.

Aurelia only observed, " We must mow it; we've got a machine, and it won't take long."

But it did take a long time. The two young men took off their coats and worked really hard, one mowing and the other sweeping up the grass, for the machine had nothing to catch it in. After they had done it all one way they thought it wouldn't be playable till they mowed it the other, and after that they rolled it with a heavy roller; when they had finished they stood mopping their foreheads, their shoes green and their trousers far from spotless. Meanwhile Aurelia was slashing wildly with a billhook at branches of overgrown laurels at the back of the court while we dived (at some peril from her vigorous but erratic swipes) to collect the branches.

" Come on in, we'll have tea now," she called out.

" Sorry," the officers answered, " we are on duty at six o'clock, and it's past five already ; we must cut off and change."

" Come to-morrow and I'll beat you both at singles," Aurelia cried; but they were cautious.

" What about marking the court and getting the net up ? "

" I've got a marking machine, but I don't think I've got any whiting, so perhaps you could bring some. We could run out the lines in no time."

" All right, we'll come and bring the whiting. We can't let your challenge go unanswered."

They hurried off, and we heard shouts of laughter in the distance. No doubt they had never before been asked to a tennis-party quite like this one.

They came next day, and after they had marked the court and fixed the net I went to fetch Aurelia, who hadn't turned up so far. She came out wearing an unevenly long black skirt, her usual boots, and no hat.

" Anyone got a bit of string ? " she asked.

Some was produced, and she tied it round her ample waist, hitching her skirt through it till it hung just below her knees, and then she looked down at her boots.

" I can't play in these, and my feet are too large to wear yours "—observing Louie and me—" but I play just as well in my stockinged feet," and she unlaced her boots, flung them away, and stood up to battle. It was an incredible sight, for she was stout, very fast, and very nimble as she flew about the court facing the slim boy in white. There was a large hole in one of her black stockings through which a pink disc of heel flickered as she bounded about. Before this game the officers had been very polite and were probably shy, but now the one who wasn't playing rolled on the grass convulsed with laughter, as did Louie and I.

It was a close match, Aurelia playing surprisingly well and hitting very hard, though sometimes rather wildly, but her opponent just managed to beat her. At the end of the second game she called to me, " Get me some lemonade."

I went back to the house and made a large jugful, which I brought out on a tray with glasses. The set was over, and Aurelia was crimson, and her hair was wet and straggling, for she had lost most of her hairpins. She took glass after glass until the jug was empty, then, seeing this, said, " I'm so sorry; perhaps my partner wanted some."

" He's evidently not going to get any," said the boy, laughing, and added, " Do you mean to tell me you are going to take on Summers now "—indicating his companion— " full up with liquid ? "

" Of course I am; I'm only getting into my stride, and I shall sweat off a lot of fat, which is such a good thing."

They started again, and this time she won.

The whole afternoon was hilarious, and the boys were amused at seeing Aurelia eat three eggs after they had refused them on the plea that it was too near their dinner-time.

" I'm sure I have lost several pounds," she said, " so I may as well eat what I like."

" Don't you always, dear Aurelia ? " Louie inquired with ironic politeness.

The morning posts produced answers to our appeal for the Soldiers' Home—small postal orders, small cheques, large ones, and one for fifty pounds. Aurelia was delighted, and would take these gifts down to the town, after whistling or singing a hymn in her high, piercing voice. The response went on for several days, and then one evening a van packed with furniture came to the door, but Aurelia was vexed and sent it off. I had gone with her, and I heard her say to the driver, " Why did you come here ? I told them to send everything to Gedge's store."

At that moment a horrible suspicion flashed through my mind : had she bought these things with the money collected ? Surely impossible.

I joined Louie and the curate, who was reading, but there was something in the girl's puzzled expression that made me wonder if the same thought had occurred to her. We were silent for a few minutes, and then she said, " Marmaduke, do attend. I'm worried."

She generally called him by some nickname, and at the sound of his real name he realized she was serious, and shut his book.

" Listen. You know Aurelia took those cheques to the bank, and not to the treasurer of the Home, and now she has bought a lot of furniture. Has she spent that money on it ? "

" Oh, impossible; she couldn't—it would be criminal."

" Would you like to ask her ? "

At that moment Aurelia came in, her eyes clear, her cheeks glowing, seemingly without a care in the world.

The curate, quite pale and with nervously clenched hands, spoke in a diffident, anxious voice, " Forgive me, I am sure it is all a mistake.   You didn't——" he hesitated, " you couldn't have used any of that money sent for the Home for any other purpose ? "

Aurelia laughed cheerfully.

" Is that what's bothering you ?   It's quite all right; I'm only paying myself back what I gave the Home to start it. You see, I was so anxious to get it going, and I had some money then, so I gave a thousand pounds, which of course was far too much for me, so as soon as I've got it back I won't collect any more."

The curate jumped to his feet crying, " You don't understand what you have done.   Once given, the money is not yours, and to replace it with charitable gifts collected by yourself—you could be sent to gaol for that."

" Don't be so silly," Aurelia interrupted.

" It's not being silly, it's deadly serious.   You are collecting money under false pretences, and I must tell the Rector."

" No, you shall not," Aurelia cried, and I could see she was shaken.   " It is nothing to do with him, and I won't have him worried."

" Yes, there you are right.   He had better not be incriminated; but God help me, I am—we all are."

" Oh, don't fuss so.   I won't collect any more—plenty of other ways of making money."

The curate was away next day, and returned late in the evening.

" I have seen the Bishop, and told him my share in this dreadful business," he said.   " He was most kind and understanding, and so distressed, and for a time uncertain what he ought to do; then he said, ' No, I won't trouble my poor friend Henry Everett, but his wife must give you her solemn promise to cease collecting and to do her utmost to make restitution of the money she has used so wrongly.'"

"I don't see that it is in the least wrong; it's quite fair to try and get some of my own money back. I gave it and worked hard to start the Home, and now it's going well. You can tell your silly old Bishop that I don't care what he thinks."

I never heard of any restitution, but the collecting ceased at that time.

Many people criticized the Rector for letting his wife do the things she did, suggesting all sorts of reasons to explain his passive attitude, but I think the truth is very simple—he just couldn't stop her. She was much younger than he was, and I think he was fond of her, and even proud of her vitality and vigour. His health was failing and he needed peace in his private life. He trained her to respect his study since one day, soon after they married, he had come home to find all its contents out of doors in the rain—books, papers, furniture, pictures and photographs of Oxford groups, all sodden. These he had carried in and dried as far as was possible, and on her return he took her by the hand, got a Bible and said, " You know the nature of an oath. Kiss that book and repeat after me that you swear before God that as long as you live you will never touch, alter, or rearrange anything whatever in my study."

She started to protest, saying she had meant to put them all back and she was going to make it look so much nicer, but he stopped her and made her repeat the oath. She kept it, and I have seen her pause like a well-trained dog and desist when tempted. In all the confusion and disorder in that house, only his study was conventional and tidy. Lizzie, the devoted servant, kept it clean and dusted and saw to his comfort as far as she could. Thus these two dissimilar people lived their separate lives in a friendly spirit.

The Rector was loved, respected, and pitied, and his wife

went her own erratic way. On occasions the Rector would protest sternly, as he did when she headed the singing of blood-curdling hymns to the accompaniment of the Salvation Army band outside his church while he was preaching.

Chapter Seven

WITH AURELIA

FEELING uncertain about my future and being reluctant to go home, I spoke to Aurelia, telling her I thought of writing to a London hospital for particulars about training to become a nurse.

" Do you want to be a nurse ? "

" No, but I want to be independent."

" What would you really like to do ? "

I explained that Lady Kenmare had advised me to study art and had said that if I was determined to do this a way would be found.

" And are you clear about it ? "

" Yes, but it's impossible, for the little I make copying pictures and doing needlework would never be enough."

" Why," Aurelia suggested, " shouldn't you go to the South Kensington School of Art here ? Lots of people do. I should like to myself, but I haven't time. And of course I would pay whatever the fee is, and you could stay with me, for I like having you."

The following week saw me at work at the local school, where the teacher was a man with a pointed beard and languid manner whose quite futile method was to make us spend a very long time stippling and finishing a study of some bust. With the technical ease I had in copying, I could carry out his ideas perfectly, and did a dreadful study, shading it to the most soot-like black in the shadows with every superficial irregularity emphasized but with no underlying knowledge of construction or anatomy.

When the School of Art closed I went to stay with some friends I had made in the neighbourhood, and while there I got a long, characteristic letter from Aurelia, posted from Switzerland, telling me that her husband had been ordered to go abroad for his lungs and had been given the chaplaincy at St. Moritz. She had taken a villa there, and would I come out at once and help her ? She would pay all my expenses.

I shall never forget my first impression of Switzerland under snow. In those days one drove the last twenty miles of the journey over the pass in a sleigh, and leaving the stuffy train and going out into the brilliant sunshine, everything around one white and sparkling, was the most exhilarating experience I had ever had. I was young, and felt that never had anything been so wonderful, so thrilling, or so happy as this adventure.

The adventure, however, did not turn out like that. Aurelia had taken a summer villa standing where the shoulder of the mountain hid the sun for most of the day, a mile from the hotel, where the Rector had been given bright, warm rooms next to the Chapel. Alas, Aurelia decided it would be cheaper for him to live at the villa and to take cash in return for his rooms and his board. It was a dreadful decision, entailing a cold daily walk to take his service and all the discomforts of that horrible villa. To others it seemed positively cruel, but I think that Aurelia, with her immense strength and indifference to discomfort, was incapable of understanding that it could be much of a trial to live at the villa, let alone a danger to her husband's life.

She had advertised for guests to spend the winter in the care of the chaplain's wife, and had had many answers. Soon after my arrival I understood why I was wanted. The guests were seething with discontent and on the verge of revolt, for Aurelia was out from morning to night enjoying herself. She would come back from the skating rink, by way of the village street, her large form face downwards on a sledge, and, being skilful at this as she was at most sports, she would negotiate corners at top speed and whirl round a wall and up to our front door in a flurry of snow, her cheeks glowing, and thinking it the greatest fun. Then she would eat a large luncheon and rush off immediately afterwards on a bob-sleighing expedition or to practise for hours round an orange for her skating test. She thought of nothing else. She explained to me that her P.G.'s had been so unreasonable, getting so cross and threatening to go away, so would I help her to see that they were satisfied, for they had paid a great deal in advance and she couldn't pay them back. This meant my running this unsuitable house, trying to keep it warm, and seeing that these unfortunate people, who were there for their health, were fed and looked after. There were no servants in the house, and I had to find women to come in at various hours to clean and cook.

I became miserable, thinking of all I was missing, and I confronted Aurelia angrily, telling her she only thought of herself, amusing herself from morning to night and leaving me to do all the drudgery. As usual, she was perfectly sweet-tempered, and said she hadn't thought it would take up so much of my time, and of course I must go out, and she would cook and serve the mid-day meal. She could cook in a slapdash and very extravagant way, but left such chaos behind her in the kitchen and so ruffled the Swiss women with orders to go out and buy this, that, and the other (generally ingredients that couldn't be got), while bedrooms were not done, that I thought it better to leave Aurelia to her sports and do my best.

Gradually things became organized in the villa, and as I was freer I learnt to skate, but was not good at it. Aurelia's tall, good-looking son came out and joined us, and as he and I were the same age we made friends. He intended to become a landscape painter, but meanwhile he enjoyed skating and playing hockey on the ice, and being, like his mother, a natural athlete, he did both well. And so the winter passed.

The Rector had resigned his living in England, and Aurelia had taken a house on the South Coast overlooking the sea, where we went on our return from Switzerland. On arrival there the Rector became very ill, and for the last six weeks of his life Aurelia threw all her inexhaustible energy into nursing him. She slept on a mattress on the floor of his room, attending to him day and night. At six in the morning she would rush out of the house, her stout figure encased in a bathing-gown, and dive from a height into the sea—for she could swim like a porpoise and was indifferent to wind, rain, or cold—returning to the house dripping and glowing with health to resume her nursing.

One morning she saw a white and shining yacht out in the bay and asked whose it was. "Lord Dundonald's," a friendly coastguard told her. She was very distantly connected with this peer and had never met him, but immediately decided to swim out and claim this nebulous link, thinking nothing of the three-quarters of a mile which lay between the yacht and the shore. She looked amusing in the water, for she had a small head, never wore a cap, and her round cheeks remained their natural bright pink, but her vigorous movements and stout body were in striking contrast to the little, seal-like head.

Seeing a man leaning over the side of the yacht she called out, " I've come to see Lord Dundonald."

He fixed an eyeglass in his eye and looking down at this unexpected visitor answered, " Have you indeed ?   Well, I happen to be that person."

" Good," cried Aurelia.   " I'm your cousin.   Will you put over a rope ladder ? "

She swarmed up hand over hand, and landed on the deck streaming with sea-water.

" You have made my deck very wet, and now perhaps you will tell me why you think you're my cousin ? "

At that moment two women dressed in smart yachting clothes came on deck and stared at her coldly.

" May I introduce a lady who claims to be a cousin but whose name I don't know ? "

Aurelia supplied it.

" And where, may I ask, is the link ? "

" Oh, somewhere a long way back.   One of your people married Elizabeth Rosette Stewart, and I was a Stewart before I married."

Then, as she told us the story, " I turned to the two women and said, ' Would one of you lend me a dressing-gown or a cloak ? '   At first they all seemed rather stiff and didn't seem even to want to lend me anything, but then one of them did get me a fur coat, and we went down to breakfast.

" I told them all about the boarding house and the Slade and the Sunday School, and of course I was hungry, and never noticed that Dundonald kept putting things on my plate.   I just ate them till he suddenly burst out laughing and said he had never seen anyone eat so much breakfast and he had lost count of the rolls I had consumed, which reminded me that I had said I would cook the breakfast for everyone.   They were all quite unstiff by this time and said, ' Anyhow, you have had yours.'

" I told them I should probably have another after my swim back.   They were so kind and nice, and waved and clapped when I dived from the bows of the yacht."

Whether she felt it much when the Rector died is uncertain. She was quite calm, and said, " I did all I could for him," and so she did for those last weeks. Perhaps there was also an undercurrent of relief at being completely free.

The Rector was to be buried in his former parish, and members of the church and officials of the town came to our house to accompany the coffin to the funeral service. Aurelia was decently dressed in widow's garb, in which she appeared very good-looking. The weather was chill, and there was hot soup ready for everyone, but when it was handed round the sombre gathering Aurelia exclaimed, " I don't want that stuff; I'll get myself some cold plum-pudding, there was plenty left," and she went out, returning with a dinner-plate on which were two large slices of suety pudding, which she ate and enjoyed. This was not done to make herself conspicuous; it was just that she was acting on impulse, and she didn't like soup, but did like cold plum-pudding. The incongruity of eating it at a pre-funeral gathering could not have occurred to her, nor would she have considered what the people present might think of her doing so.

Aurelia knew of my wish to study art, and directly after the funeral she said, " I have always longed to go in for art; let's all three go to the Slade School," the third being her son. Every difficulty melted before her enthusiasm. The seaside house could have visitors and a manageress, and she would take rooms close to the Slade and perhaps take in other students. All perfectly simple; the first thing was to go up to London and look for somewhere to live. We would go together.

We were to leave at midnight and arrive at five in the morning, and there never was such an exhausting twenty-four hours.

" Why, why, Aurelia, start at such an hour ? " I cried.

" But of course it's far the best way; then we have a clear

day before us and no time wasted. I went all over the Continent like that, had a full day in each place and no hotel bills. When it was a short journey I spent the rest of the night in the waiting-room, where one sleeps quite well."

She could sleep anywhere.

When we reached the station we got into a third-class carriage, but just as the train was about to start she changed at great speed into a first, where a naval officer in one corner was the only occupant. Aurelia immediately took off her boots, explaining that they would make an excellent pillow and adding as she looked vaguely round, " If I could have a piece of newspaper. . . ."

The naval officer politely handed her the outside sheet of the paper he was reading.

" Thank you so much. You'd better do the same and have a good sleep."

" I never make a pillow of boots or shoes in trains," he answered gravely.

Aurelia stretched herself on the seat, saying, " Wake me at Clapham Junction," and immediately went to sleep, never moving except to snatch at the newspaper under her head and throw it on the floor.

The night seemed long; the naval officer dozed in his corner. We reached Clapham Junction at last, and I touched Aurelia, who woke instantly, her eyes bright and her cheeks rosy, though one side was slightly blackened.

" Come," she cried, " no time to put my boots on."

She was out of the first-class carriage and into a third-class in a flash and, hurrying after her, I saw the naval officer watching the manœuvre with interest.

The day in London remains in my mind as a blur of running to catch buses; of hammerings in vain at six in the morning at a Temperance Hotel; of adjourning to a cab-men's shelter and drinking hot, sweet tea and eating thick slices of bread and butter while Aurelia cracked jokes with the men; of an interview and prayers at a Salvation Army centre; of a long wait in a city solicitor's office; of walking through every room at the Academy, where Aurelia was determined not to miss a single picture, and then an endless hunt for rooms near the Slade School. We wandered down Gower Street, through Charlotte Street, and through many by-ways in that neighbourhood, all seeming depressing to my tired mind. In the end Aurelia decided on an unfurnished house near Fitzroy Square which had one large, well-proportioned room for our living-room. We spent a long time at the house agent's, and ended the day with another visit to the Salvation Army Centre, by which time I was too dazed to take much in, but Aurelia enjoyed leading an entertainment with recitations, hymns, and prayers. When I tottered after her to the return night train I had learnt what she meant by night journeys giving one a full day.

Till the term opened at the Slade, Aurelia was busy and happy collecting a quantity of furniture at auctions and second-hand shops. She seemed to have plenty of money, but it transpired later that, her last trustee having died at that time, she had appointed the eccentric old artist I had met at the Rectory and a follower of the Salvation Army, neither of whom knew anything of trusts or had any means. They signed whatever she told them to, and she was selling this trust capital freely.

With this money we were able to move to London and furnish the large gaunt house in Fitzroy Street where we were to live.

Chapter Eight

THE SLADE SCHOOL

AURELIA was too busy receiving vans of furniture to think of going to the Slade on the opening day. Each van as its contents were disgorged added to the chaotic confusion of the London house; but her son Herbert and I decided to leave her to deal with it all, knowing she would be completely happy in the general muddle, and we were determined not to miss a single day of the session.

At this school it soon became clear that whatever dexterity I had in accurate copying was of no value here. Working in the Antique Room on what I thought was a good finished shaded drawing of a figure, I heard a voice saying, " Are you trying to do wool work ? "

It was Professor Henry Tonks, who stood behind me, very tall and severe-looking.

" Get up," he ordered, and sitting in my place he gave me my first lesson based on anatomy, illustrating it with a convincing drawing showing how the muscles clothed the bones.

" You had better do a fresh sketch every hour till you get the idea," he added as he went on to the next student.

So began my first contact with this great teacher, a teacher who guided his pupils more to an understanding and appreciation of art than to personal performance. After I married I got to know him quite well, and he explained his views. He thought personal vanity should be suppressed when it took the form of a wish to paint and to disfigure walls with valueless and generally offensive productions, and he believed that in our age not more than two or three in every thousand students would ever do anything intrinsically worth while, though a very large percentage could be made into critical and cultivated people. He advised us to go every day for ten or fifteen minutes to the National Gallery, the South Kensington Museum, or the Print Room of the British Museum, to study one picture, make a sketch of its pattern and rhythm, and buy a postcard reproduction and pin it up at home.

Later on he advised us to get an understanding of periods and the links between the arts, architecture and sculpture, paintings, textiles, porcelain, silver, and iron work. All these in their different mediums express the spirit of their age, and that spirit varies in different countries, as the Renaissance reached them at different times. He thought everyone should and could learn to draw, not as an end in itself, but as giving discrimination and insight, and he urged us to sketch and observe and memorize and to keep the waste-paper basket within reach. His method developed one's critical faculty so far beyond one's capacity that very few Slade students did desecrate walls with their efforts. I followed his advice, and have been grateful all my life for his guidance. He was also the kindest teacher, and took infinite pains to help anyone who was intelligent and hard-working.

One morning Aurelia arrived in the Antique Room carrying a Gladstone bag and a large Bible. It was a quiet room, and her voice rang out startlingly when she called to me, " Where am I to sit ? "

I found her a donkey—a kind of low stool—which was almost overwhelmed with her massive person, and she was given the regulation board, on which to pin her paper.

" I want one twice as big as that," she announced loudly.

I begged her to keep quiet, for everyone was watching her. She opened her bag and turned its contents on to the floor : two old-fashioned gold watches, a slice of bread, a box of charcoal, a china figure, a miniature, a quantity of tracts, and a parcel of thick sandwiches which came undone.

" I shall do that man," she declared, pointing at Hermes, and I went back to my own seat.

Tonks came in, sat on my stool, and said, " You can carry your next drawing a little farther," and he made a sketch on the corner of my paper before passing on to the next student. When he reached Aurelia and stood behind her his hand went up to his mouth to hide a grim smile. " What do you think you are doing ? " he asked.

" Drawing that thing "—pointing at Hermes.

" Yes, I surmised that, though I might have imagined a gorilla drawn by a savage; but why do you want to do it at all ? "

" I want to do pictures," Aurelia answered cheerfully.

" Well, take my advice and give up that idea."

" I have never tried to draw a naked man before, and you oughtn't to discourage me. I have come here to learn, and you must teach me."

No student had ever dared to speak to Tonks like that, but all he said was, " Well, get up."

" This stool is so low," she said, laughing and extending her hands for help.

Tonks, looking rather baffled, heaved her up and sat down himself, and then he saw the floor littered with her many things. The large Bible was open at the Prophet Ezekiel, and the page was crossed with red-ink lines. Tonks sat still, taking it all in—the watches, the miniature, the china, the Bible, the tracts, and the box of charcoal which Aurelia had trodden on and got mixed with the sandwiches.

" What's all this for ? " he asked.

" I have discovered a new prophecy no one has ever thought of."

" You can't think of it here."

" But drawing seems to help me to see a new point of view. Let me explain."

" No . . . that's a very bad miniature."

"Is it? Then I shall pawn it instead of one of the watches."

"Pawn the Bible, too, and as you are supposed to learn drawing and have told me I am here to teach you, perhaps you could attend."

"I'm longing to," Aurelia asserted eagerly.

He began his careful elementary lesson. But she wasn't really attending and said plaintively, "I don't care about bones; I want to make beautiful pictures."

Tonks gave it up and left the room.

Aurelia was popular with the students from the first day; during an interval she was the centre of a group, asking them all to a prayer-service in her room on Sunday afternoon, and suggesting that some of them should take rooms in her house, which several did.

The next day Aurelia arrived rather late, with even more paraphernalia, including a large board and a double-sized piece of paper, a whole loaf of bread, a spirit lamp and saucepan, the Gladstone bag, and a dilapidated eighteenth-century volume about art printed on thick paper with long s's. She opened the book at a picture of a nude man who was apparently divided into sections, and started her enormous drawing (if drawing it could be called) with a head like a football; then she measured seven lengths of the head, made a black line and drew two club-like feet on it. With constant references to her book she drew thick black lines with arrow heads pointing to the various parts of the human body, one to the nipples, one to the navel, and so on, connecting these indications with thick black outlines. The result was an indescribably grotesque indecency. She was completely absorbed, and had cut her loaf in half with a Spanish dagger she had extracted from her bag, using it freely to rub out her violent charcoal strokes, which she then put in again. Occasionally she ate a bit of bread.

Tonks was making his usual tour when he caught sight

of this appalling drawing.   He got up and stalked over to her place, undid the drawing-pins, and tore her paper in half, saying sternly, " I don't allow abortions of this kind to be done here."

Instantly Aurelia's face puckered up and tears ran down her cheeks, which were so black with charcoal that they made pink rivulets.   Tonks muttered something and went out, signalling me to come.

" She's a relation of yours, isn't she ? " he asked.   " Is she mad ? "

" Oh no, really not."

" Well, I can't have her disorganizing this place.   I shall speak to Professor Brown, and she'll have to leave."

I pleaded with him, assuring him she would give up coming if no notice was taken of her, and he relented enough to say, " Well, we'll see.   Meanwhile I shall send her down to the skeleton room, where she can draw and disturb nobody."

Could she ?   Before long, as we were going out for luncheon, we heard Aurelia's high-pitched voice (which was by nature quite a good one of the Gracie Fields type, but untrained) singing lustily, " Oh, make those dry bones live again, great Lord of Hosts ".   She seemed to know only that much of the hymn, for she repeated it over and over again, to the delight of the men and girls outside the skeleton room, who clapped and joined in with ribald variations.

Tried as he was by Aurelia's brief stay at the Slade, Tonks later on got endless amusement out of watching her. He discussed her character at length, and announced that she was the only completely primitive adult he had ever known, and that although she could read and write, she had no knowledge about anything : Art, literature, history, values—all were a total blank.   She had no code of conduct, knew neither shame nor self-consciousness, and responded only to unreasoning impulses.

[77]

Though completely ignorant of periods, Aurelia had instinctive taste of a rather garish kind, and she made that cellar room decorative. At one end she had a small organ with gilded pipes but squeaky tones. She slept on a couch of Empire design, covered on occasions with vivid silks and shawls, and in one corner she had a stuffed peacock with tail-feathers spread and a figure in brass of Buddha in front of it. Branches of evergreens in an immense Chinese vase stood on the floor, and there was also a depressed-looking palm-tree, suggesting a large dying spider, growing out of a Victorian white-and-blue china pot which evidently did not agree with it, and on this palm she hung several texts ornately decorated on cardboard. She never had cut flowers.

For electric light she had many lanterns with coloured glass slides, and the floor covering was a very worn Aubusson carpet on which stood two grandfather armchairs with gold-encrusted priest's vestments pinned over their rather tattered coverings. She also kept several dogs. Every Sunday afternoon Aurelia held what she called her " Sunday School ".

I have become confused about her various brands of religion. The Salvation Army would have suited her best could she have been made a general. At the time of the Sunday School she was an enthusiastic exponent of the tenets of an American gentleman called Doctor Dowie. His teaching seemed to be based on rapturous enjoyment of Salvation and a conversational, light-hearted intimacy with the Almighty, and a complete certainty of His approval of Doctor Dowie on all points.

Perhaps I am wronging the Doctor in making these statements, but Aurelia varied her religions so often that it may have been under another banner that she expounded this point of view.

I can remember her standing, dressed in a sort of Indian dress, with a gold net over her hair, expressing in herself the idea that Salvation was a matter of delightful enjoyment, not to say fun. Words never failed her, and she would interpose lamentable verse into her extempore eloquence. Around her, mostly sitting on the floor, those intelligent boys and girls enjoyed it all, especially when Aurelia, seated at her squeaky organ, gave out hymns which she led in her resonant voice and in which they all joined, but in shocking parodies of the rather primitive doggerel lines which she sang with such gusto.

" Now for old Blood and Thunder," they would call out, this being their paraphrase of one of the Salvation Army hymns into which Aurelia would launch with enthusiasm.

Throughout the session many of the students would be sketching her in strange situations and strange costumes or in none, preaching her special gospel now to City gentlemen in top hats, while she had dispensed with clothes, to aborigines dressed in a few feathers, or on the Island of Patmos to some strange fishes. The hymn-singing would be interrupted by the boiling of a kettle on the fire and cutting up of loaves of bread spread with plenty of jam, and serious talk or chaff would carry the party on till late in the evening.

Aurelia was able to make any social gathering she inaugurated successful, enjoying it so much herself that every-one else did; she never minded being laughed with or at, was never tired, and was always good-tempered. There were endless discussions with the students, some quite serious, about her religion : did she believe everything or nothing ?

" Of course; I not only believe, I know," she would assure them, and in saying that she was sincere. She had no idea of logic or any understanding of the dogma of Christianity or of any of the great religions, reacting entirely to emotional impulse, and the latest impulse would possess her completely for the time being to the exclusion of previous ones. At one time she was a Baptist; I can be sure of this because she took me to the Caledonian Baths, which were engaged for the ceremony of her total immersion.

We stood on the edge of this grey-green basin of water, Aurelia robed in a modest long bathing-gown, accompanied by a small man in a semi-clerical outfit and knee-high rubber boots, who put his arm behind her back and said, " Place your hand, sister, on my shoulder." When Aurelia, who was stout and well-muscled, flung her arm round his neck at the critical moment, he lost his balance, and total immersion came to them both. Aurelia bobbed up bubbling with laughter, and the solemn atmosphere was shattered, for we, too, were thoroughly wetted and were shaking out our hats and coats. The little man showed no Christian spirit of forgiveness, for he was extremely cross as he crawled out on all fours, nor did he leave any blessing behind him as he went muttering and dripping into the nearest cubicle. After swimming round the bath and getting out, Aurelia only commented, " Well, that was a funny baptism."

She was happy with her circle of art students, and had several to stay with us when we went to her boarding-house on the South Coast for vacations. There, too, she threw the glamour of enjoyment over our holidays. Many of the students would bathe and sketch, and sometimes go for moonlight walks along the cliffs, catching fire-flies, which they put into their hair and hers.

On these holidays it fell to me to see to the catering and to maintain some kind of order in the house. On our return to London, Tonks would enquire what Aurelia had been up to, for outside his teaching sphere he was amused by her, and would comment, " Well, anyhow, you should welcome having the medieval luxury of keeping a jester in the home."

Chapter Nine

BRITISH COLUMBIA

AFTER attending the Slade School for only a short time
Aurelia gave up the attempt at learning to draw. Her
son Herbert and I attended regularly, but our background
in the Fitzroy Street house was casual and uncomfortable,
as indeed was living anywhere with Aurelia. In contrast,
my Aunt Louise Berens' house in Eaton Square was for me
a refuge where I found a kind welcome, in orderly and
luxurious surroundings.

No three sisters could be more different in looks and
character than Louise, Aurelia, and Katherine, my mother.
In the 'nineties, when it was the fashion to call people " professional beauties ", Louise was regarded as being in that
class. She was middle-aged when I knew her, but still
beautiful, as indeed she remained to the end of her life. As
well as being clever and enterprising, she was one of the
kindest people I have ever known. My Aunt Louise had
taken no notice of me when as a child I was living in Ireland,
merely regarding me as one of " Kate's vipers ", but after
we met in London we became lifelong friends.

One evening during my second session at the Slade, she
startled me by saying, " I am thinking of going to America
and British Columbia for some months."

" Why do you want to go there ? " I exclaimed.

" Why not ? " she answered. " Unimaginative of you
to be so surprised. I know Europe, Egypt, and Tangier so
well, I want to see new, young countries. I have been
reading about British Columbia; it sounds interesting and
lovely; and now there is all this excitement about the
Klondike gold rush."

Some days later I got a telegram saying, " Everything

arranged about journey to America. Starting next week. Shall be away for about six months. Would you care to come with me? Should like to have you, and of course all expenses paid."

The suggestion put my mind in a turmoil. On the one hand, what an exciting adventure, and with someone I liked so much; and, on the other, ought I to give up the training I had desired so ardently?

I went to the Slade, unable to decide. Meeting Professor Tonks on the stairs, without pausing to think, I blurted out, " Oh, please advise me; do you think I ought to go to America? "

Tonks stood quite still and said nothing for some seconds, and I realized how imbecile my question must have sounded; then he remarked, " How should I know if you ought to go to America? "

" Because I cannot feel sure if I ought to give up my work here and travel with my aunt for six months."

He smiled, saying, " So she's off to upset the other side of the world, is she? "

I explained that it was another and quite different aunt; then he became helpful and serious, ending by saying, " I hold that an art training is largely a training for life, so that fresh experience, seeing new lands and new points of view have much value, so my answer is, yes, go to America."

A week later we were on the liner *Lusitania*. How my life does change! I felt; it seems to go suddenly from one extreme to another. So short a time ago I thought of little except of how to express the human form, and had Aurelia's muddled home as a background; now here I was with waiters and stewards rushing about, crowds everywhere, music playing, bugles sounding, lavish tasteless decoration all round, and much time spent in trying to eat quantities of food.

We could spend the daylight hours playing games or

listening to an American reading " Uncle Remus ".   In the
evening we were expected to attend dances, concerts, or
lectures, and finally on the last night sing " Auld Lang Syne "
while crossing hands with complete strangers.

Our stay in New York remains a confused blur in my
mind.   My aunt had many friends, who were so kind and
hospitable they made us feel we would be welcome to spend
the rest of our lives in their homes; but we both wanted to
get away from this tiring, exciting town, where from luncheon time till the small hours we were taken from place to
place.   In one super-magnificent mansion I observed some
little gilt chairs with box-like seats made of glass, through
which you could see jewel-framed miniatures and gold
ornaments.   I pictured a heavy guest sitting on one of these
chairs and finding his behind suddenly encrusted with
splintered glass, diamonds, pearls, and filigree gold.

I also remember with gratitude finding in my bedroom a
large bunch of red roses with stems eighteen inches long,
with a card attached on which was written, " From one
American in the name of many others who have seen and
loved Killarney."

After a final party we got away to Montreal, breaking the
journey to see the Niagara Falls.   There we behaved as
tourists should, and allowed the determined attendant to
dress us in mackintoshes and hand us over to a relentless
guide, who insisted upon our being photographed, once
under a wall of water and again emerging through a mist of
spray.   The resulting pictures made us both look slightly
cretinous, but the guide, after prolonged examination,
remarked, " Not as stoopefied as some."

We reached Montreal in bitter cold weather, and my dear
aunt immediately fitted us both out in raccoon fur coats, in
which we looked like the native bears, and were just as well
protected.

We had an introduction to Mr. Hosmer, the head of the

Cable Company, and made friends with him and with other people with whom we had a link, and as usual met with much kindness and hospitality.

Montreal was our starting point for the long journey across Canada, and when we left we were seen off with flowers, fruit, and chocolates, and given books of cable franks. The train felt like a temporary home, going slowly over that vast prairie, pausing every evening for twenty minutes to allow us to take exercise on the platform and see a rather theatrical Red Indian—or someone dressed like one —trying to sell souvenirs. The approach to the Rocky Mountains was inspiring after days of watching waving grass and flat plains, and I was allowed to travel over the pass in the cab of the engine-driver, who told me all the wonders of this line and the stupendous difficulties overcome in crossing so great a range of mountains. As one looked down the immense ravines below us, these difficulties were not hard to imagine.

On reaching British Columbia we left this train in order to see more of that most attractive country, and also to meet an old friend of my aunt's, who, as the head of a large electrical engineering scheme, was supervising the construction of a dam. First we had to take a sleigh and drive to a lake, a great sheet of water where we picked up a paddle-boat which went chuffing along from one primitive landing-place to another. Occasionally there would be a solitary passenger to take on board; more often a barrel of something, or a package to be picked up. The lake was surrounded with snow mountains, and pine-trees came down to the water's edge; it was a lovely scene, silent and empty, and everything sparkled like a frosted Christmas card.

Towards evening we came to a slightly larger landing-place, from which a little mountain train was to take us up to the camp. It was a funny-looking little train; the engine was very small and could draw only two carriages, one open like a cattle-truck, and the other, which we were to occupy, upholstered in faded red plush. We were told this train had been bought second-hand in three separate lots and that our carriage had been made originally for Brigham Young's wives. The engine would puff along for a few miles and then stop to be fed with wood, until finally it stopped intentionally for us to get out. It was a brilliant, moonlit night, and we could hear the rushing river near by and the sighing of the wind in the pine-trees. Half a dozen men were waiting for us, and helped us to scramble on to the rough verge.

The little train was puffing away when suddenly there was a shout, "Where the devil is he?" It appeared that a Chinese cook who had been engaged to cook for the two invading guests had been seen to get out of the rear carriage, but perhaps had not liked the look of this wild country, for while we were shaking hands he must have slipped back again and gone away in the train. The men thought his loss a catastrophe, for they had made great preparations for us, and now the most important part was missing, but we tried to make them understand how little we cared.

We spent ten wonderful days at the camp. The country was lovely, the sun shone, and we picnicked out of doors. I went about on snowshoes, often with a Scottish engineer, a sad man who told me tales of his hard life here. He was surveying the area, and one day, when taking a sight, he clutched my arm, saying, "Quiet—look!" and just ahead of us was a big brown bear with a baby bear at her side.

"Don't move," he whispered. "I won't be long getting my rifle. She won't hurt you, but if you move she'll take her cub away."

The bear heard him as he went quickly down the hill, and, standing up on her hind legs and extending her front paw, she drew her baby to her side. It was such a maternal gesture, so like a fond human mother putting her arms round her child, that it seemed murder to shoot either of them, and though rather frightened to do so, I moved, and immediately the bear shuffled off, heading the baby in front of her. The engineer was disappointed, and said in his pessimistic way, " My luck always is out. I'd have made a fine rug of the old one, and the young one would have been tender eating."

Our next stay was at a mining camp, where we put up at a primitive hotel, surrounded by shacks and huts, with snow mountains all around. Escorted by friendly guides, I went down mines, saw others now disused, their machinery rusting, and heard all the talk of the various assays of ore from the shafts that were being worked. The mining business seemed dishonest : a prospectus would be sent out with glowing accounts of the profits which might be expected from some mine which the men on the spot knew had no future, while some of the good ones were not put on the market, but held by groups in the know. To me it was a new adventure, and full of excitement. Standing in a rough crate and holding on to a rope, I went down a mine, and was then allowed to work a compressed-air drill. The rock I cut was collected, and later on I was given a pin-point of gold and told I had mined it, which I doubted, but pretended to believe.

When I was in Montreal I made especial friends with Mr. Hosmer, the head of the Canadian Cable Company; before leaving he gave me several books of franks, to use for sending cable messages free of cost, and said, " I want to know all you are doing on your travels." When staying at the great dam I used one of these franks to tell Mr. Hosmer what the engineers thought about it, and its working capacity; he answered asking other questions and adding, " When you get to the gold mines let me know anything you hear about them ", so I used more of my franks to tell him all the news that I had picked up, even repeating some

of the current jokes. Then I got a letter from him headed
" Business ", the gist of which was that after my aunt's
return to England he was prepared to offer me a post to stay
in Canada, to act as his personal agent, and to report to him
all the information I could gather about the development of
certain projects he was interested in. The salary, and commission on profits he made with my assistance, seemed to me
very large.

Once again my mind was in a turmoil.

All my life the lack of money had haunted me. As a
child I believed my poor father's cry that we would " all
be in the workhouse soon ", and was terrified at the idea.
Since I had left home my precarious earnings and my
allowance of twenty pounds a year kept me perpetually on
the brink of a financial abyss. Now if I liked I could earn a
lot of money and save most of it. With this in my mind I
hurried to show my aunt the letter. After reading it, she
looked at me and said, " You can't possibly do anything of
the kind; he shouldn't have asked you. Don't you see
that it is all very well for you to run about with a lot of
young men and gain their confidence, with my eye always
upon you, but it would be quite another thing to do this as a
commercial business once you were alone ? No, my dear,
you must refuse such a post," and so I did.

It was the time of the great Klondike boom, and on
leaving the mining camp we went to Victoria, where we had
introductions and where everyone was in a state of wild
excitement about this discovery of gold. After travelling
in lands of snow it felt like coming to the west coast of
Ireland, the air being mild and soft, though the climate was
actually much better, having far less rain and being less
relaxing. On seeing Esquimalt we were so enchanted with
that lovely coast that we took a small furnished house close
to the shore.

To my dear Aunt Louise, accustomed to living in a large,

well-staffed London house, it was a comic relief to find our one marvellous Chinese servant able to buy our provisions, cook admirably, keep the house spotless, wait at table, dig the garden, mow the lawn, do all our laundry, move quite silently, look immaculately clean himself, and sleep on a straw mat in a shed outside.

" But I must have someone whose time I can waste," she exclaimed.

Suggesting the idea to Sing was difficult, and he was offended.

" The Missis not satisfied with how I do ? " he asked gravely.

" Yes, quite satisfied," we assured him.

" I have not enough to do. Why, then, another ? "

The question sounded very reasonable, so we tried to make him understand we only wanted a boy—someone he could train and whom we could use for messages.

I think he thought us wanting in common sense, but, with his unfailing good manners, he only said :

" Ladies want boy, me get."

Ching, the boy, was untrained and very young, and in awe only of Sing. With us he would shout with laughter at the smallest joke and, squatting on the floor, would rock himself in admiration of flowers which he produced in quantities. We thought the cost of these went into the household accounts, and only knew better when a guest at dinner, looking at the lavish display on our table, said without resentment, " Ah, there are my tulips."

Ching, who had been sent with our note of invitation, had cleared her garden while waiting for the answer.

" They will do it before they are trained," she explained. " He feels he has done you a good turn, but I daresay your head man will beat him."

" Quite right, too," my aunt agreed.

One day we returned a call on a stout and highly refined

lady who, after preliminaries, said, " I hear you have got my late cook; he behaved very badly to me."

" We find him excellent."

" No doubt you do, but he left me without a word, and when I went into my kitchen, naturally expecting to see him there, I found an inferior creature in his place and something written on the wall."

" What was written ? "

" I'm sure I don't know, but I'll show you if you like."

It was written in beautiful Chinese characters down one side of the wall in scarlet, and looked like a decorative banner.

I asked Sing about it, and found him unresponsive, but on being pressed he said, " I write lady character."

" Do tell me what it was."

At last Sing said with his quiet smile, " I write, ' Woman she talk too much; she pay too little ' ! "

" Did you send the man she found there after you had gone ? "

" I honourable man. I not leave lady lurching, but send less good man as me."

He was an honourable man, and served us with perfect dignity.

We had an American lawyer friend with whom we went as far north as we could to see the start for Klondike. On this high ground snow was deep, and sleighs were piled high with provisions for the terrible journey. The men looked bulky in their thick, rough clothing, and there were many teams of dogs—ten or twelve, harnessed in pairs, all eager for their work. One man told us a lot about these husky dogs, saying they had characters as varied as men.

" Now look, ladies. This fellow is my leader—the cleverest dog I ever had : he never makes a mistake. But do you think he'll put up with another taking his place ? You watch out ! "

He harnessed the leader fourth place in the sleigh, and then put another dog ahead of him. Immediately it was as if a fiend had entered the displaced leader, who struggled to get at his usurper, snapping his foaming jaws, his eyes bloodshot, his hair on end, and his limbs trembling with strain. When replaced in his rightful position he lay down exhausted.

His owner brought him a piece of dried fish, patted him and soothed him and said, " You see, he can be as jealous as any woman, and he'd have murdered that other one if he could have got at him."

We were told many stories of the hardships of the great trek northward. Financial success seemed to come to those who did some essential work and didn't try to wash for gold. One man was said to have made a fortune by soldering, receiving a sovereign's weight of gold for every kettle and pot he mended. Another man did as well with a mending outfit, taking up needles and coarse thread, buttons and patching material, and charging so much pure gold for each job. Yet another took up whisky and sold it by the tea-spoonful, but got drunk himself, and his whisky and his profits vanished. In those pioneering days the roughest type had the best chance of surviving the hardships, the climate, and the fights.

Coming back with gold, though many failed to do so through theft and violence, they usually spent it in wild orgies. One man, having hired a special train and a brass band to go back to his home town in splendour, had spent his fortune when he got there.

We left British Columbia quite sad at heart, and came home by way of Seattle, Chicago, and Quebec, landing at Liverpool in fog under a grey sky, but our memories were many and varied, perhaps the happiest being of our toy house on Esquimalt Bay, a setting for Sing's trim figure in his clean white suit, never hurrying, yet accomplishing everything.

Chapter Ten

MARRIAGE

MY father died, aged eighty, while I was in America, so on my return I thought I ought to go and see my mother. She had left Cahirnane and taken a house in Dublin immediately opposite a church which held High Church services. On seeing what she had chosen, when free to go anywhere she liked, I was appalled. This ugly, expensive, semi-detached house, with its run of cats' garden at the back, instead of Cahirnane! I did not care for living at Cahirnane myself, but it had its dignity, its seclusion, its extensive lands, and its beautiful views and trees.

She chose and liked this house on a street, with its iron steps leading up to a hall door, its upper half made of coloured glass in a geometrical pattern, that led into a passage hall.

My mother, after this long interval, seemed as alien from me in thought as her house was from my idea of a pleasant dwelling. I saw that she was too self-centred even to see that it was odd that she should ask me nothing about my American tour, my work at the Slade, or my life with Aurelia. She talked exclusively of "the Parish", its activities, its choir, and, above all, its vicar.

As she was not interested in anything I had done, I told her nothing of all that had happened to me. On the other hand, I was not interested in "the Parish" and had never seen the vicar, but she talked of nothing else. She seemed in better health and happier, and not so difficult in temper. When she said with obvious reluctance, "Do you perhaps want to live here now?" I could answer without any doubt in my mind, "No, I only wanted to see you before going back to London."

I did go back to Fitzroy Street. I had been away for the best part of a year, I had seen a great deal and had lived in luxury, except at the camps where I found so much to interest me; my Aunt Louise and I had associated with rich, hospitable Americans, and we always stayed at the best hotels. After all this I found it hard to adjust myself to the casual discomfort of living with Aurelia. I went back to work at the Slade, and found most of my friends had left; but even there I could not quite recover my old enthusiasm.

For about three years before going to America I had seen a great deal of Herbert Everett, and we had become attached to one another. He was a good companion, and we enjoyed going off together on a double bicycle, I sitting on the back seat, while he guided it through the London traffic from the front. Once out in the country no one could be more appreciative than he was of the passing scene; we would watch the clouds as they swept across the sky and the shadows they threw on the earth, and would compare such an effect with the work of old English landscape-painters. To enjoy such things together may seem a trivial bond, but I have found seeing things that are loved in harmony with another person, whether it be a distant view or a fine work of art, is a sound basis for friendship, and I have little in common with those who care nothing for such things.

Herbert was thought to be one of the most promising students at the Slade; this was in part owing to his having previously worked with a painter trained in Paris, where they taught the technical handling of oil paint, which was not done at the Slade. Mr. Steer, who was the professor responsible for the life class, was an inarticulate person who would come slowly into the room, stand looking at a canvas and move on without making any comment, leaving the owner uncertain whether he had thought the work needed no correction or was too bad to bother with. After a time he would sit down and look in silence at some student's effort, saying little or nothing, and then would take up a brush and do some painting on its canvas with real mastery.

Mr. Steer did, however, speak of Herbert's early landscapes as being full of promise. Tonks thought them mature and excellent. When therefore I returned to Fitzroy Street, and we had resumed our old relationship, I transferred to Herbert my personal ambition regarding work, and never doubted his having a great future. That hope was not fulfilled. My own belief is that he was by temperament akin to the masters of the eighteenth century, some of his early sketches having something of their quality, and his enthusiasm was for Crome, Turner, and the watercolourists of the Norwich School and suchlike. Living in an age when new and subversive ideas were sweeping over the world of art, he forsook his own bent and tried to adjust his work to current thought.

But full of confidence in the future as we both were at that time, we soon decided to get married. I made one condition : I was prepared to have very little money at first, but we must be free of liability towards Aurelia.

Solicitors were consulted, her tangled finances examined, and the remaining trust funds divided between her and her son, securing her just sufficient to live on, or so we believed.

I wrote to my mother to tell her about my plans; she answered, asking me if I wished to be married from her house, in which case she would entertain the Parish and also give me a trousseau; or, if I preferred to be quietly married in London, she would send me a hundred pounds. I chose the money, and with it bought some of the family silver from Aurelia and some necessary comforts for our rooms in Fitzroy Street. We meant to have the big room as our sitting-room, with an adjoining bedroom, and a very small kitchen.

We were to be married privately in a near-by church. I

wore a plain coat and skirt, but Aurelia turned up in a tight bright blue dress that made her look stouter than ever; she had gay beads round her neck, and wore a blue hat, on which she had pinned something shiny which looked like rather battered decorations left over from a Christmas tree.

Walking on our way to the church, we met a tiny little man, whom Aurelia greeted warmly, asking him if he still worked for the Salvation Army; on his saying that he surely did, Aurelia cried, " Then of course you must come and see these two being married."

The little man edged away and protested that he " reely couldn't " and indicated his shabby clothes, but Aurelia swept his excuses away, urging, " Don't you see, you have been guided to meet us on this particular day, at this particular hour, when I haven't seen you for such ages, so of course you are meant to come and pray for them both." The little man succumbed and, murmuring, " The Lord be praised," followed us into the church.

No one can go through their own marriage service without emotion, but my emotion was turned to panic on coming out behind Aurelia after the short ceremony. She was standing on the steps beaming at the onlookers who had collected in the street, looking enormous in her bright blue dress beside the little man in his bowler hat. Then I heard a wheezy voice say, " Gord bless you, deary," and in Aurelia's charming, ringing tones the answer, " And God bless you all, dear people."

I clutched Herbert's arm and whispered, " There'll be a crowd here in a minute, and they'll start a prayer meeting; do let's slip away quickly."

As we went we heard a man's Cockney voice call out, " Best of luck, Ma, for yer unimoon; look out, though, as you don't step on 'im, and not know you done it."

Chapter Eleven

HONEYMOON AT SEA

IN the spring Herbert and I decided upon a plan which we called the Honeymoon Journey, little knowing how ironic the name was to turn out.

Herbert loved the sea, and believed he would do good work making a voyage in a sailing-ship. I was sure he could, and thought the idea exciting, so we arranged for a passage to Australia on a 700-ton barque.

I took with me a number of old-fashioned books, thinking that they would fill the many gaps in my education and that I should have plenty of time to master them. I also provided two large sacks of onions, with vague ideas of averting scurvy, a sack of wholemeal flour, a kettle and spirit lamp, and plenty of tea. In addition, not realizing what sea-water and exposure would do to them, I took materials to make large embroidered curtains.

We went on board on a fine evening in early June, and a tug took us down the river, past barges and ships, and past Greenwich, looking like an eighteenth-century print in a golden mist and backed by stately trees. At that point a black cat, feeling the call of the land, jumped and swam for it. Wise cat! At dusk, clear of the land, this tug cast off, and shouts of farewell were drowned in the rattle of the sheets as sails were hoisted and our small barque gently heeled over to the pull of the wind. Our journey had begun. We were to have one hundred and seventeen days of it with no possible hope of escape, no possibility of acquiring anything beyond what we had—not so much as a postage stamp—and with no sight of land but for a distant view of Tristan da Cunha, looking no larger than a bee's wing on the horizon. Variety we had, but it came from the elements: storm, hurricane, rain—tropical or merely enveloping and penetrating—cold, heat, and calm, which, in an unfortunate moment, I said I liked. The utter horror with which this avowal was received was genuine, and when we stuck for a week, helpless and motionless, in the neighbourhood of the Equator, in an atmosphere like hot porridge, I was not allowed to forget my expressed liking.

I had walked on to the ship carrying my kettle and spirit lamp, both of which the captain removed, saying, " On my ship no lamps or lights are allowed."

" What do you do when it gets dark ? "

" Sit in it or go to bed."

And so it turned out. We had our first meal with the captain and his wife, who was the only individual other than the crew on the ship. Both were elderly Liverpool people, and were not a nice couple. He had started before the mast, and was surly and gross; she was of the same type, and although she had voyaged in her husband's tramps to various parts of the world, she knew nothing but the quality of the fare at the nearest eating-house. Her large, red face would expand when speaking of chops and steaks and liver.

The food that first day, served by a barefooted boy, was just edible, but the mate, who came in as soon as the captain had finished, explained, " It's all first rate now, but wait till you get the condemned stuff. The Old Man puts the all right in front for the Inspector to see, and the rest he gets on the cheap and makes his bit. You wait; you'll find out soon enough."

I liked the mate, who was a middle-aged, small, dark working-class man with a master's ticket, very efficient, having to serve for his living under an old man for whom he had the utmost contempt.

" Driving his ship on dead reckoning, the old blighter ! Half the time he's out on her position," he would explain.

The mate amused himself by trying to frighten me.

" She's a rotten old tub anyway, and you know he's out to lose her, for she's been through her third survey, and the owners reckon the insurance would pay them better than selling her abroad."

" Really ? How odd ! "

" He's done it before for them, and that's why they employ him. He got his ticket suspended over that other one, and was a year ashore. He put her down nice and handy on a low reef off Tasmania, where he and the crew could get away while she broke up slowly."

Whether the ship was really destined to this end I cannot say, but on the voyage subsequent to ours, under the same captain, she was lost with all hands off the coast of Tasmania. Evidently the spot was not so handy.

I had not long to wait before verifying the mate's warning about the food. It was revolting. The large tin of tea brought in at breakfast was a curious metallic black colour and tasted as I should imagine cuttle-fish ink must taste. As it was made at five in the morning and served at eight, the pot seemed able to add its own tinny flavour. When I asked for hot water, I sensed for the first time the old woman's antagonistic feelings towards me, for she snorted and said something that sounded like " la-di-da ". Bacon, swimming with grease, was brought in, and Herbert whispered :

" I wouldn't take it; it's very rank."

I had no wish to, and had a slice of bread and took some butter which suggested rancid cheese and drains. It was worse than anything I had ever dreamed of, and I hurried away to spit it out and rinse my mouth. When I returned, a dish called " scouch " was on the table, which looked like short bits of rope and gristle swimming in greasy water. I never tried it, the smell was enough. The captain, who had no inhibitions, took a large helping, crumbled bread into it, poured fat bacon over it and scattered on top enough pepper

D   [97]

to grow seeds in. No doubt this, helped by large flicks of mustard, was a successful disguise of decay.

The other meals were of the same character, the dishes having names I had not heard before. "Strike-me-blind" was a rice pudding of a quality more suitable for ammunition than for eating. "Dogsbody" was a pale, greasy suet with bits of high meat inserted. "Crackerjack" was ship's biscuits, freely seasoned with weevils, pounded in a canvas bag with a belaying-pin and soaked with hot water and pea-flour. "Slathery Jack" was a mould of such glue-like consistency that once it was bitten into, one's teeth couldn't part. The mate ate little and abused the food, but the captain and his wife ate with gluttony and no manners. I gave up the contest, and throughout those months lived on a little tinned milk and hot water, wholemeal bread and boiled onions, and occasionally some burnt and lumpy porridge.

Having vaguely thought of my voyage to America when agreeing to this one, I found the contrast painful. We may to-day, under rationing, think a good deal about food, but when it comes to the edge of hunger and the monotony of a daily onion and dry bread, food, despite one's effort to forget about it, becomes an obsession. Thinking of apples made one's mouth water too much, and once, longing for tea and scones and real butter and jam, I found myself on the verge of tears. One can be beautifully indifferent in times of plenty, but if anyone thinks himself above such cravings, let him try real austerity.

There were two bunks in my cabin, one narrow with high sides like a coffin, and the upper one wider, with no sides, like a large tea-tray, and unsafe in heavy weather. In the lower bunk not only was it difficult to bend one's knees or avoid being bruised, but there was a rat which I called Richard, who gnawed and gnawed, close to my neck, and then I could hear him scurry down the side to start near my toes. I begged the mate to get rid of him, but he said he couldn't, adding :

" He'll get out all right, and if you're asleep, he'll eat the soles of your feet."

He lent me a sheath-knife, but I never used it on Richard; when he sounded too near I climbed to the tea-tray, risking being flung to the floor. To add to this, when the ship rolled there was a frightening banging in the hold, then for a few seconds a rumble like distant thunder, and then thud against the side, pause, rumble and thud again. The mate explained that this was an agricultural machine that had broken loose in the hold.

" The Old Man won't let me try to fix it, and perhaps I couldn't; there's a lot of cargo down there, as like as not she'll get a hole stove in her side. Christ ! I'll be glad to get out of this death-trap."

Three weeks out we ran into heavy weather, and the wind rose and went shrieking through the rigging. The Old Man was in his cabin. It was the mate's watch, and he was very efficient, turning out all the crew, giving sharp orders, and himself going aloft like a cat, furling sails blown stiff as metal till we had only one small sail left. Running past me as I clung to the rail, he shouted, " You must be lashed if you want to stay here. We'll be taking in seas any moment, and you'll be swept away like a cork."

I should have been had he not lashed me under a weather cloth, for towards dusk the sea rose even higher, and our little ship would at one moment seem engulfed in a seething valley, dark and violent, and would appear in that vortex almost helpless to climb the approaching foam-crested mountain. Nor could she completely, for at one moment she and the sea would seem one as the crest of that mountain swept over her, leaving the deck awash and the scuppers streaming. Then she would shudder and slide down again into the dark valley to face the oncoming giant mountain once more.   There was a bang from aloft, and our sail flew from the ship looking, for the few seconds we could see it, like a child's pocket handkerchief—a little white square against the cloud-torn sky.

The Old Man was on deck now.   " Get below ! " he ordered as he passed me.

Sheets broke loose and went cracking like whips, wood splintered and the companion door was wrenched off.   The mate found time to free me.

" Anything may go in this gale.   Wait till just before she rises to the next wave, then get across on your knees and hold on where you can."

That night I lay in the coffin bunk while the ship rolled and groaned.   Sleep was impossible, for though everything was secured in the cabin, something was at intervals crashing and rolling back and forth.   In the hold the rumbling and banging went on, and to stay in that narrow bunk became intolerable.   Though no lights were allowed, I knew every inch of my surroundings, and clinging to anything I could hold on to, I went towards the stern of the ship on the level with my cabin and sat on the floor, leaning against timber.

Could the small vessel survive this nightmare struggle ? She took on personality, and through the uproar of strains and bangs seemed to say, " This fight is too much for me. I am old, I have fought the sea for more years than you have lived.   My strength is past."

I ceased to think of the ship, and my thoughts turned inwards on myself.   What was I doing in this alien and horrible place, in this waste of water ?   What folly brought me here ?   Was it just to help Herbert to paint—the one thing he had not done and never did on that voyage ?   Or was it personal vanity that made me adventure something unusual that other people hadn't done ?   Was it vanity that made me dream of educating myself while in truth I hated those heavy books full of conflicts and tortures and only wanted some easy reading to help me to forget my present plight? Was it vanity that made me bring admirable necessary foods and none of the nice, sweet things for which now I craved? I felt myself to be a perfect self-deluded fool, and there was no escape: there was nothing left but endurance and courage; and for how long? Many weeks certainly; possibly months, and in sheer misery, cold and bruised, I wept there in the dark, leaning against the shuddering side of the ship. I wept as I had not done for years and, eased somehow by that breakdown, I staggered back to my coffin bed and slept.

Days passed, weeks passed, and the sea grew calm, the weather hot, but dull and sunless. All sails were set, but they hung lifeless.

"We're not making two knots," the mate grumbled. "We may be stuck round here any old time."

"Whereabouts are we?"

"Bothered if I can tell you. Something like twenty to fifty miles from the Equator, but I haven't been able to shoot the sun these days. See if you can get anything out of the Old Man."

All I got was a grunt and the news that we were fifty miles farther from Hobart than we had been a week earlier.

Interminable days passed, and as I came on deck one morning everything was wet as in a steam bath. The heat was awful, there was no visibility beyond a few yards of oily, porridge-coloured sea, fading into a porridge-coloured sky, and we lay inert, as in some nightmare lotus-land. The ship swayed back and forth, very slowly responding to an invisible ground-swell, when suddenly the air was torn by our fog horn, and fainter came an answering hoot. Another ship—a thing we hadn't seen since we left England—looking perilously close, smoke pouring from her funnels as she sheered away.   Gazing up at her huge bulk and tall sides, we realized our insignificance—a mere minnow compared to this leviathan.

" Wasn't she enormous ! "

" Just a tramp of six or eight thousand tons; remember we are only seven hundred."

In this heat I felt ill and asked to have my food, such as I could eat, on deck.   The old woman was rude about it, as she often was, asking such questions as :

" How do you gut a herring ? "

" I never have," I would answer.

Or, " Which end would you begin skinning a rabbit ? "

" I have never tried at either end."

" I suppose your lady's maid does it ? "

" Lady's maids wouldn't either."

And she would mutter something about " such airs ".

When I asked the mate why she was so unpleasant to me, he burst out laughing, saying, " It's as good as a play to watch you.   You keep being polite whatever she says and it makes her mad.   We had a Lancashire woman on the last trip, and they'd slang each other every day and make it up every night.   That's what she looks for."

One day the old captain came to my side and said, " Not feeling well, I hear."

" It's only the heat."

" I'll send you a black draught."

" Don't trouble; I shouldn't take it."

" But I order it."

" I'm sorry, but I shouldn't take it in any case."

He stumped off and returned with a book.

" Here, sign there."

He put his large thumb on the page on which was written, " Passenger refuses drugs at captain's orders."

" Why should I sign that ? "

" Because if we bury you at sea I'm cleared."

I signed.

Life would have been easier if this old man had been less inhuman. He would not allow us to speak to any of the crew or go fore or aft on the deck, making us stick to our own small strip. I begged him to let me cook, for I could have made reasonably good milk-puddings with tinned milk, but he got angry and said on no account was I to go into the galley. The old cook, whom everyone called Abraham, was a biblical figure with white hair and beard and a thin, mahogany-coloured body, and wore ragged blue dungaree trousers and nothing else. He had come aboard, with hair and beard trimmed and dyed black, as an A.B. aged fifty, but he was nearer seventy-five, and quite useless on deck, so he was made cook, though he had never cooked before. I am writing of a ship as I knew it fifty years ago, when the crew lived in appalling conditions and came near to starvation.

At last a faint breeze filled the sails and we moved, and week by week it strengthened until at last we picked up the trade winds. What a change! The ship heeled over and cut through blue water, the sails bellied out in the sunlight, flying-fish flashed around, and with widespread wings albatross and mollyhawks of dazzling white sailed by, diving to water level to pick up scraps thrown overboard and rising with scarcely a movement of their great wings to float, apparently without volition, in the sparkling air.

We were leaning over the rail watching porpoises playing round the bows and seeing curious lilac-coloured jelly-fish floating past, when I looked up at our sails towering against the sky, and at once recalled a strange incident that happened years earlier, when I was sixteen. The wife of one of our tenants was believed to be a witch. She was an old woman with grey hair and bare feet and lived in a hovel on Lochetane bog, where we went to see her.

" We want you to tell our fortunes," we began.

" Whist now, it may be stockings you'll want me to be knitting; come in, then."

We went into the dark, earth-floored cabin.

" I wouldn't have you talking abroad of fortunes; 'twould bring trouble on me."

She drove out some chickens and shut the door; the only light came from a very small square window.

" Will I look in the crystal ball for ye ? "

She sat on a low stool and put a clear-glass globe about as large as a cricket ball in front of her on another stool, holding her hands round it without touching it, and told us to stand one at a time behind her.   My eldest sister went first.   The old woman swayed slowly backward and forward.

" The glass is dark," she murmured.   " I can see nothing, 'tis all a great darkness."   She turned to us.   " Wisha, that's nothing; 'tis often that way."

That sister died young.

" Now let the other one stand in her place."

The witch of Lochetane spoke.   " The light is coming. I see great journeyings for you." (Hopeless, I thought; I am chained here.)   " Round and round this world you will be going, and I see water.   Oh, glory be, there's the grand yacht—the finest yacht ever I see, and you leaning over the side with a fine big gentleman.   Oh, she's a great ship and all, and white sails up to the blue sky, and big white birds flying round.   Would you see it yourself ? "

I looked over her shoulder, but all I could see was a milky mist which dissolved quickly, leaving a clear crystal ball.

" 'Tis gone," the old woman said; " but I'll tell you what it is.   You'll get married to a grand rich gentleman and he owning a great yacht.   It's travel the world with him you will."

The deduction was quite wrong, but not the vision, for I was seeing it in actual fact.

Now it was October, and we were near the end of our journey, and one marvellous day we saw the land! I felt just like a Victorian heroine about to swoon, for it was the heavenly vision : there were trees—green trees—a gate, a cow. No, I was too excited to swoon; I was nearer hysterics. Herbert took it more calmly, for fundamentally he liked the sea, and I didn't, which in the majority is one of the differences between men and women.

We reached Hobart one hundred and seventeen days after leaving England, and I waved farewell to that ship, hoping never to see her again. But the next day, discovering that a rug had been left on board, we went back, and found the captain bargaining with a man from shore over a quantity of tinned foods, galantines, tongues, sardines, jam, and fruit; all, no doubt, sent by the owners for us, for we had paid a good price for our passage. That unpleasant old man by withholding these things was again making his bit.

From Hobart we went to Sydney on a luxury liner. The food was superb; the weather was very rough, and other passengers faded away, so we sat alone at one table, and the officers at another. As we ate our way through the menu from soup via lobster to the ices, we heard a whisper, " They seem hungry." When we explained that we had just come off a sailing-ship the ice was broken and they couldn't do enough for us. We sat with them late into the night, telling and hearing stories of the sea.

Chapter Twelve

AURELIA AGAIN

WE arrived back in England after a year's absence, having spent several months in Australia, where we had rented an attractive little house on Lavender Bay in Sydney harbour. We interviewed the owners, a nice young couple, and asked what we could do about getting a servant.

"Would you take a man and his wife if they did everything for you and kept the garden?"

"Certainly, if they are not too expensive. Do you know of suitable people?"

Yes, they did, and, naming a very modest sum, asked if it was too much. It was happily settled that we should come in at once, and when we arrived this pretty young woman brought in our tea.

"We mustn't bother you," I exclaimed.

"You see, Tom and I are the suitable couple," she replied, laughing. "You don't want all the rooms, and we can look after you perfectly."

So they did, and we became good friends. Our rent, which we paid three months in advance, was immediately spent by this enterprising pair in hiring an open-air sports stadium for forty nights and organizing bicycle races, boxing bouts, gymkhanas, shadow plays and all kinds of entertainments.

"If every night plans out well we shall be quite rich," they said.

"But suppose it rains?"

"Rain! Of course it won't rain for months."

It never did, and the ceaseless sunshine remains my special memory of those hot months. It affected the atmosphere: everything was edge clear and there was no mystery in that charming landscape of islands, bays, and woods; no greys and half tones, and the people whom I met seemed imbued with that atmosphere. Doubts, whether of themselves or their country, like the mists in the landscape, were not there; they were sure of themselves, carefree, and not introspective.

We came home in a liner, pausing for a few hours at Capetown.

We were surprised to find when we settled into our rooms that Aurelia had let her cellars and was living at the back of a shop she had taken near by. She gave evasive answers to our questions, and it was always difficult to get any clear statement of fact out of her. At last she burst out, " I want you to lend me one hundred and fifty pounds for quite a short time."

That was a large sum for us, and we told her she ought not to ask for it, as she had as much to live on as we had.

Then she started talking of other things, of some fine chandeliers she knew of that might be worth five hundred pounds, and as she stood up to go she said, " I may as well tell you I haven't an income now, but if you will lend me what I asked you I shall be all right."

Finally we extracted the truth : she had disposed of her life interest in return for a lump sum, which she said she had spent in stock for her shop. We said we must see a solicitor and find out whether this disastrous transfer was legal. Who was acting for her ? She only urged us to lend her the money, which would enable her to manage perfectly and free her from debts. Debts, too ! It was despairing, but, seeing we were determined, she ultimately went with us to her solicitor.

" I was going to tell you," he began, " how this lady became my client, and perhaps you won't think much of my business acumen when you have heard me. She came in, a stranger out of the street, and was so earnest that I should join her in prayer—and I believe in prayer—that for the first time in my legal career I was on my knees in my own office . . . and she went away with ten pounds of mine, leaving no security. I was so overcome with my own conduct that I went straight to my partner and told him exactly what I had done. He looked at me intently—I suppose to see if I was in my right mind—and said, ' Where's that Deed of Partnership ? I may have to reconsider it.' Then he asked, ' Was she young and lovely ? ' and I answered truthfully, ' No, a stout and comely forty-five or fifty.' ' Well, then, she must be a remarkable, not to say a dangerous, woman.' Now, having heard this, are you prepared to let me try to help you ? ''

Aurelia interposed, " I don't need any help. All I want is for them to lend me one hundred and fifty pounds, which would free me from debt, and then I could earn my living quite easily."

The solicitor interrupted sternly, " Would you repeat that statement that given one hundred and fifty pounds you would be free of debt ? "

" Yes, I would ; I should get on perfectly."

" And yet "—he spoke slowly—" you know that in this drawer, under my hand, I have unpaid bills of yours amounting to over five hundred pounds."

We were staggered.

Aurelia, not the least abashed, said, " Of course I know that ; but with one hundred and fifty pounds I can buy stock —all sorts of things I know of—and sell them and clear it all off."

That was the beginning of years of effort to disentangle her hopeless affairs. Mercifully, as debts were paid off by the solicitor for a diminishing amount in the pound, so her credit diminished, and the losses in which she could involve herself grew smaller. The decline was gradual, for she had inherited, in addition to capital, a great deal of good furniture, silver, and china, and gradually she sold or pawned it all.

When I had to find funds for her, I made her give me pawn-tickets on which things could be recovered. At one pawn-shop there was quite an exhibition of family silver, and I not only redeemed as much as I could afford, but recovered some pieces of antique furniture, all of which I have to this day. Later, when we had settled in the country and our home contained these things, Aurelia, who had sunk into poverty and owned practically nothing, showed no envy or resentment, but accepted the reversal of position with her habitual sweet temper.

Soon after we came back from Australia, and while Aurelia was still in her near-by shop, my dear Aunt Louise, with whom I had gone to America, came to see me.

" I want you to do something really important for me," she said. " You know Pearl's wedding is going to be a tremendous affair, an immense gathering, and Princess M. is coming. The wedding is on Monday next, and very mistakenly, I think, Pearl's mother, on the strength of cousinship, has sent Aurelia an invitation. Will you look after her and keep her away ? She does look so extraordinary now, and it isn't as if it was only ourselves; there are all his people to consider."

I promised to do my best, and early that Monday afternoon I went round to Aurelia's extraordinary shop, which was filled with a jumble of old clothes, furs, crockery, and furniture. There I found Aurelia and a small boy. I thought that the best way to divert her from the wedding, which she seemed to have forgotten, would be to say I wanted to buy something, and I suggested a washing-stand. She rose at once to the proposal, and saying she had several in the cellar, propelled the small boy in front of her and led me down some stone steps to the basement. It was rather dark and very dirty, and furniture was piled to the rafters in confusion. Aurelia pointed to something with four legs sticking up at the top of the mass and urged the small boy to climb and extract it.

He climbed well, but couldn't dislodge the thing, so Aurelia went after him, breaking a chair in the struggle and dragging down a large, awkward washing-stand.

" It has a marble top somewhere," she said.

" That's cracked, missus," the boy volunteered.

" Anyhow," I said, " it's far too large; I want something much smaller."

Time was getting on, I thought hopefully as the scramble started again; but Aurelia, engulfed in junk, turned suddenly and asked, " What day is it ? "

" Monday, missus," said the alert boy.

" It's dear Pearl's wedding. I must go at once."

" You can't. Besides, it's over—it's for half-past two, and it's three o'clock now, and look at the state you're in."

" I'm going," she answered calmly. " I can wash."

" But it's over," I persisted.

" The church part is, of course, but I can go to the reception."

" Aurelia, don't," I begged. " There will be lots of smart people you won't know, and you have no suitable clothes. Please, please don't go. Come back and have tea with me."

" No, dear, I'm going. I can't see why I shouldn't. Clothes don't really matter, and I mean to go."

I saw she was quite determined.

" Well, will you wash—really wash—and I will run back and get my tidy black silk skirt and some safety-pins ? You couldn't get into anything else of mine."

With my skirt pinned round her she still looked very odd, and her nails were all in mourning, but she wouldn't wait; she wanted to get off quickly, and nothing more could be done.

Just as she got to the door she exclaimed, " I've never sent Pearl a present." She looked vaguely round the shop, and picked up a small, shiny china lamb with black painted eyes, such as children used to buy for twopence in village shops.

" I'll take her this lamb."

" Your gloves," I cried.

" I can't stop to look for them."

She went, and I returned home defeated. At six o'clock my Aunt Louise came to see me, looking beautiful in violet-coloured velvet, old lace and diamonds.

" Oh, my dear, how you failed me ! " she said.

" What happened ? "

" It really was awful. The bride and bridegroom were standing under a bell of white flowers, with Princess M. close beside them. Just as they were about to cut the cake with the bridegroom's sword there was a scuffle at the door. My heart stood still, for I saw Aurelia's charwoman-like bonnet in the centre of a sort of scrum. She hadn't brought her invitation, and when the detectives seized her, as of course they did at once, she screamed at the top of her voice, ' I'm the bride's cousin.' Several relations then freed her, and explained to the detectives, but Aurelia, taking no notice of anyone, pushed her way through the crowd, elbowed the Princess, to whom everyone else had curtsied, out of the way, and flinging her arms round Pearl's neck, presented her with a ridiculous china lamb. Pearl really did the best thing she could : she subsided into helpless laughter, and somehow after that it didn't seem so dreadful. The last I saw of Aurelia she was eating, talking, and laughing with a crowd round her. You might have spared me."

I explained the efforts I had made, and then Aurelia came in with her charwoman's bonnet very crooked over her beaming face.

" I did enjoy that," she told us. " I stayed till the very last."

" My best skirt ! " I cried as I saw an enormous tear and a trail of muddy silk.

" I'm sorry, dear, but the pins came undone, and I put my foot through it getting off the bus."

About this period Aurelia became secretive about her enterprises; money leaked away, and she lived in great discomfort. Once more, with the help of her solicitor, we tried to probe into her affairs. As a result of his persistence we found she had two other shops, served apparently by casual vagrants, except for an old French lady in one who looked quite distinguished in heavy widow's weeds, but, as she could speak no English, we did not feel she could be a successful saleswoman in a muddle shop in a shabby back street in Bloomsbury.

" I had to take her in," Aurelia explained, " because she has nothing, and nowhere to go. Her husband died quite suddenly, and she hasn't the money to get back to France."

We firmly insisted that these secondary shops must be given up. There was also a room she had hired which was full of books, and we learnt that she had gone to Ireland and bought whole libraries.

" I am sure some of them are very valuable," she told us.

" But you wouldn't know if any of them were."

" No, I shouldn't; but I advertised in a wonderful magazine that teaches healing for a Christian man who really understood the value of old books, and I have got such a charming young man who has been going through them for a fortnight, and only charges three guineas a week. He really does know about their value, and is putting them in two cases, one for very precious books and one for good saleable ones. The rest, he says, will be rubbish."

" You can't go on paying him three guineas a week," I said; " or have you paid him ? "

" Yes, I had to. He is an expert, and wouldn't come

unless I paid him in advance, but I owe the rent for the room."

We went to that room and found the door open and an immense heap of books on the floor; but the Christian young man was not there, nor were the two cases containing the books of value he had so carefully selected. He was not seen again.

Aurelia gave up the two extra shops and took the French lady to her own shop where she lived, but she was summoned over the transfer of one of them, and asked me to go to the magistrate's court with her. To my surprise, she was dressed in complete widow's black, her face shrouded in a long black veil.

" Yes," she explained, " that nice old French woman lent me these things and dressed me herself. She was quite agitated when I got her to understand that I had to go to a trial, and she kept on saying I must look *comme il faut*."

We sat in the court awaiting our call while drunks and petty thieves were tried, sentenced, or released, until Aurelia's case was called and the clerk said something that sounded like breach of contract.

A little man started speaking : " I took over the lease of this shop in Little Charlotte Street from this person "—then, looking at Aurelia in her long veil, he corrected himself— " this lady, who agreed to hand it over for the sum I paid her, complete with stock."

" Had you a contract to that effect ? " the magistrate asked.

" No, that's where I made the mistake; I trusted that person's word."

" I left what I could," Aurelia murmured.

" All she left, sir," the little man resumed with passion, " was a dirty tail of 'uman hair."

" I told you they were Queen Victoria's combings, and valuable," Aurelia again interposed.

People giggled; the clerk called silence and the magistrate

said, " You mustn't interrupt the plaintiff. You can state your facts later."

" When I took over that shop it was in a fair mess, but some things were in it, which I reckoned to have when I paid her."

" Were those things specified ? "

" No, sir, they was understood."

" That will do. Now let the defendant state her case."

Aurelia, in her charming voice, spoke clearly and well.

" I am a clergyman's widow, and not a business woman."

I agreed with her fervently, and wished she really held that view.

" When I gave up this shop several people were anxious to take it, but this man was so eager to have it that I let him have my lease for very little, and, partly out of kindness, I said I would leave him what I could, so I left him the linoleum."

The plaintiff, stung to fury, hissed, " Just a little bit of rag, and I suppose you will say it was King Edward's bath mat."

" Sit down, and don't interrupt."

People laughed, and the clerk ordered silence again.

Aurelia resumed, " I never thought of that, and of course I shouldn't have said it if it wasn't true. Other things he saw were my underclothes; he couldn't expect me to leave those to him."

This produced more giggles. The magistrate gave Aurelia a questioning look and snapped, " Case dismissed; a trumpery affair which should never have been brought, and if I hear any more laughter I shall order the court to be cleared."

But he did hear more laughter, for as Aurelia passed the unfortunate plaintiff she threw back her veil and said in a clear voice, " I had a skull in your shop, and if you like it I would give it to you."

He looked furious, but was hustled out of the way as the next case came on.

As we went out Aurelia said, " I'm sure the widow's dress was a help; I shall keep that sort of thing for occasions."

I feared the French lady's chances of getting her veils back were slender.

Usually Aurelia was indifferent as to what she wore and her clothes were deplorable, but when she wanted to make an effect she would dress herself up. She had a collection of odd bits of silk and some shawls, and when reciting—as she loved doing—she could be a striking figure, if one didn't look too closely. Dressed in an orange-embroidered Chinese coat, gold sandals, an Indian shawl and wearing a veil over her hair, she would enjoy the sensation she caused in some dreary mission hall.

Aurelia had gone to the Slade School intermittently for a few weeks, then, as she told us, " I said to Mr. Tonks, ' I don't really care for drawing, but I want to paint.'

" He answered in his abrupt way, ' Well, you can't.'

" How could he know that I couldn't ? I explained to him that I loved nice colours and was sure I could make beautiful pictures, but he wouldn't even listen, and spoke quite sharply, saying, ' No one here is allowed to paint till they have learnt to draw, and I am satisfied you will never do that.' He isn't a very nice man, for before I could answer he had marched out of that antique room which I had got so tired of."

Though Aurelia gave up going to the Slade, she kept up with the students who had been there with her, among others Augustus John, his sister Gwen, and William Orpen.

At that time John was a beardless, shy youth; he developed a very different appearance later, but his exceptional power as a draughtsman was soon recognized.

With his long upper lip and odd little face, Billy Orpen

looked like James Stephens' description of a leprechaun. He was only seventeen and very small, with a great sense of fun and a gift for caricature, and even then his work was mature, for he had studied in Dublin from the age of twelve. Later he rented the cellar in our house, where he painted his little picture, " The Mirror ", which was hung in the New English exhibition and sold at once. In our sitting-room he painted " The Fracture ", a large and less attractive work, a Slade student acting as the patient, and Willy Gore, an Irish doctor who was also studying there, posing as the surgeon. Billy Orpen, with his great sense of fun, enjoyed Aurelia. He painted her and made some comic drawings of her, but unfortunately, though with many intermittent jokes, they came to a disagreement over a serious portrait he painted of her. An amazing piece of portraiture it was, showing her fanatical side : she is looking up with her faded blue eyes into the distance, while her gnarled hands rest on an antique Bible. Into the painting of the hands and this Bible, with its thick yellow-grey leaves and old leather binding, he put the most wonderful genre painting. He thought it the best piece of work he had done so far, and meant to exhibit and sell it, and then Aurelia claimed it as hers. Orpen was outraged, and said she had agreed to sit in return for the sketch he had done of her on the island of Patmos.

The wrangle went on and on until Orpen, who came of solicitor stock, and had an Irish fighting spirit, sued Aurelia for the return of his picture, which she had secreted. He lost his case, and after it was over he came to see us, rueful and very angry, but despite this real anger, astonished and almost amused at the show Aurelia had put up.

" My God, what a woman, and what a liar ! She looked the oppressed, injured gentle widow, and they believed every word she said, while I, who told the truth, was looked on as a dirty little Irish liar. And the cunning of her ! She bought a frame for my picture and brought the receipt into Court and said in the most innocent way, ' You see, I shouldn't have had it framed if I hadn't been sure it was mine '—and she bought this frame when I was telling her very plain that it wasn't."

Orpen walked up and down our room with his hair standing on end, and then exclaimed, " Wait till I tell you what she did then. She sprang a chest of drawers at me— a rotten old thing I wouldn't give you a thank-you for, and never knew was supposed to be mine—and she ups and says she paid for the picture with a valuable antique chest. She thought out that lie after she got the summons, for she came and cleared things out of the drawers just then and never said a word of its being hers or mine."

" Yet," I said, " when we wanted her to sign a life insurance paper in one of our efforts to settle her affairs, she read the clause that she agreed to take reasonable care of her health and exclaimed, ' I can't sign that; it might not be the absolute truth, and I am always truthful.' "

" Well, that's the biggest lie she's told yet," Orpen remarked.

Aurelia would have been hurt and surprised had she heard this conversation. Her dramatic instinct was strong, and before an audience such as a court of law provided she could not resist making a case for herself, throwing accuracy to the winds for the sake of effect. Having won her case, she wanted to be on happy terms again with Orpen and to compensate him for the loss of his picture and his costs. At first he would not be placated, but ultimately, however, Aurelia succeeded in healing the breach, and their complicated barter deals began again and their friendship was re-established.

Chapter Thirteen

DORSET

I DISLIKED towns and wished to live in the country, and fortunately, a year or so after we came back from Australia and had done what we could to straighten out Aurelia's tangled affairs, Herbert decided he wanted to paint in Dorset. So we left London and went to Wool, where we rented the Manor House, which overlooks the river and the bridge and is on the edge of the Purbeck country. My son Henry was born there.

The Manor House was large, built of stone and charming to look at. It belonged to Mrs. Drax, an old lady who had a prejudice against water being laid on in any of her houses; the place was cold and damp and most uncomfortable. The rent, however, was only twenty pounds a year. Discomforts were nothing to the agony of anxiety I went through in this house during the first four months of my little son's life. When I first saw him he looked like a new-born pigeon plucked from its nest. Infants had never had a great attraction for me, and I was quite taken aback when this poor little bag of bones awoke a protective love in my heart, such as tigers and other wild beasts might feel for their young.

When the monthly nurse was going she advised me not to make myself sick worrying over the child, for anyhow he wouldn't live, and fearing another professional would also hold this view and show such indifference, I decided to take care of my baby myself. A specialist came from Bournemouth and diagnosed no fatal condition, but said his life hung on a slender thread, and urged the importance of sleep, adding comfort by assuring me that if the child survived infancy he might be perfectly strong and healthy, which indeed he is. This was a relief, for I had resigned myself to dedicating my life to the care of an invalid, picturing him dressed in Jaeger woollies and living on Bengers' Food.

Finding he slept best in an upright position with his head on my shoulder, many nights were spent walking or sitting with the little creature in my arms, but still he did not thrive, and at three months old weighed little more than at birth.

A despairing letter to my Aunt Louise Berens brought one of her lavish telegrams in response, to the effect that she was sending me a French " nou-nou " to nurse my boy, and I was to meet her and her child at such and such an hour and day. The woman arrived, accompanied by a revolting infant with long black hair. Alas, she proved a complete failure, for when my poor baby was pressed to absorb some of her ample fount of nourishment, he showed resentment with a vigour I had not thought him capable of, arching his back and shrieking, while the French baby howled in chorus.

In another letter to an Irish friend I had referred to my troubles, and she advised asses' milk. This acted like a miracle, and all was well from the very first bottle. I felt quite light-headed with joy and relief. The milk came every day by train from London at a cost of six shillings a bottle. I called it " Ba's champagne ", and would have sold my wedding ring or anything else to procure it, seeing him gain weight and sleeping peacefully, but I felt it would be more sensible to keep a donkey. A lively young brown donkey and her foal were bought, but she was a wild, skittish creature, and had to be tied fore and aft before anything could be done. Then she had the gift of withdrawing her milk and only releasing it for her foal, so an older staid grey donkey and her offspring were hired; this mother was docile and a complete success, if a little too intimate, for she would come into the house when the door was left open. While these conditions prevailed in my household I saw a carriage stop at my gate and a large middle-aged woman and a chinless young man emerge, evidently coming to call.

The Manor House had a wide stone porch, which was a favourite place for the grey donkey, whose every whim was indulged. Seeing my visitors approaching, I hurried to the door to find, as I feared, that they were confronted by this massive obstruction.

" I am so sorry," I said as I dragged the donkey out of the way by her mane. " She will insist on lying here."

" Is she a pet ? " the lady chirped.

" No," I answered, " she is acting as a foster-mother for my little son."

At that moment the skittish brown donkey raced past, kicking up her heels, followed by an excited foal, both painfully close to my visitors, who asked nervously, " You keep other donkeys ? "

" That one," I explained while showing them in, " is no use because she withholds her milk."

I was handed a card, and, seeing the name, realized that this was the rich woman of whom I had heard, who had married her son's young tutor. We had barely started a rather strained conversation when shrieks resounded through the room.

" Is your little boy crying ? " the lady asked, when the noise could no longer be ignored.

" It's the French baby . . ." I began, when the door burst open and the " nou-nou ", in a dreadful state of dishevelment and exposure of person, rushed in and, taking no notice of my visitors, poured out a torrent of French to the effect that " la petite " had the colic and would madame come at once.

" No," I answered; " give her dill water and pat her back. I'll come presently."

Feeling some explanation of this intrusion was necessary, I told them that the woman had been engaged before I had the donkeys as a foster-mother for my baby, but that he wouldn't let her nurse him. I then saw that the chinless young man was trying to suppress giggles, and I would have laughed with him but, glancing at his wife, I realized that she was feeling outraged and had risen to go. The situation had got out of hand, so I took them in silence to the door. Alas, the large matronly grey donkey was again lying in the porch, this time on her side, exposing her pale stomach in a far from refined way.

Watching my visitors drive off, it came home to me that they must have felt that they had been in a lunatic's home. Well, it had all got to stop; the French woman, whom I had kept at her own wish for weeks, must be put into the train and made to go; the brown donkey and foal should be sold, and the grey treasure confined in a nearby paddock. I, too, must return to ordinary life and cease to focus solely on saving my baby. I went into the nursery, where he lay pink and well, and I murmured to myself, " Mad or not, it's been worth it." Shortly after these plans had been carried out my husband came home and life continued on normal lines.

The Manor House had been the home of the Turbervilles, and it was here that Thomas Hardy came to see us. He was a simple, unpretentious man, who told us tales of the early Turbervilles, upon whom he based his great book. He believed the rather crude fresco pictures, which he found on an upstairs wall, to be portraits of Turbervilles, and these I copied for him, and they were reproduced in his novel. He sent me a copy of this book with a kind inscription of thanks for my work, but to my great regret the book was stolen and I could not trace it.

Driven away by discomfort, we left the Manor House, and after spending some months in Paris, stayed for a time at Swanage, where my son Anthony was born. But even as long ago as the time we first went there the place was spoilt by many ugly red-brick houses, and an old labourer to whom I talked, looking regretfully at the town, said, " An' I do mind when Swanage lay like a grey cat under the hill."

We left Swanage and went to Corfe Castle, where we rented Arfleet, a charming old mill house which was approached through a courtyard.   On one side of this stood the actual mill, housing immense grindstones and wooden wheels, on the other a walled garden and, facing, the small three-storied house.   All were built, both roofs and walls, of Purbeck stone, so that my old labourer friend could with satisfaction have compared the little settlement to a grey cat, but this time set in a flat green field.

I gardened at Arfleet, growing flowers in the walled garden, working a kitchen garden for vegetables with some idea of becoming a vegetarian, for I had a horror of the suffering and fear inflicted on animals to provide us with meat; and this dated from when I was five years old.   I had wandered through the yard at Cahirnane, past the new stables and down a lane flanked by old stone buildings, at the open door of one of which I saw a man holding a sheep. Having no idea of what was happening, I stopped and looked in, and suddenly a second man slashed the wretched creature's throat with a long knife and blood gushed out.

" No, no, you mustn't ! " I shrieked and rushed away, blinded with tears.   Instinctively I made my way to the kitchen, where I hurled myself into the cook's arms and, still sobbing, told my incoherent story.

" Whist now, dote," she responded soothingly.   " How would we get a leg of mutton without killing a sheep ? "

This logical statement linked food with death for the first time in my mind, causing many struggles with nurses and governesses over my refusal to eat meat.   Though thinking of becoming a total vegetarian when I was at Arfleet, I was doubtful whether in my case it was practicable, as I found it hard to live on nuts and lettuce, and I also wondered whether by doing so I should become a crank. This fear was emphasized by my friendship with some neighbours, Mr. and Mrs. Tigh, who were dear, nice, absurd people.

They would kill nothing; not a mouse, not a mosquito, and they had trained birds and red squirrels to engagingly intimate habits. Mr. Tigh died, and the bereaved widow, less sensitive on art matters than on the suffering of animals, ordered a memorial to her husband to be carved by a local monumental mason, who was an animal lover, but not very expert in the craft of sculpture. He decorated a large tomb-stone slab with the figure in relief of the late Mr. Tigh, dressed in a tweed coat, the pattern of which he represented with much care by diagonal grooves on the stone, and carrying on each shoulder a ferocious-looking creature, purporting to be a squirrel, but much nearer the size of a tiger. Having started the head and shoulders on heroic scale and added to the sense of weight by the massive creatures encircling the neck of this lover of squirrels, the sculptor got into difficulties. Finding the stone too short, he disregarded human proportions, and reduced the size of the knickerbocker-clad legs, making them appear painfully unable to bear their massive burden.

Mrs. Tigh seemed quite undisturbed at this curious rendering of her husband's figure, only remarking sadly, " I do wish he had given the squirrels kinder faces."

After her husband's death Mrs. Tigh left her home and bought a house and a hundred acres of land, which she intended to make into a sanctuary for wild life. Some years later I received a letter asking me to come and see her, as she was in trouble and was sure I could help her. I started off on my bicycle. It was a long ride through woods and fields to her isolated home, but at last I came to a six-foot-high, fine-meshed wire fence, no doubt the protection for the " sanctuary ", and there was the locked gate and the bell I was told to ring. An old man came with a key and let me in. The drive was dusty, and what had looked like brown heaps of dead leaves disintegrated and turned into rabbits; on one side the field was the colour of wet sand, showing no blade of grass, and on the other side the trees were barked for varying lengths up their trunks. I passed an orchard of young apple-trees, all apparently dead and with peeled bark. It looked most melancholy.

Mrs. Tigh had aged, and seemed to be in a flutter of distress.

" It is so good of you to come," she said when I was shown in. " Everything is dying except the rabbits, and I don't know what to do. There are thousands of them, and they have eaten everything—all the grass, the shrubs, the vegetables and the flowers, and even the trees; for my rabbits can climb trees. I have to buy food for my three old horses, which I still have, as there isn't a blade of anything on the place for them to eat, and the people aren't even kind here; they don't like me because I wouldn't let the hunt on to my ground and the fence keeps everyone out. I thought I could make it so lovely for the animals, but instead the rabbits have made it a desolation."

She was on the verge of tears.

" You must get rid of the rabbits," I assured her. " They breed so fast and they can't get out."

" I know I must, but I couldn't bear to have them slaughtered by men on my place ; I feel I would rather have it done in God's way. Can you find me someone who has a lot of ferrets or stoats or weasels ? I would buy them, and they could just get rid of the rabbits in a natural way."

I thought over the problem on the way home. Mrs. Tigh had once told me that she had to give up going to church because she was so sensitive to auras, and if a butcher was in church she knew it at once, and, because of his dreadful work, his presence turned her faint. The only man I knew who kept a lot of ferrets was a sporting butcher whose house

I passed on my way home, and as his aura would not affect me, I decided to consult him. In answer to my knock, the butcher himself opened the door, and I told him my story and said, " Could you help this poor lady to buy ferrets or stoats or weasels ? "

" No, ma'am," he answered firmly, " I wouldn't be party to such cruelty. I've dug half the night sooner than leave a ferret down a hole to eat part way through a rabbit and not finish him perhaps for hours."

He then made practical suggestions for clearing the place, offering to come along with a couple of men on any Saturday or Sunday and do it himself. I hesitated to distress Mrs. Tigh by telling her what the butcher felt, but I did so, thinking she ought to know, and hoping she would draw the deduction that I did—that you cannot set yourself against the scheme of creation—and adding that if she could not accept his suggestion it would be advisable to take her palings down.

Mrs. Tigh wrote and told me that she had done this, and that the rabbits had poured out and devoured everything in the villagers' gardens. She ended her letter by writing, " They were angry with me for putting up my fence, now they are angry because I have taken it down. How difficult it is to do right."

At Arfleet I distributed seedling plants to cottagers, not to make them give up eating meat, but hoping to wean them from the ' cabbage only ' habit. By doing so I saw the conditions in which the country people lived, their bad houses and low wages, and I wrote articles to the Press on this subject. I also took to the House of Commons a deputation of small-holders, who had been given a very shabby deal. They were nice, simple countrymen, and going up in the train, I coached each one of the six in what they were to say, heading them off from the irrelevant side-tracks they were only too ready to wander down. On the way home one of the men asked me anxiously, " Did I speak un proper ? " They all did, for Mr. Runciman, the Minister of Agriculture, came to see the conditions for himself. He was really shocked, and put the whole matter right.

I heard subsequently that some angry ratepayers had called me ' a poisonous woman ' for the part I played in the affair.

Chapter Fourteen

PAINTERS

MANY of our Slade School friends came to paint in the neighbourhood while we were at Arfleet.

One day I received a letter from Henry Tonks, asking me to find suitable lodgings where he, Mr. Steer, and Professor Fred Brown could spend the summer. It must, he said, be within very easy reach of a good landscape for Steer to paint.

I found a perfect setting in a farm overlooking Poole harbour and wrote describing it, saying they must come and see for themselves before making so important a decision.

They duly arrived, and lunched at our attractive old stone mill house. To reach the farm we had to cross a field with no special view, and Professor Brown went on ahead with Steer, who shielded the sun from his head with a large white cotton umbrella, and about half-way across the field he turned and said, " Tonks, this is dull."

Tonks stopped.

" If Steer thinks it dull it is no use going on."

This was really too childish; they must go on, for they weren't going to live in this field, so in gloom and silence we pursued our way. When we arrived at the farm with that enchanting country between Corfe Castle and Studland and across the water to Poole lying below us, Poole harbour with its creeks and inlets and tree-fringed islands and cloud shadows breaking the foreground of heathland and pines, Steer stood entranced.

"I could paint here for a lifetime," he said almost under his breath, and Tonks beamed with relief and pleasure.

All three spent that summer and a subsequent one at this farm. Steer painted several large landscapes almost from his door, and only once was beguiled by the magic of the blue Poole to go farther away when, having started a picture, he unfortunately saw a snake, and although assured it was quite harmless, he never went again.

On the day of their arrival Tonks came to thank me for finding their rooms, and I took him to see my garden. As we went I reached up to pick a rose which was trained over an arch, and Tonks, exclaiming, " Hold that pose ! " produced materials and did a sketch and showed it to me; it was quite charming and pleasantly flattering.

"Would you stand for me if I were to do an oil picture ? " he asked. " It is such a perfect setting : all those flowers and the twisted apple-trees with the castle showing above the wall and you standing there, would make it a balanced composition."

Hesitating, I agreed, because I wanted to help him, but I wondered how I should find the time, and hoped it would not prove long. Had I known that the whole summer would be taken up with the painting of this picture I should have refused. Tonks was enthusiastic, believing he could put all he knew about painting into this work. He was full of all sorts of theories, one being that without plagiarism one ought to assimilate what other painters had done, and thus he could emulate the careful detail practised by the Pre-Raphaelites in his painting of the flowers, not forgetting the French " Plein Air " school and their feeling for light. Such light, he hoped, would diffuse his whole picture.

Suddenly he commanded in the sternest manner, " I forbid you ever to criticize what I am doing," adding more gently, " You see, if I am depressed about my work or shaken in my confidence as to its success, I can't go on, so I want no one to see it till it is finished."

Months went by, and it was not finished; tulips bloomed, petunias glowed, dahlias blossomed, but the painting went on. Some mornings I hung my white dress under the pergola and escaped, and although I never criticized, yet I felt more and more that the painting was becoming a confused failure. This sense of confusion was not helped by my little son Tony running towards me with outstretched arms, his pale gold hair looking silver in the sunshine.

" Perfect," Tonks murmured. " Can you make him repeat the movement and stand for quite a short time ? "

This was difficult for a baby barely three years old to understand, so every morning I had to hold a toy while Tony, loosed at the garden door, was told to run for it with arms held out.

The other painters kept asking me about the picture, and Ronald Grey did a caricature of Tonks pulling back a curtain to expose his masterpiece while they all fell flat on their faces, consumed with jealousy. Alas, this was not what happened, for I subsequently received a letter from London, saying, " The scales have fallen from my eyes, and now I see that the picture is all wrong. "

He sent me a landscape in water-colour as a gift, and I regretted he had not chosen instead the first attractive portrait sketch which had suggested the fatal picture.

The following summer Tonks painted a village girl wearing bright clothes who posed in the dusky and mysterious interior of the mill. This work was attractive, well painted, and executed with ease.

The painters often came to our small house in the evening for talk and music, and we went for excursions with them. During those summer months Tonks found amusement from the occasional visits of Aurelia, who would come to stay with us at any hour of the day or night, alone or with some odd dependant.

Once, arriving at three in the morning, she shouted under my window, " Can we have something to eat and beds ? I've got a monk with me."

" A monk ! " I gasped, putting my head out of the window.

" Yes, come down."

A stolid young man, no longer dressed as a monk, was standing behind Aurelia. He was a Belgian, and spoke broken English.

When I enquired about him, Aurelia explained, as if it were the most natural thing in the world, " He escaped from some monastery and had nowhere to go, so I took him as my maid, and he does other things."

Aurelia ate heartily, and seemed in the best of spirits, but her monk was limping, and said he was too tired to eat.

Next morning Tonks was painting in the garden, and I told him about them. They came out and joined us, and after greetings Tonks, looking at her mud-caked skirts, his rather grim mouth twitching with the amusement he always found in her doings, remarked, " Your lady's maid seems to have neglected his duties."

At this criticism the monk burst into speech.

" I not a pony "—he called it a ponee—" she work me that way with meo-gany wardrobes on my back I stagger."

" Sounds hard for a maid," Tonks stated gravely.

" That not all. I fetch coals like a ponee but he has carts to him, but I sacks to my back. When I go to her and say I help her shop and keep order in her clothes, and she say yes, she never explain she need ponee."

E [129]

" He does talk rubbish," Aurelia said, sitting down on the grass.

" But appears obsessed with his equine-like trials," Tonks put in.

The monk had more to say and, flinging up his hands, he exclaimed, " And last night before God she walk half England, and my heel one big hole, and she care not how I suffer."

" Go away back to your room and I'll send Mr. Tonks, who really is a doctor, though he paints, to look at your heels," said Aurelia.

" Oh, will you ? You told me you were a healer and medicine was all wrong : why don't you cure his heel ? "

" Because he doesn't co-operate.   He wouldn't sing with me or enjoy himself on our walk last night."

" That fellow has not been a monk," Tonks observed, watching the retreating figure.   " A monk wouldn't talk so much. He was probably a bottle-washer at some monastery."

On another occasion while Tonks was still painting in the garden, Aurelia arrived, this time in the morning and in an incredible state of dishevelment.

" Good gracious ! " he said, " you seem more in need of your monk maid than ever."

" He's gone to be a waiter, but I had to sleep in a flower-bed last night."

" What ! "

" I really had to ; that's why there's some earth on me."

" There is indeed ; there's earth all over you, even in your hair.   But let's get this clear : why did you have to sleep in a flower-bed ? "

" It was like this : I was coming here last night, but missed the connections, and thought I'd walk from Bournemouth."

" But that's over twenty miles."

" I didn't do it, for soon after I started it came on to rain and simply poured. I was very sleepy, so I went up to a villa and knocked and asked the woman quite politely whether I could spend the night there, saying I could sleep in any chair; but she wasn't at all kind, just saying ' Certainly not ' and shutting the door. I thought it so un-Christian and so dreadfully wrong to refuse anyone shelter when it was raining. I didn't mind so much for myself, but felt she ought to be helped to see how cruel she had been."

" I suppose you would take anyone in—even a burglar ? "

" Yes, of course. As it happens, I did only last week."

" How did you get hold of him ? "

" I didn't; he just came."

" Do try to explain consecutively what happened," Tonks ordered in his most determined manner.

Sitting on the grass, and leaning against a tree, Aurelia told us the story.

" I was sitting up very late behind the shop because I had been to a meeting about British Israelites and the Lost Tribes and had brought back a lot of pamphlets explaining it. All so very interesting——" She looked up eagerly, but getting no response, went on, " I hadn't noticed the time, and I had taken off my boots because my feet were tired after walking such a long way from the meeting. Then I heard someone at the door and went into the shop, which was nearly dark, making no noise, of course, with only my stockings on. I could just see someone was there, and hearing that it was a very wet night, I said, ' Do come in out of the rain and shut the door.'

" I saw it was a man, and that he was startled and about to make off, so I took hold of his arm and said, ' You're soaked through; come in and get dry.' He tried to wrench himself away, muttering, ' You're in with the cops, I reckon.'

I laughed, and said I wasn't, and I thought that they interfered with people too much. Then he asked me if I was
alone. I took him into the back room, where there was a
fire and a light, and saw that he was young, but dreadfully
wet, so I made him take his coat off and gave him an old cape
to keep him warm while it was drying. He looked hungry,
so we had some supper—cold meat and bread and cheese—
and I made tea. When I asked him how he had opened
my door which was locked, he said it wouldn't keep out
anyone who knew how, and I asked if he had come to get
something. He was quite nice about that, explaining that
he had fixed to pinch something, but he wouldn't go away
with a thing of mine now, so then I talked to him about the
Lost Tribes and British Israelites, but nothing I could say
would make him take any interest in them."

"I don't either," Tonks remarked. "But what did your
fellow say?"

Aurelia laughed. "All he said was, 'Blimey, missus,
I'm no sheeney, nor more aren't you.'"

"In fact, the irrefutable answer for your society."

"You are quite wrong. You see, the Lost——"

"I don't want to hear anything about them! What did
you talk of next?"

"I asked him if he'd been in prison."

"Just like that—as you might ask him if he'd been to
Brighton?"

"Yes; why not? And he told me all about it, and said
he came out worse than when he went in. I am sure that
was true, and if only people would be kind to burglars I
think it would do them more good than sending them to
prison. He was a nice man, and came next day and changed
my lock so that it would be a hard job to pick. I think he
really was a nicer man than you are." She said this quite
simply, adding, "Could you get me a brush to get this earth
off with?—it's quite dry now."

"First tell me, did you really sleep in that woman's garden?"

"Yes, and quite well. The earth was soft and the rain stopped, and I do hope she was sorry when she saw where I spent the night because of her unkindness." Here she gave a gurgle of amusement, adding, "Anyhow, she couldn't help seeing, because a funny thing happened: this mantle was trimmed with sequins, and when I got up the earth was covered with black spots. I suppose the damp had melted them off. I must go now; I have a meeting at Swanage, and am going to London by the night train."

Tonks, looking at her as she wandered away, said thoughtfully, "Who but Aurelia [everyone called her Aurelia] would have imagined that a knock-about turn like sleeping in a garden bed could induce religious conversion? Imagine the middle-class owner of a small Bournemouth villa coming out in the morning and seeing her tidy front garden bed depressed and covered with an irruption of black spots, and all surrounded with bits of broken geraniums, being moved by such a sight to Christian repentance."

Tonks paused and gave his sudden rare hoot of laughter.

With the departure of Aurelia, the fantastic atmosphere she always brought with her faded and normal life was resumed.

We spent several years at Arfleet, but there were claypits close to us, and when excavations there threatened to undermine our house we had to leave it. Soon after we went the whole little settlement vanished completely—just as responsibility for Aurelia and other ties in my life were to come to an end.

Chapter Fifteen

BECOMING A BUILDER

WE decided to own our next house, and to this end we bought land, not on the Purbeck ridge where Steer had painted, for there the view faced north, but on the opposite side of the bay, near Broadstone. It was a heather-covered slope with some pine-trees, and looked towards Poole harbour.

I told the builder what we wanted the house to look like and did a rough outline plan of the rooms. At that time I believed in the William Morris tradition, that as much as possible should be done by handcraft. The builder had quite other ideas, and every time I went to see the work I found something regrettable, such as an odious terra-cotta cock-eyed ornament on the end of the roof-ridge or a high mean cement step to the front door in place of the massive slab of Purbeck stone I had asked for. Exasperated, and never knowing what vandalism he might perpetrate next, I decided to camp on the site to circumvent him. Many small houses and villas are unattractive through having been built by men who have seen little better work and are obsessed by meaningless conventions, like people who think they are scarcely respectable if they do not possess bedroom suites or net curtains.

While living in a tent near the house I made friends with the workmen. The builder came from Swanage, but the men were local, and not members of his own staff.

We moved into the house before it was finished, and while carpenters and painters were still at work Colonel Elwes came to see us. We gave him luncheon in the loggia, which overlooked the attractive view and got all the sun. There was a hatch to the kitchen, and he said the whole place reminded him of where he used to spend his leave in the Himalayas and that he would like to buy our house. Later he came again and offered us a price which gave a good profit.

Telling the carpenter about this, I said, " I feel I cannot begin a struggle with a builder again from the start."

He was silent for a moment, then, giving me a shrewd look and speaking slowly, he answered, " Why shouldn't you be your own builder ? "

Completely taken aback, I retorted, " How could I possibly be a builder ? "

" If you could draw the plans we could see you through, and by doing it that way you'd save a lot of money."

While I was thinking of the idea and feeling uncertain of its feasibility, the men came to see me, evidently having been talking it all over between themselves. They were confident of being able to carry out the scheme.

We laid out the plans of the finished house, and a brick-layer explained clearly what the lines represented, pointing out which were foundation walls, which air cavities were external, and which walls were only party ones, carrying no weight. A carpenter took up the tale, indicating how the roof-timbers and joists were shown, and the puzzle of the cross-section was cleared up. By the time they had finished I had grasped the meaning of the drawing and agreed that I could do plans which they could work from for a larger and a better house.

I took a long time over the effort, making a first attempt on squared paper, allowing each square to equal a foot, then reducing it to reasonable size before tracing and colouring, but this first drawing taught me something.

Then there was the question of quantities, and on this matter, too, my advisers helped, giving particulars from their books of measurements used for calculating piece-work, such as so many bricks to a superficial yard, so many joists and floor-boards to a square, and so on, until gradually I achieved a theoretical understanding of the problem I had undertaken. We bought another lovely site, but before starting building went to Holland for a holiday, where we collected many things to build into the house, such as carved stone heads to act as corbels to the lintels of windows, and panelling for the interior. An old dealer called everything he sold us " A vonderful hot egg "—meaning Gothic. To-day I should not try incorporating such things into a modern house; I rely on simplicity and proportion.

On my return I got in touch with my men and, on their advice, bought the necessary scaffolding plant. In order to be on the spot from the first, I had set up in a pine-wood on our ground a large, heather-thatched hut, which would be useful afterwards for garden things, and close by a tent for my boys during their holidays. I never felt so near Nature as when I was living in that hut. Just above my bed a wren made a nest, in which she brought up a family, and as I watched these tiny creatures feeding every day, I felt quite maternal towards the fledgelings. I would breakfast in the open air under pine-trees, sharing my meal with many enchanting birds, while red squirrels would come and chatter and sit up and nibble bread.

It was a fairly large house that we were building, and doing it myself with the foreman and his set-square, up to the last finishing touch, cleared up many mysteries. The men, feeling themselves sponsors of the whole thing, took pride in it and were most helpful. I went with my foreman bricklayer to order bricks, and was instructed by him in distinguishing wirecuts and flettons and cast, over-burnt bricks, and with my carpenter to select timber. The latter advised me to reject what he called blue and twisted stuff. They told me I must have printed business cards and paper. I felt a complete fraud in calling myself a builder, but saw at once how essential it was, as it entitled me to a large commission on all I bought. The dishonest side of these commissions was also exposed, for some builders' merchants would print a two-and-a-half commission to show clients and give perhaps twenty per cent to the builder, stating this concession on a separate sheet.

Before this house was finished I had many requests to build for other people in the neighbourhood. My bricklayers having done their work—a stage which is reached about half-way through a building—and tilers, carpenters, plumbers, and plasterers being left to complete the job, I bought another site and made plans for a smaller place, and also acquired seven acres for elderly friends who wanted a small-holding. In this latter building I wished to demonstrate how high the cost of Council houses was, so I planned mine to be of the same number of cubic feet as a pair built by the local authorities. Theirs cost eleven hundred pounds; my single house of the same size came to five hundred and fifty pounds. I gave my old friends a life lease, and recently, thirty-five years later, heard from my tenant saying, "Labour is difficult to get, so I am earthing up my potatoes, but as I am ninety-one, I begin to feel it is rather hard work."

I had these three houses to supervise, and loved the work, finding satisfaction in seeing my own ideas take form and in creating something useful and permanent; and also in sharing friendly contacts with good types of working men, for they were craftsmen, and they, too, felt the pleasure of making something of essential value.

I kept time-sheets and accounts, which proved conclusively how much cheaper building by direct labour was—even including the plant I had bought : scaffold poles, planks, ladders, and rope—than when done by contract.

I discussed this with my men to see if they could explain it. Country builders do not make fortunes, so why should their prices be so high ? All sorts of suggestions were put forward. The foreman's was that a builder reckoned to pay his own rent and to keep himself and his family through his work, while " you allow nothing for that. Then he has an office, a clerk, and a van, and the more work he takes on, the more overheads he has to meet. With your three houses you can manage the paper work, buy all the materials and see they get delivered, and," he added with a wink, " keep a sharp look-out that we don't waste time. None of that is reckoned in your costs."

" There's all the idling on a job," another man suggested.

" Why should there be any ? " I asked.

" Look at it this way : a builder has a dozen places to get round. He'll miss a thing or two, something that's wanted and not delivered; lime may be getting low, or fittings held up on rail, and the men have to fill up time."

" See, too, some of the timber I have to work, unseasoned twisted stuff," a carpenter added. " It takes me hours to cut it down, and that happens because a small man will start out without enough capital, and when he can't pay what's owing he has to take whatever's sent him. It's the same way with some big firms, too. And then there's discount; some don't get it as you do, where they can't settle for a long while."

They all agreed, however, that work went slowly when there was bad feeling. I asked what caused it.

" All sorts of things," they explained. " Often it will come through a bad foreman, who reckons he'll do himself a bit of good; if he's for ever at you and blast your eyes here and damn you there, he may think he'll get the job to go faster that way; but it don't, it goes slower."

From my own experience in building in England, Ireland, and Italy, I think good relations with one's men is of vital importance, and apart from its being right, and making for happiness all round, costs are reduced. I have on occasion let the men choose their own foreman from among themselves, telling them to select the man they think most capable and even-tempered. Their choice has always been right. I expected discipline and they responded; time must be kept and off-time not extended casually, as they were inclined to do over tea-drinking.

Sometimes they would argue, " You wouldn't be hard on us for five minutes."

" Yes, I should," I told them, " and I have done this sum for you : five minutes twice a day for twelve men for eight months equals thirty-seven pounds when paying time, and I should get no thanks for it."

They assured me they would never have guessed how much it would cost, and now they would get going directly the whistle went.

Another point I made when starting work was, as I told them : " I won't hear complaints about any of you; the first man who tries to make trouble goes. I shall know well enough what's right and what's wrong, and there won't be anything wrong if we all pull together."

I knew my men individually, and found older men more satisfactory than younger ones.

An older man, talking about piece-work, said, " Paid that way, a man took a pride in what he could do."

" What about the man who couldn't do so much ? "

" We'd help him, and the lazy chap soon got out of such ways. But now it's pull down to the slowest instead of pulling up."

" It's argued that piece-work puts too much strain on men."

" That it doesn't; it's steady does it."

We had discussions on all sorts of subjects : trade unions, State direction, insurance, and doles. I remember one argument between my foreman carpenter and a young bricklayer.

"No interfering, if I could choose; I like to stand on my own feet," the carpenter declared.

"And I," the bricklayer countered, "like to lean up against the State or the employer, or anyone else who will pay me for doing nothing."

Many of the cottages in which the men lived were old, small, and in bad condition. One day I said, "Since we build cheaply, could we have a co-partnership scheme, buy a plot of land, and you men build houses for yourselves?"

It was pathetic to see the enthusiasm with which the idea was received. For weeks we talked of it in the dinner hour, thrashing out every aspect of the plan. Finance came first; the men agreed to put their savings into a common pool, each man to be credited with the amount of his contribution when paying off the cost of his house. My bank was ready to advance the bulk of the necessary money, holding some of my stock certificates as guarantee until the houses were built, when a mortgage could be arranged. The men had to live while working on their own houses, so it was decided they should have trade union rates of pay from the bank fund for a forty-two-hour week, and do overtime evening work voluntarily and at no charge. Listening to them talking it was clear that a great deal was going to be done in those long summer evenings—we proposed beginning the following spring, 1915. Each man was to pay off the cost of his own house, plus a proportion of the price of the land; some thought they would be able to pay it off in six years, others said eight or ten. I promised to help them in every way. They needed education as regards aspect and layout for this scheme, but soon accepted the points I made. We had found land we could acquire with a fine group of pines on it, which I said must stay, and the houses should be grouped on the outskirts, each having a separate garden at the back but a communal front of lawn with flowering trees and seats, a well-hidden drying-ground for all, and a wired-in babies' play-place. It would have been a scheme in keeping with William Morris' idea of how a socialist country would function.

I have always regretted that the idea was never attempted, but all our plans were dashed by the outbreak of war. It was difficult enough to complete the houses under way, and impossible to carry out the commissions I had accepted. The workmen's dream of owning their own houses made by their own hands was shattered, although we tried to hope we might start again in a few months' time.

The long years of war were to pass, and when peace came I was in Ireland and some of my men were dead.

Chapter Sixteen

NURSING

THE national calamity was temporarily overshadowed for me by a personal one, for at the start of the war my marriage foundered. In the past if things had been uncomfortable, as for instance directly after my babies were born, Herbert went away, perhaps to Paris or to Cornwall, or I might not know where he was. This time he informed me that his disappearance was to be final.

I was very unhappy and distraught with anxiety, for I had been fond of him, and thought I had done my best for him, and now I was faced with complete failure. In addition to emotional distress, my financial position was desperate. My income was just enough to pay for my boys at their preparatory school, and allowed no margin.

Before the war I could have earned all I needed by building, having secured several orders, but now nothing of the kind could be done. I applied for paid employment, and was offered one or two suitable posts, but naturally these would not admit of my being free to look after my boys during the holidays, and this I felt to be essential, fearing that Herbert might intervene. I need not have worried on this account, for he made no effort to see or interfere with the children, and from then onwards I looked after them exclusively, but at that time I had not realized that this would be the case. Ultimately I worked for three terms as a V.A.D. in hospital, which at least secured free meals for me, and I lived in the smaller house I had built, and to which I had transferred my furniture.

Nursing the wounded was, I think, good for me, for seeing so much pain, often allied to such good spirits, put my own troubles into perspective, and being kept busy I could forget them, but I never became hardened to the suffering I saw. There was a big, rough youth with a shattered knee to whom the dressing and probing under the patella were agony. His efforts not to cry out, then his groans and, after it was over, his shamefaced tears, which made this great creature look like a miserable bewildered child, were touching, and I determined to try to help him.

On the morning I was to wait on Sister at this dressing I went to him when Sister was well out of the way and said, " Listen carefully; while your knee is being done I shall put my hand on your arm and press it hard and take most of your pain away."

" How will you do that ? " he asked.

" I am very strong, and I shall will your pain to flow away through me. What you must do is to believe and know I can do it. Shut your eyes and say over and over, ' It's gone away, it's gone away.' "

It actually worked wonderfully, and the Sister praised

him for being so good.   It happened a second time, and then
I was off duty and he announced stubbornly that he wouldn't
have his dressing done without me, though he kept his word
not to say why.   Of course it was done, and it hurt him as
much as ever.   The Sister was annoyed and suspicious of
some mutual attraction, but although I couldn't tell her the
facts, feeling that she would have disapproved of anything
so unorthodox, I assured her there was nothing of that sort.
Then I gave the boy my indiarubber to squeeze when I
wasn't there, and he said it helped, but not as much as my
hand.

I had many jokes with the wounded.   One Sunday
afternoon I asked them all to write to their mothers, and
gave them pencils and paper.   One convalescent youth,
looking up with troubled eyes and grasping his pencil,
exclaimed, " Writing do make I sweat."

Indeed, everywhere the letter-writing seemed very halting.

" How many of you have written, ' Dear Mum and Dad,
I hope this finds you well as it leaves me.   I hope Mary is
well and I hope Bob is well and so on ' ?   Your mothers
won't want any of that; they will all want to know what
your wound is and how it is getting on, what the ward is
like and whether you are happy, and what your nurses are
like, whether you have books and games and flowers and
what you have had for dinner.   I'll write for Jim, as he can't,
and I'll say, ' My arms are still bandaged, but will be as good
as ever when I leave here.'   Now, each of you say what you
like about your own wounds."

" What am I to say ? " asked a boy who had had a quantity
of shrapnel splinters in his behind.

" Say ' I'm lying on my face because I can't yet lie on my
embroidered pincushion.' "

This simple jest became a catchword.

" Now describe the ward and the games you play and so
on."

[143]

My finished letter went from bed to bed, and was laboriously copied. They were such nice boys, and they could talk of things with interest, but writing seemed to clamp down on their capacity to express themselves.

We spent the holidays in my small house, and then I had an offer to let it furnished for three months, and at the same time I heard that a slum hospital in Dublin was in need of nurses. On hearing from the matron that she would welcome me if I would live in and work in the wards, so many of her staff having left to serve abroad, I decided to go there.

Mercer's Hospital was a complete contrast to the hospital for the English soldiers, where everything had been new, very clean, and very strict. Here the house was old, with heavy oak staircases and doors, and in one of the latter could still be seen the hole which the founder had cut over a hundred years earlier for the convenience of her cat. The patients, too, were different : there were men's and women's surgical and medical wards, accident and out-patients' departments, and I worked in all of them, being directed by matron wherever there was most need. This hospital, no doubt, is very different now, with ample means from the State lottery, but in those days they were very short of money and depleted of staff.

All the work seemed directed to one point—the hour of the doctor's coming. By ten o'clock everything must be in perfect order, and to this end the whole ward was roused at five-thirty or six in the morning, according to the number of patients in it. Some of these had perhaps only dropped off to sleep in the small hours, yet lights must be on, washings got through, beds made, floors swept, dressings done. Night nurses were changed to day nurses, but the tumult went on. Breakfasts must be eaten and quickly cleared away. At the sacred moment everything must be finished and calm must reign, nurses must be spick and span, with previously turned-up sleeves pulled down, starched cuffs and belt adjusted, and cap and apron immaculate. Flagrant faults of junior nurses were overlooked: they might be rough to patients and use their meagre allowance of milk in entertaining medical students, be casual in sterilizing instruments and bandages, say they had given medicine when they hadn't, or write up pulse or temperature chart without taking either. Such things when found out would get a reprimand, but when a patient was wheeled out for the doctor's examination and was found lying on a blanket and without the regulation sheet, a storm broke out afterwards that vibrated right through the hospital. The probationer's excuse that the sheets below were all so damp she was in dread to put one under him, was brushed aside. The ward was disgraced, the Sister was disgraced, and the wretched probationer made to feel disgraced for ever; her tears couldn't wipe out such disgrace, and so on and on and on.

This row and the veneration for the doctors made me remember Tonks' sardonic views of nurses.

" They are a menace," he declared. " So trim and clean and sweet and charming; they put the innocent doctor on a pedestal, they listen to his words with unconcealed admiration, and with every breath they flatter him, they almost worship him, and all for one purpose : they intend to marry him. Their purpose achieved, they knock him off his pedestal, they shut him up when he speaks, they are off with their own pure, sweet uniform and on with tawdry finery that completely transforms the creature and removes all her charm, and that at his expense. Instead of the submissive, delightful attendant of the hospital, the wretched man is saddled for life with a domineering woman of limited intelligence, with no resemblance to the seeming gentle nurse he thought he knew."

A harsh view, no doubt, but the " put him on a pedestal " attitude was certainly taken. Nevertheless there were

Sisters in that hospital who worked with untiring devotion for the benefit of their patients.

People often came to the hospital extremely dirty, and I would be told to give them their first bath. After I had bathed one woman the water was like black bog-water, and thinking she had better be rinsed out, I gave her a second bath. When I had dried her hair and put her into a clean nightgown and dressing-gown I remarked hopefully :

" Don't you feel nice and fresh now ? I am sure you will want to take a bath often after this."

Then I took her to sit by the fire, and as I left the ward I heard her say emphatically to another woman, " That baaath will do me for a year."

Another time a very large driver of a Guinness' brewery van was brought in with crushed ribs. The doctor was to see him that evening, and I was told to give him a blanket bath and to see to his nails on both hands and feet. He looked grey and shaken, and kept muttering to himself, sometimes murmuring, " Holy Mary, take me out of me trouble," and then fretfully, " Putting water and soap on me."

He bore it all till his toe-nails were being cut and cleaned, then, looking at me with hatred and raising his large, cropped head off the pillow, he exclaimed :

" Bad cess to you. After the day I'm through, crushed by me lorry, the breath drawn out of me, waiting below in the cold till the teeth in me jaw was rattling, and you come sponging and washing, with me helpless stretched in the bed under you and not satisfied "—he paused, almost trembling with fury, and added—" till you have me toe-nails clipped." He hissed these last words with venom.

He little knew how completely I agreed with him, but it was a case of the patient's comfort versus the doctor's pedestal, and in that juxtaposition the patient's feeling would not be considered.

Down in the out-patients' department I saw many and various cases. A notice said, " Ring for the house surgeon when required." Ring one might, but nothing ever came of it.

It was curious that the many bruises and contusions needing dressing were always said to be caused by falling down the chapel steps, though probably being drunk the night before was nearer the truth. The principal work was cleaning and disinfecting such wounds, or sometimes, as in the case of a man with a bad cut, sewing it up, after ringing fruitlessly for the house surgeon.

Asked how he came by his injury, the man with the cut answered, " A friend hit me on the head with a hammer."

Many children came in with sores on their legs and arms, which would be cleaned and bandaged, and then later they would be seen cutting about the streets with their nice white bandages the colour of the mud. These children would come into the hospital as tuberculous patients at adolescence and die before maturity.

One day a specialist on tuberculosis, standing by a girl in bed who had little chance of ultimate recovery, said, " They could all be cured if they could be put out on the Hill of Howth in the wind and the sun early enough. Early enough," he repeated. " As it is, treatment is useless."

" How many sleep in your bed at home, Norah ? " he asked.

" Six," she answered. " The three young ones at the bottom and me and me sisters at the top."

" And is that the bed you're going back to when you leave here ? "

" It is so, sir."

" And you are the eldest and live in those streets down by the river, back of St. Patrick's ? "

" That's where we do live, sir."

[147]

He shrugged his shoulders and murmured, " Perfect inoculation of the disease for the rest of the family."

I was glad to have experienced the routine of a hospital, but also glad that I had not trained as a nurse and made it my life's work, as I had thought of doing when I saw no other way of escape from my home. The setting had the effect of shutting out all other interests; one was too close to death and the breakdown of the body to feel interested in anything outside the walls of the hospital.

When holiday time came round once more I left Dublin not to return to nursing there, for I was afraid of falling ill, as the food was bad, the work hard, and I had lost weight and sleep. I couldn't afford to be ill, and I felt sure I ought to take an easier, outdoor post, but I said good-bye to the patients and the staff with regret, for I had liked them all.

The humble sick had been touching in their gratitude for the least kindness shown to them. I remembered a patient who when in great pain was being rather roughly fed by a probationer whose place I offered to take, suggesting she had so much other work to do. I gave the poor man a rest, and we got through the meal quietly, and as I laid him back he whispered, " Thank you. The first day you walked into the ward I knew you were the only lady in the place."

" How could you know that, for my uniform is so shabby ? " I said.

His eyes lit up for one moment. " I should know," he murmured, " for I was a butler once." He died the next day.

I was impressed by the Roman Catholic service for the dying. When the priest had come and carried out the ancient prescribed ritual and given the final absolution, the patient seemed withdrawn from this world and able to await the end in peace.

I can never forget Mercer's Hospital.

Chapter Seventeen

GARDENER COMPANION

A KIND friend who had heard of the sort of post I was looking for suggested a position that sounded possible; this was to be gardener-companion to Miss Nelly Baring, who lived at Burley in the New Forest.

"You will be very comfortable and well fed if you go there," she wrote, and added, "Nelly goes to Scotland for much of the summer, so you could put the boys with someone in the village and see them every day."

I was advised to write suggesting an interview, which I did, and was at once invited for a trial week-end. I was met at the entrance gate by my would-be employer, accompanied by six wildly yapping Pomeranians, who all seemed to be suffering from attacks of hysterics.

"I hope you like little dogs," she screamed above the tumult.

"I hate them," I screamed back, "when they behave like that."

Now I've lost my chance, I thought; but she told me later that it really made her feel inclined to engage me, as she dreaded a pussy-purring person who would sit with her, knit, and agree with everything she said.

We went round the gardens, which were extensive; they consisted of a rose-garden, a rock-garden, and two long, deep herbaceous borders on either side of a wide, mown-grass path. I asked what labour was available.

"Before the war I had three men," she said. "Now I have only one left, and he's a bit of a fool; that's why I wanted someone like you."

"I'll do my best," I answered, "but don't expect too much."

I thought that the gardens were well laid out, which was not surprising, as Miss Gertrude Jekyll, a cousin of Miss Baring, had planned everything, and had wisely left two fine, tall Scotch pines standing, ordering ericas and azaleas to be planted under them.

" Gertrude wouldn't come here," I was told, " as she was getting old, but she made me send her a measured ground plan, which I had to get a surveyor to do, as I couldn't make one myself. Then she arranged it all."

Miss Baring knew nothing about flowers, but wanted to have a first-rate garden; after dinner she showed me a list of elementary horticultural questions she had sent to her cousin. Miss Jekyll's answers were amusing, some being clear and instructive and others a terse "nonsense" or "don't be silly " or " do use your head and consult my chart ".

The next morning I was asked whether I would come on a permanent basis, and I agreed conditionally. First I made her come with me to see the greenhouses, which were in a deplorable state—full of dead or dying plants; and I said that I proposed clearing out this rubbish from two of the houses, shutting them up and having them lime-washed inside by the remaining gardener during the wet weather.

" I can keep one house properly," I explained, " but I can't keep three."

Miss Baring was a sturdy figure dressed in very Scottish tweeds, with a tendency to champ her teeth if thwarted.

" I've always had three," she protested.

" Yes, and three men," I countered. " Now, with one fool of a man, and, you may be thinking, one fool of a woman, you must be satisfied with one well-kept greenhouse instead of three derelict ones."

After a momentary pause she gave in.

" No, I don't think you are a fool by any means," she told me, " nor are you the sort of doormat person I feared I should get."

I laughed at that, and said that anyhow I would try to be a good gardener if she would be reasonable.

I settled in, and soon found that if Miss Baring was not a clever woman, she was a first-rate housekeeper. During the first Great War there was no austerity for those who could afford enough and cared enough to secure luxuries. My employer cared passionately. She had venison and game sent from Scotland, salmon from Ireland, butter, cream, eggs, and poultry from her farm tenant, and had a standing order every month for a one-tiered wedding cake from Buszards. She kept an excellent cook, with whom her morning interview sounded like a battle—a battle she always won, and from which Mrs. Baines, the cook, would retire white-faced, to vent her outraged feelings on the kitchenmaid.

My employer remained exacting, and said she couldn't live without hothouse flowers all the winter.

" I can give you some, but not a great many," I explained.

" Well, I want a great many, and I am ordering these seeds."

She showed me a list which, if grown, would have decorated Buckingham Palace and several hotels. I scratched out three-quarters.

" You couldn't get in at your door if all these were grown, and you'll be very lucky if I manage half of what I've left you," I told her.

She was very nice to me, but the horrible little dogs were a daily trial. She encouraged them to bark, and they needed little encouragement; they were all fed on luxuries, and if after being over-gorged, one turned away with curled lip, she would exclaim, " Oh, my Sweet, did Aunty forget the bread sauce ? "

Sweet, who was particularly fat and frequently sick, would then vomit on the carpet, and when this happened repeatedly the vet would be sent for.

" He is very expensive," she said, " and has to come from a distance; but it's worth it, for he really does understand her constitution."

A genial vet arrived in a car with a dog-basket, and after examining the fat, lethargic, yapping pom, he said, " I must take her home and look after her for a week."

When her owner, on the verge of tears, had seen her bundled into the basket, I went with him to his car and he said, " I hate to see dogs ill-treated like that well-meaning lady does, feeding them to death."

" She says you understand this one's constitution."

He answered with twinkling eyes, " That's right, and my treatment's right. I shall leave a bone hung just out of her reach and let her jump for it, and give her a bowl of water and a little dry bread for three days, followed by a low diet of biscuit for another three days, and so I'll bring her back a decent dog. By the way," he added, " don't let the old one bite you, for his teeth alone are enough to poison you."

" He tries to bite my ankles every day, and he has torn all my stockings."

" I'll be putting him out soon; the sooner the better, I'd say, for I suspect an internal growth."

The vet was quite right; the vindictive, evil-smelling old Jacko was taken ill the day before Sweet came back. My poor friend sat up with him all night and tried to put brandy and hot milk between his clenched teeth, but the next day he had to be put to sleep. To get his owner away at the fatal hour I persuaded her to go to Bournemouth, and she busied herself choosing hats, for she loved clothes almost as much as food. On our return Jacko was dead.

The house was hushed. His owner took to her bed, and she and her maid prepared a box lined with white satin; in contrast, the shambling gardener rejoiced openly.

" He tore all my trousers, that varmint did. I never harmed him; give him a bit of my dinner once and he bit my finger for it and I had to go to the doctor, for it was poisoned. He'd no sooner see me than he'd come tearing at me; he even has me Sunday trousers torn, but he'll do it no more, for he's lying dead there in the shed."

"I can't bear to see my darling Jacko put in his grave, so I shall stay in bed," poor Nelly said as she gave me the white satin box and some flowers. "Come and tell me about it afterwards. I'm glad it's a lovely morning and the birds are singing for my little pet."

I went out to the shed and called the gardener.

"We are to put him in this box," I told him.

"We ain't, not yet; I'm a-carrying him on this shovel." And carrying the shovel on which lay the prostrate Jacko, he addressed him: "Aha, you little varmint, I've got you now; no more tearing and biting and barking for you, you set-up little brute. I've liked well digging a hole for you."

"He must be put in his box."

I had scarcely lowered him into it when the gardener rattled in earth and stamped on it with his large splayed feet. Then more earth.

"That will keep you down,"—and another stamp, more earth and more stamping. "Now you won't get out."

I was about to put the flowers on the grave when he said, "Wait, I must firm it down."

After vigorous stamping he announced, "Now, varmint, you're finished and done for," and he shambled off.

"Was it a lovely funeral?" the poor mourning owner asked me.

I felt justified in giving her comfort by telling her the birds were singing, he was in the lovely box she had made him and her flowers were on his grave, but I did not tell her of the words spoken at his funeral.

My days were arranged on routine lines, and I always spent an hour or more before breakfast working in the garden, or in the greenhouses when it was wet. I enjoyed the quiet and freshness of the early mornings, and my employer thought it must be a dreadful hardship but also a token of my zeal to be at work so early. After breakfast I would look at the newspaper, laid out and beautifully ironed, and then go to the garden and arrange work with my underling, who was a big, shambling creature with feet that turned outwards in such a strange way that he was rejected for the army. He was no fool, but only had a slow brain, and when given sharp, quick orders, could not take them in. Like many elementary working gardeners, he was devoted to vegetable-growing and really disliked flowers; I think he bore them a grudge for sometimes wasting his time and taking him away from the things which he thought really mattered.

I had my own sitting-room to read or write or work in when I had finished gardening for the day, but after dinner Nelly, as she asked me to call her, liked me to stay with her. She told me much of her past life, from which I felt that hers was an affectionate nature. Perhaps the horrid little dogs filled a blank in her heart. Until his death she had been a devoted companion to her father, with whom she had fished Scottish rivers and stalked deer in Highland forests. She also told me of the splendour of Norman Court, their Hampshire home where they had given house parties and balls.

" All gone now," she would sigh, then her eyes would light up again and she would explain, " We did things properly at my home; we always had a French chef and a truffle man and his hound, so you can see I must have everything well done even here."

It may have been her devotion to Scotland that made her tolerate a lazy elderly ghillie she had imported to drive her car and whom she haloed with the glamour associated with their days on the moors. He was a counterpart of Queen

Victoria's John Brown, and was inclined to give orders to everyone. He was fond of his whisky, drinking large quantities of it, and when he suffered from lumbago or influenza, he believed it to be the best and only cure.

Kind as Nelly Baring was to me, she was determined to have everything up to the mark, and I began to feel the strain of the work, for I could never catch up with what needed doing, and the lazy chauffeur, who did nothing except point out what should be done, annoyed me.

For the Easter holidays, I had placed my boys in rooms in the village in the care of a governess, and one afternoon as I was putting peat round some azaleas on the drive I heard a scuffling outside the front gate. At first I took no notice, then, thinking it might be one of the little dogs, I went to open it, and found my little boy Tony flat on his stomach, breathing heavily.

" Darling, what is it ? " I cried.

He leant up against me, his face grimy and tearful, and said, " I want you."

Those three words went straight to my heart. I knew they both wanted me, and I was tied. What should I do ? What could I do to make a home for them ?

The solution came quite unexpectedly. I always corresponded from time to time with my cousin and godmother, Olive Ardilaun, and it was at her suggestion that I had gone to nurse at Mercer's Hospital in Dublin. Though I had not mentioned the incident, my letter to her after finding Tony trying to see me from under the gate may have seemed anxious and tired, for I received an immediate reply asking me to come and see her at her house in Carlton House Terrace.

I went to London for the day. The house was in the very grand style, with marble staircases and marble statues, French furniture, much gilding, brocade hangings in strong yellow and many mirrors; not altogether in good taste, but opulent. My cousin was a striking person of sixty; tall, dark, very upright, good-looking, with charming, expressive grey eyes, and dignified in a manner that was slightly alarming. She questioned me closely, and in the end I told her everything : my wish to look after my sons, my difficulties as to means, and my present position with its advantages and strains.

During luncheon we chatted of other things, and she reminded me of the time when I and my eldest boy stayed with her when he was five, recalling that when he saw a Guards' detachment going past the house with their band playing and pennants flying, he had asked were they guarding my godmother.

"He was a dear little boy," she added.

After luncheon she was silent for some time and then said, "I have a plan, but I don't know if you would care for it. There is an empty house at my Irish place, about a mile from St. Anne's. I shall give up this London house and live most of the year in Ireland, and I should like to have you and your children near me, for I am lonely wherever I am since my husband died."

I knew at once it was what I ought to do, for not only did I admire and like my cousin, but she was the only relation who with her large means could, if she wished, help my sons if I failed. Instead of battling alone on the edge of insolvency, I should feel anchored, and I could sell my house in Dorset and send the furniture to Ireland.

So it was settled, but when I had to tell my poor dear employer that I was leaving her and all about my cousin's offer, we had a painful scene, for she got angry and seemed offended. When she showed that she was hurt and distressed I really minded, and when she subsided into tears I went and knelt by her side, saying, "Dear Nelly, do try to understand my position and let us remain friends,"—which we did for as long as she lived.

At last her worldly common sense came uppermost and she agreed.

"I hate your leaving me, but of course you are quite right to go, for Lady Ardilaun might do anything for your boys," and then she added after a pause, "and one ought never to neglect really rich relations."

Chapter Eighteen

LIFE IN IRELAND

MY furniture had arrived, and I was being shown over Sibyl Hill by the caretaker, an untidy but friendly old man. This house Olive Ardilaun had lent to me as a permanent home. It was a large Georgian building, the front door of which opened into an oval with four recesses in the walls. Mahogany doors led to the inner hall, from which a wide, shallow flight of steps went up half-way. Above the landing where these steps divided there was a high window with heraldic arms in badly coloured glass of a much later date than the house, and under this light stood a cracked black stove, probably put in at the same time as the stained glass, and with the unsuitable name of " Pansy " in raised letters across its rotund front.

The rooms on the right and left of the oval hall were built in half-circles on the south side, the tall sash windows following the curved line. All the shutters and doors had pleasant moulding round their panels.

No domestic architecture is more satisfying than good early Georgian, for the quality of the work is excellent, the materials good, and the taste restrained but always fine, and, in really good examples, splendid. But much as the house appealed to me, my heart rather sank when the old caretaker threw open a door from the inner hall and said, " This is the dining-room, and we put your furniture here."

It was a room close on forty feet long, and my furniture looked a mean little heap in such vastness. My heart sank farther when, on my asking where the kitchen was, he took me down a long, stone-flagged passage with a number of smaller rooms off it, round a corner and into a cavernous kitchen with an old rusted range going right across one end. There was no electric light anywhere.

My first night in that gracious and charming house brought home my practical difficulties. It rained, and the rain came through in many places, so that part of the night was spent in putting basins and buckets to catch the worst floods. No servants had been engaged, as the house must be put to rights first, and the old caretaker and his wife, who lived in a near-by cottage, did their best to help. The kitchen was the first problem : could they light the range ?

" This many a year 'tis not been lit."

Would there be water in the boiler ?—and anyway that's cracked.

The water turned out to be from a well in the yard, and the old man pumped it, but explained, " Summers it do be very low, 'twould be as well to give a shilling to him as takes the cows water round in his cart and maybe he'd tip a couple of barrels in."

This plan was carried out, but after the well had been fed from above and pumped from below there was still no responsive gush when the taps were turned on in the bathroom, and the explanation was : " Them muslin pipes wastes a good part; I'd be pumping the whole day before I'd fill the tanks."

I felt prejudiced against muslin pipes on seeing their sweating, rust-pocked state. The day's distress culminated in finding that none of the three old-fashioned w.c.'s functioned at all, and that the vast kitchen range had a cracked oven, a leaky boiler, and took a hundredweight of coal to fill. Realizing that immediate repairs were essential and that besides the roof being repaired the old kitchen must be abandoned and a modern range put in a smaller room near the dining-room to take its place, I decided to go to my cousin, who owned the house, and explain matters.

As she had a cold she could not shake off in her own vast and very chilly home, she was staying in the Shelbourne Hotel with her maid and her secretary. I was taken through a palm-filled, over-heated hall, up thickly carpeted stairs to her suite, where she was in bed, looking charming, with cream lace over her dark hair and the same over a warm rose dressing-jacket and bedspread. I found her most gracious and kind and pleased to see me until in reply to her query as to how I was getting on, I told her of the manifold needs of the house. Instantly she stiffened and I felt her alarming side.

" Well, my dear, if you don't like it, you had better go back to England," she told me.

" I don't think anyone can live without elementary essentials : water, a dry roof, and means of cooking," I said.

" Our agent and his wife lived there quite contentedly for many years, but as I say, there is nothing to oblige *you* to stay there."

Shaken by this attitude, I decided, on my way home, what I must do. Retreat was impossible, for I had sold my house, brought over my furniture and given up my job. I must realize sufficient capital to engage men, buy the necessary materials, and make that charming house habitable; this I did. Meanwhile, wondering that the agent and his wife had been able to live there contentedly, I asked the caretaker how they had managed.

" For water they'd never turn a tap, they had the drop they'd want brought in in a bucket."

" And for cooking ? "

" They'd do that on an open grate and a bit of an oil stove; they'd not use the range."

" But why ? That must have been very uncomfortable."

" God rest their souls, they was old and in dread his lordship would turn them off and they troubling him, so they thought best to pull along and take all easy."

Soon my cousin wrote asking me to come and see her and tell her if I had done anything about the house or if I meant to leave it.   I had kept accounts and time-sheets, and taking these I went to that luxurious hotel, showing her my papers and explaining exactly what I had done.

" Was it all really necessary ? " she asked.

" You wouldn't like us to have to seek cover in the bushes, like well-trained cats, or cook on two bricks and never have a bath or indeed wash at all except with water that came through the roof."

" No, dear, I wouldn't."

She went to her writing-table and wrote a cheque, which she handed to me, and I saw it was for £100 more than I had spent.

When I exclaimed at this she said, " You may want some extra furnishings or carpets," which indeed I did.

Later I understood her first reaction. Like many very rich people, she was a magnet for sycophants, and in guarding herself against being imposed upon she was often suspicious of quite innocent people, but she was most generous, and since that first encounter I have never had acute financial anxiety.

I enjoyed furnishing the rooms I used in that house, and would haunt the quays of Dublin, where I bought several pieces of antique furniture. The dining-room was a problem, for the boards were rough and my carpet looked a

BANTRY HOUSE

FAMILY GROUP AT BANTRY HOUSE

(*Left to right*): Uncle William (3rd Earl of Bantry); Lady Elizabeth White (m. Egerton Leigh); Aunt Jane (Countess of Bantry); Lady Ina White (m. Earl Ferrers); Viscount Berehaven (4th Earl of Bantry); Lady Olive White (m. Sir Arthur Guinness, Lord Ardilaun); Sir Arthur Guinness

LADY ARDILAUN

minute island in the middle. One day in a tiny shop in a narrow street off the quays I found an immense roll of carpet with only the back showing, but of such weight that the price seemed reasonable.

"But I must see it," I said.

"For goodness sake how could you see it in this place? 'Tis a grand carpet. Why wouldn't you chance it?"

"I won't chance it; it may have some hideous pattern all over it."

"Wouldn't you like a bit of fancy pattern?"

"I wouldn't."

"If that's the way of it, sit down quiet awhile whiles I'll be watching the door. Guinness' vans be often down this way, and for the price of a drink the men will stretch it in the street for ye."

It happened as she planned, and two large draymen struggled with the carpet, which reached across the street, holding up the traffic, and attracting passers-by, who were interested and encouraging. The carpet became mine; it was a pleasant, faded plain dull gold colour, of soft, thick pile, and it fitted the dining-room perfectly.

We spent the next eight years in that house. My boys loved it, and I was quite content acting as lady-in-waiting to my cousin, both for her social and charitable efforts, and, in addition, doing a good deal of building work for her and for other people.

Olive Ardilaun had a unique position in Dublin. She had married Sir Arthur Guinness when she was nineteen, he being then the head of the brewery, but later selling his interest to his younger brother for a large fortune, which was invested in the family business. He became member of Parliament for Dublin, whence he spent his whole life, devoting his time and money to the people's benefit. His statue stands in St. Stephen's Green, which he converted

F   [161]

from a dreary enclosed square into a charming public garden.
Later in life he took a peerage.

It had been a happy marriage, but childless, and when he
died, two years before I came to live at Sibyl Hill, Olive was
a lonely woman, and this loneliness was emphasized by her
living at St. Anne's. It was a vast building in pseudo-
Palladian style, the huge portico being flanked on either side
by seven high plate-glass sash windows and surmounted by
fourteen others. Externally its great size and fair proportions gave it a certain dignity, but nothing can be said in
favour of the interior. The dark, enormous hall was
intersected midway by a wide, cold, white marble staircase,
and on the landing where the steps divided to ascend in two
flights sat a female figure, also in cold white marble,
hampered in her clearly expressed desire to appear modest
by the lack of any rag of clothing.

A London firm had furnished this mansion throughout,
and the effect achieved was of an out-of-date luxury hotel.
The reason for this wholesale method was that after the
house had taken seven years to build and was still not
finished, a date for completion was fixed so as to get the
workmen out, and it was arranged for the furniture to come
in on that day.

Olive hated the place in winter. I can see her now in my
mind, a tall, slight, black figure, flitting across that cavernous
hall, and when I joined her she would say, " Listen ! The
wailing and crying never stops. Can't you hear it coming
from a long way off ? "

" No," I would reply. " I hear the wind whistling in that
dreadful decayed and leaking winter garden."

The house was built around this depressing failure, and
rain coming through its faulty glass roof made the water
seep down into the cellars, where the central heating, which
never functioned well, was often put out by flooding. St.
Anne's may have been a good setting for very large formal

parties, but for my cousin it was more like living in a mausoleum than in a home.

With this thought in mind I suggested to her that she might take a house for the winter in Dublin instead of going to the Shelbourne Hotel for short spells. She told me she had thought of doing that, but there was another possibility. She owned two houses in St. Stephen's Green of which the leases had recently run out. She would like me to go over them and report whether they could be made into one comfortable house. They were dilapidated, but having been built in mid-eighteenth century, had the grace and character of their day. I was commissioned to do them up, and enjoyed the work. I connected the two houses on each floor. It made a perfect small town house, and I was pleased when I was allowed to furnish it, having permission to take anything I wanted out of St. Anne's. That limitless depository provided all utility things, and I found some Waterford glass, plenty of delicate early Irish silver and some good pictures brought from Muckross. For other furniture I secured the best that the many antique shops of Dublin could provide.

The Ardilauns had owned three large houses : one in Carlton House Terrace, one called Ashford near Galway, with extensive shooting and, of course, St. Anne's, four miles from Dublin, but I think no one of these places gave Olive as much pleasure as her small house overlooking St. Stephen's Green. She was touchingly delighted when connoisseurs admired her rooms, for she had never before enjoyed informed appreciation of her great possessions.

During the summer garden-parties were given at St. Anne's, but in the winter the small house in Dublin was the setting for many dinner-parties. The furniture in the dining-room was black lacquer, and old Hicks, a well-known dealer, altered an antique mahogany table of no great value for me, reducing its width, giving it oval ends, adapting its own cabriolet legs and staining it all black and polishing it till it really shone and gave back a lovely reflection of delicate silver and glass. The curtains and table-mats were of rose-red silk. The afternoon parties were given in the drawing-room.

In 1917 the Castle and the Garrison were still English, and we saw many soldiers and officials. Dublin lawyers and doctors came to see us, also professors from Trinity College, and country friends would sometimes appear. Another group of people we knew, though not intimately, were the outstanding figures in the Sinn Fein movement. The Abbey Theatre was our link with them, for Lady Ardilaun was interested in this venture, which she supported with large subscriptions from its start. She also gave luncheon-parties, after which she would take a dozen or more of her guests to fill the stalls and enjoy the plays, making, at Lady Gregory's request, as spectacular an entry to the theatre as possible. We would, in fact, make several entries, going in at one side and out the other, and then round again, being urged to do so with the idea that if an audience was seen hurrying in it would attract other people.

We could be amused or interested in a play without being in sympathy with its political implication, and would go and see Douglas Hyde and his handsome cockatoo in the little red-brick villa, never guessing the exalted position he was to reach, and would ask him whether he really believed it possible or desirable to resuscitate a dead language.

" Dead ! " he would exclaim. " It has never died, and will flourish again."

We told him of the cry of the troubled school-teacher who said to us, " How will I tell young Pat to wipe his nose in talk he doesn't understand, and forbye how will I tell him how to name a bicycle or a train or any such thing ? "

" It will come, it will come," he assured us. " The Irish

once had a great art and literature, and when they speak the Gaelic and are a free people they will have it again."

No doubt George William Russell (" A.E.") ardently hoped for and believed in the independence of Ireland, but it struck us that his mind was more fixed on mystical union with a spiritual centre than on any earthly fever. His painting suffered from this other-worldly absorption, for all sorts of angels and winged figures appear in his landscape, and are regrettable, though no doubt to him they were as " real as in a dream ".

Sometimes to entertain our guests we had musical afternoons, or actors from the Abbey, and very good they were. I remember Sara Allgood's charming voice as she enacted funny scenes with that perfect absence of self-consciousness characteristic of the Irish players. Another time Olive thought it might result in a wonderful experience if she ventured to ask W. B. Yeats to address us and to recite some of his own poems; this he consented to do. A very mixed gathering awaited him : soldiers from the Phoenix Park, some Castle people and other Dublin friends, and an old and deaf peer from the country. Talk was general when Yeats arrived late, and when he was announced he remained standing in the doorway, voices being hushed while everyone looked at his sombre figure. Then, as he did not move, Olive came forward to greet him with charming kindliness, asking if he would prefer to have tea before we were to have the pleasure of hearing his verses.

" I'll speak now," he answered.

There was some confusion getting everyone to sit down, but at last Yeats stood alone in silence in the centre of an expectant circle, his lock of black hair falling over his forehead and his eyes on the floor. After a pause which made for discomfort, though I suppose it lasted for less than two minutes, he looked past us all as if seeing some distant vision and said, " I speak of the moon."

He spoke a lot about the moon in a slow, chanting voice, sometimes as if she were a siren to allure and destroy, again as a medium of strange magic, or as a cold menace, and nobody understood any of it.

When he had stopped as abruptly as he began, Olive said, " Perhaps, Mr. Yeats, you would recite ' The Lake Isle of Innisfree ' for us." But he seemed not to have heard and announced, " A verse to the moon."

This verse had only four lines, which he half said, half sung, and then he bowed and backed towards the door, saying he wouldn't stay for tea.

When he was gone and chattering began again with varied comments, an officer was heard saying in a clear, clipped voice, " Quite batty, I suppose, poor fellow," and the deaf peer rumbled :

" Couldn't catch it all, but there's no moon to-night."

In front of me was sitting a quite bald parson, and beyond his egg-like dome was a vase of pink flowers blossoming on bare branches. James Stephens whispered to me, " Wouldn't it be well for him if some of those rosy buds would grow on his head," and this remark seemed quite in keeping with this odd party. I think Yeats was sensitive to atmosphere and could not adjust himself to the people he was addressing, for when he came to see us later, he was easy to get on with and interesting to talk to.

We were opposed to the nationalist movement, and felt utter horror at the murdering of British soldiers and loyal Irish policemen, and so we were debarred from friendship with any of the people who were fanatical leaders, suspecting that they tolerated, if they did not actually approve, these crimes in support of their cause.

Our life, whether at St. Anne's, Sibyl Hill, or in Dublin, was not all spent in social affairs. My cousin did a great deal for poor people, and every week we went to a hospital or some other charitable institution. I would tell her she made these efforts as a " heavenly fire insurance ", and that it wouldn't be valid after all as it was made too easy for her.

" If other people take flowers to a hospital," I explained, " they have to pick them and tie them up; but it's all beautifully prepared for you."

" The head gardener would be hurt and offended if he was not allowed to do them," she told me.

" You don't have to make the cakes or sacrifice anything for the making."

" Of course they are made in the stillroom."

" And other people don't have the matron and the secretary warned and awaiting them on the steps."

" Don't be silly; I don't do it as an insurance, and naturally someone is there to receive me."

She actually was truly kind and sympathetic to all her poor friends. Once, during the time when Sinn Feiners were stealing cars, she was looking from the window of an upper ward in the slum hospital where I had worked and, not seeing her car, exclaimed, " What should we do if it has been taken ? "

An old man who had on his locker her gifts of tobacco, cakes, and sweets, said eagerly, " But, my lady, the tram passes your gate."

" I've never been in a tram."

This statement caused a sensation. " Never been in a tram," was murmured from bed to bed.

" Nor in a bus," she added.

" Would you always be going in your car ? "

" Yes, except for a long journey."

" How would you be going then ? "

This question was put with profound interest, and she sat down and told them how she used to go to London.

" My husband arranged it all. Our head coachman— he is pensioned now—always went three or four days before I did, with a carriage and a pair of horses and a groom, then the second coachman would drive me down to Kingstown, where our agent met me and took me to the cabins engaged for me and my maid, which were full of flowers from my own garden. The footman who had been on the box driving down travelled on the same boat, so that when we reached Holyhead he was there to look after us and take us to our reserved carriage on the train. Then at each stopping place he would come to the carriage window—at Chester and Crewe, for instance—and when we arrived at Euston there would be dear old Horton and my own carriage to meet me."

It was pure fairy story to the eager listeners, who took a vicarious pride in the performance, without a trace of envy, and wanted it repeated with every detail filled in. The next time we were in that ward they hoped for more stories and started the ball by asking, " Tell us, my lady, did you ever see the King ? "

She responded with stories of jubilees and drawing-rooms, of commands to garden-parties and dinners at Buckingham Palace, and of coronations ; and, with her real Irish gift for description, she brought the splendour and tradition of an Abbey coronation as a reality to these men lying in their beds of sickness.

Loath to let her go, they asked : " Did you ever see Queen Victoria ? "

" Yes, of course, often in London ; but the old Queen didn't treat Ireland too well. When she was young she and the Prince Consort came and stayed with my mother's people at Muckross, in the south, and about fifty years later she came again and paid me an afternoon visit."

" Did you give her a cup of tea ? " they asked eagerly.

" Yes," she laughed, " and a bunch of flowers."

" And she'd like a cup of tea as well as any old woman, wouldn't she ? "

The description of this visit reminded me of a quick-witted old lady to whom a doctor's wife complained that my cousin's garden-parties were very mixed socially.

" Yes, she does mix her parties," the old lady agreed. " I was asked to meet Queen Victoria."

Sometimes we went to a home for old governesses where on opening the front door we were met by a smell of cabbage, mutton, and linoleum. This was a tiring effort, for we had been told there were hurt feelings and jealousy if anyone was missed, and so we went from room to room. In each of these was a gallery of photographs of late pupils, and as some of the governesses were very old, we would be amused at identifying some elderly general as a little boy in a sailor suit. A holiday or any change was difficult to secure for these poor old things, so I offered to take some who had nowhere else to go for a week at a time. They were no trouble, and I found their overwhelming gratitude oppressive. One old lady, a tiny hunchback, deeply religious on evangelical lines, was determined to repay me by converting me. She used to dart out and beg me to kneel with her in prayer and, though I was patient in listening to her exhortations, kneel in the drawing-room with her I would not. She was to be returned to the Home in a seedy, old-fashioned carriage, the cheapest thing I could hire, which was driven by an old man wearing a top hat like a concertina but which had a cockade, and on seeing this grandeur my poor tiny friend was overcome.

" It is too much," she cried, pressing a tract into my hand; " but I can do this for you. Promise me that you will read it. It might be the means of saving you : it saved King Edward before he died."

The tract was an irritating and lurid description of the effects of drink and an unctuous appeal to abstain. I don't drink; if I had been so inclined I should have needed a stiff one after keeping my promise and reading that tract.

A very different visit from that to the governesses with

their photographs was to a vagrants' shelter which my cousin helped to support. All sorts of derelicts found their way to this large cavernous room, where they could cook a bit of food and find warmth and a roof for the night for nothing, and by paying twopence, have a mattress on the floor to sleep on.

The matron who supervised this mixed but cheerful crowd told us stories of their strange lives, often unattached and carefree, but sometimes tragic. One was of an old woman who, when cooking at the stove, suddenly saw a policeman at the door, and no doubt knowing that he had a warrant to arrest her, like a flash was lying on a mattress with a blanket pulled over herself, her old head in a rusty bonnet sticking out at one end and a dirty pair of boots at the other.

" I'll defy ye to lay a hand on me in my bed," she announced with spirit.

" If ye can call where you are, being in your bed, you have the law of it," she was told.

"And honest paid for," and fumbling in a bag hung round her neck, she extracted twopence.

" Queer and rare for yourself to be behaving honest, but for all as I say you have the law of it, and I'll be going on my way ; but I'll have you yet."

As soon as she felt safe she emerged, putting her twopence back into its bag, and muttering, " Sinful waste 'twould be to be paying the price of a mattress, for I'll be out of this before the night's through, and when me fine boyo is at the door to meet me he can cool his heels while I'll be travelling the mountainy roads with my reels and bootlaces."

Over all we did, whether we were visiting poor people, entertaining, or peacefully gardening, hung the threat of what amounted to a war, and hardly a day passed without our hearing of some cruel outrage or the murder of someone we had known.

Chapter Nineteen

WAR IN IRELAND

I HAD come to Ireland after the 1916 rebellion, when
Sackville Street stood in partial ruin and murders and
burnings were still frequent. Lloyd George had sent us the
Black and Tans as auxiliary police, and although I hold no
brief for the plan, or for them, I think that when people in
England condemn the violence of his force, they do not
realize their provocation. The English, unlike the Irish,
forgive and forget all injuries done to them or hatred felt for
them.

The first brake full of gay young men drove from Kingstown to their barracks singing songs which were abruptly
checked when a man, stepping off the pavement, hurled a
bomb into their vehicle and disappeared. He was shielded
by his friends while the first victim died during his first hour
in Ireland and his comrades were wounded and spattered
with his blood. Again, in the first week of their arrival,
a rifle-bullet ploughed through the brains of one of the
players during a game of football. Were these Black and
Tans gentle ? Of course they were not, but the pattern of
the fight was set by the Irish, and took the form of attack
from a place of safety and the quick disappearance of the
attackers. As in all movements of violence, it was
organized by a small minority who, with eloquence and
bribery, roused in their followers the sleeping tiger which
lies deep in us all.

My house was a mile and a quarter distant from my
cousin's vast mansion, and, as she was lonely, I would go
and see her after dinner, and stay until midnight, or sometimes even later if she could persuade me to. The later it
grew the more brilliant and amusing she would become,

while I would be increasingly dormouse-like and drowsy, but on any sign of my going she always had something she wanted to show me.

"My dear, have you read this interesting diary of our great-uncle, all about his rides through Wales?"

"No, and I don't care where he rode; I'm going to ride home on my bicycle."

"You can't go yet; it's quite early."

She was very interested in genealogies, and if she saw me rolling up my work she would say, "I must show you a delightful print of the old Countess of Desmond, who comes into the Herbert family and who walked right across England when she was one hundred and ten. I think you have a look of her."

"Whatever she did, I'm going to bicycle more than a mile for home and bed at once."

Ultimately I would escape, be shown out at the huge portico by a sleepy footman, and be greeted by the night watchman who patrolled the house. The avenue ran perfectly straight for a mile, and midway there was a deep underground tunnel, constructed when the drive was made, to prevent people using an existing right of way, and being seen in the open crossing the avenue. This passage was a hiding-place for Sinn Feiners, who had a system of lights from torches or lamps by which they signalled from the sea road south of the big house to the road north of mine. I would bicycle quietly down this avenue and suddenly be picked up by the beam of a torch, which would flicker and follow me as I sped along. At the end of the mile this arrow-straight road curved round to my house, and the signal would be picked up and another light follow me down that last quarter of a mile. My nerves stood it well as long as I was moving, but I felt a tremor when I had to get off, lean my bicycle against the steps, and fumble with my key at the front door while that beam of weak light played on my back, and then pick up my bicycle and get it into the hall and lock up.

One night as I was approaching the underground passage nine men emerged and stood across the road holding revolvers. I got off and faced them in silence, while one man stepped up to me and said, " You do be very late on this road. Take warning that if anything is said of our being this way or of your seeing lights or hearing whistles, your place will go up."

Looking at the speaker, I saw he was a mere boy, and, indeed, despite their rifles and revolvers, the others appeared very young, and after the first recoil I felt no fear.

" Now you have said your piece," I said, " get back to where you've come from and let me get back to my bed."

They made way, and as I rode off they called after me, " Good-night to you, Mam."

When I told my cousin about this she said, " I wish you would take the night watchman with you."

" No," I said; " that would be dangerous : he has a gun. Going alone, unarmed, and showing I'm not afraid is, I feel sure, the safest way."

Incidentally, soon afterwards the night watchman was tied to a tree and his gun taken from him, in spite of his protesting, " That gun wouldn't kill a sparrer."

" I told them so," he explained, " but for all they took it off me and left me tied to the tree all night."

I was pleased one night, coming home in a thick white ground-mist, to have succeeded in frightening one of the haunters of the tunnel. He had just crept out, and, seeing a dim shape, I rang my bell sharply before he saw me. I suppose he thought it was police, for, throwing up his arms, he gave a wild cry of " Christ ! " and hurled himself into the trees.

In the old outhouses of my house many men on the run hid and slept, and one night, hearing constant whistle signals,

I felt worried, for there were so many cases of these men breaking into houses demanding food and blankets with threats. Getting out of bed without striking a light, I knelt at the window-sill and saw furtive, stooping figures crossing the garden. I called the couple I employed and got them to come to my room, where we watched figures still creeping past the house.

After a few minutes the woman said in an agonized whisper, " What'll I do if they take my lovely young cocks ? "

The idea of this calamity steadied me, and I sent them back to bed. Not that there wasn't tragedy through these men. They made a hole in the brick wall of the vegetable garden behind my house, which gave on to the road, and through it shot a man dead. The police made a vain search, and the hole was built up only to be broken open again, for at that time they were shooting our troops from ambush wherever they could.

I was anxious, because I had an old friend whose only son was quartered in Dublin and drove past that hole on his way to see his mother. At a party one day I warned him under my breath while pretending to look at a flower : " Go the other road; there's a man with a rifle behind the hole in my garden wall."

Not very long afterwards a man was found lying dead on the garden side of the wall, and it was much later that I heard what had happened. The young officer, far from going home the other way, was determined to get this gunman and, putting the brakes of his car hard on just short of the spot, had got out, saying loudly, " Dash it, steering's gone wrong again," and had lobbed a bomb into the hole.

That was the kind of war it was, and the British soldiers hated it. Friends we had known were murdered, reprisals were taken, and one atrocity followed another. Then came capitulation from the British Government, and emissaries from the gunmen went to London to negotiate a treaty, which, after some months, was signed. Loyalists felt that if it was to be granted it should have been done either long before the crime wave had grown to such violence, or not until the terrorists had been beaten, which the commander of the troops believed could have been done in a comparatively short time had his hands not been tied by the Home Government. It was painful to hear boastings of how little Ireland had brought England to her knees, and it also set a precedent that others have not been slow to follow.

No sooner had the negotiators of the treaty returned in triumph than they were met with bitter hostility from the extremists in their own party, who screamed of betrayal and vowed revenge. They formed themselves into the Irish Republican Army, and civil war broke out between the I.R.A. and the Free Staters; burnings and shootings were worse than ever, though now ostensibly directed by Irishmen against Irishmen.

One day, having heard that the lovely Customs House had been set on fire after street fighting, I went into Dublin to see, and found a shrieking crowd watching flames lick up towards the dome. It was utterly horrible that these savages should enjoy such vandalism. A loyalist whom I met reproached me for feeling the loss of any building so bitterly, implying that by doing so I minimized the much more important loss of life the movement had cost. It was impossible to explain in that crowd that it was not a matter for comparison, for I felt that any real great work of art represented one of the highest expressions of man's spirit which remained to rejoice the heart and inspire countless numbers of those who had eyes to see, long after the bones of the creator had turned to dust. The value of human life is a totally different thing, and cannot be assessed in the mass; the death of certain people might be a good thing, and a great saint might be of more value than any great work of art. It certainly was shattering to hear a howling mob exulting in the destruction of their own heritage, though in fact the fire was put out before the whole structure was destroyed.

Later the I.R.A. barricaded themselves into the Four Courts—another beautiful building—from where they could safely snipe their enemies, and the Free Staters were driven to beg the British garrison to lend them a big gun to dislodge them, thus partially destroying this fine structure. However, they got into trouble with it, and had to ask for the gunners, who, when they arrived, were enraged to find their precious weapon so badly handled and men trying to fire it from a safe distance with the help of a long strand of wire.

Hate, rage, and bitterness flamed ever higher between the two factions. If one side occupied a house or barracks, the other side tried to eject them, and then they would burn the place down, or perhaps the occupiers, before getting out, would burn any place they could to spite their enemies. Both sides blew up trains and bridges indiscriminately.

During this civil war period we heard that Macroom Castle, Lady Ardilaun's old home in County Cork, which she had inherited, was full of I.R.A.'s, and almost immediately afterwards rumour reached us that it was burning. When people have been born and have grown up in a house on their own land, where their forebears have lived and died for generations, they may feel not only love for it, but a bond which ties them to every stone and tree and sod of the place. That was how my cousin felt. The day the rumour of the burning reached us was made more anxious and unendurable in that there were no railways, posts, telegrams, or telephones functioning between Dublin and the south to confirm or to give any particulars of the situation.

There was no leaving Olive that night; she walked from

room to room wringing her hands, sometimes weeping and murmuring, " My place, my own dear, dear home," then with rage she would add, " The brutes—if only I could get news."

Feeling sure the rumour was true, I tried to make her see that it was better burnt, cleansed by fire from all the horrors it had seen, and in an effort to make her take this point of view I talked of the immediate past. It had been the stronghold of that area for the Black and Tans. At first a series of stiff, polite letters had come from the commanding officer to my cousin, which she had answered with anger, so deeply did she resent her property being commandeered. The last exchange was a request for the coal cellar to be unlocked by the caretaker, who had refused to do so.

" What do you want it for ? " was wired.

" To put coal in," was wired back.

Such skirmishes were overshadowed by the swift tragedy that overtook the Black and Tans. While on the way to one of their first patrols they met what appeared to be a company of British soldiers in uniform, who called their brake to a halt with a polite request for help, and then immediately opened fire at close range. Seventeen were killed and their bodies terribly mutilated.

Soon after this incident I went to the Castle by train to collect some things my cousin wanted saved. I arrived in the early afternoon, intending to stay for a night at the local inn. I found the place darkened, an order having been given that windows were to be closed and blinds and curtains drawn. Kneeling on the floor, I peeped under the blinds, and soon saw a gun-carriage driven at speed over the rough road and with a coffin bouncing on it. Black and Tans were standing with rifles at the ready, and at a signal the massive oak gates of the Castle lodge were opened, the gun-carriage without slackening speed dashed through, and the gates were closed again. That evening I saw the commanding officer, and found him almost distraught with anxiety. It was arranged to have a picture by Claude and a few pieces of furniture—all now in my possession—removed.

"The prisoners can do that in the morning," he agreed; "we have half-a-dozen in the coal cellar."

"Then you did want it for more than coal?"

He gave a wan smile. "When I first came here I little knew what I was in for. I can trust no one. Already I have lost twenty-five of my men, and they are getting hard to hold. I can't give them any exercise—can't even allow them to knock a ball about in the park, lest they are sniped at from over the wall. They can't walk a yard or go into a shop without danger, and they are savage for revenge."

I reminded my cousin of all this, saying, "There were too many tragic things done there. I cannot forget the poor woman in her long black cloak going down on her knees to entreat me to speak for her son, who was a prisoner in your castle. When, with clanking chains round his legs, he was carrying out your picture I did speak for him, you know, asking if there was any hope for him, but the Colonel thought there was none. 'He was caught with a gun just after one of our poor chaps was shot, and was certainly one of the gang that got him.'"

"I can't help anything that has happened there," my cousin replied. "It was my trust to guard and care for. It withstood Cromwell's siege and has seen plenty of trouble ever since. My dear, dear home."

"Nothing in the past has been like these recent horrors. Only the other day we heard of those four young officers being caught by the I.R.A. and tortured in those cellars till they died. Such things leave a terrible atmosphere, and if it really is burning, I feel it would be a purification."

"If I could only know: to be helpless to do anything is

killing me. Even if they have burnt it, some of the things might be saved if someone could see to it."

"Would you like me to go?" I asked. "I am sure I could get there with my bicycle."

This idea gave her a little comfort and, borrowing night things, I went to my room.

The next day I got as far as Limerick by train, but beyond that the line and bridges were damaged. It was two o'clock, and I had sixty miles to go. Advised that all that country was in the hands of the I.R.A. and a pass from them would be necessary, I applied reluctantly at their headquarters, and obtained one from a seedy-looking young man in a stained yellow mackintosh. A couple of men with a side-car also applied, and as they were going my way they offered me a lift.

"Hop up now, and we'll tie the bicycle behind."

"No, thank you all the same," I replied. "I'd sooner go on my own."

Off they started, and about two miles down the road I came up with them, the car on its side, the horse out of the shafts and a big hole in the bridge ahead of them, but there was room for me to pass.

"You were not so foolish for all," they shouted as, waving to them, I went on my way.

It was a lovely soft day, and the country looked peaceful. After going for a couple of hours I came to a white cottage, and went in, asking if I could have a cup of tea.

A woman, with bare feet but perfect manners, welcomed me, and while laying the table she asked me, was it far I was going, and when I told her my destination she exclaimed, "Holy Mother! you'd never reach it the night."

"I might stop off in Millstreet, and go on in the morning, but the days are long, and I might get there yet."

"I wouldn't be wishing you on the mountain and night falling, for terrible things do be doing; one of my boys is out this minute."

" With the I.R.A. ? "

" Indeed, yes; and I have another a Free Stater. My heart's scalded, for didn't I lose my eldest in the war."

" Which war ? "

" In the English war with the Germans, of course. I'm heartsick with wars; all my three boys were good boys, but, God help me, with a great taste for fighting."

I thanked her for her excellent cup of strong tea and wished to pay for it.

" To take the price of a cup of tea after having a pleasant chat ! No, indeed and I will not."

We parted with kindly feelings, and in the golden light of the late afternoon I pushed on, looking towards the mountains, which were violet in the distance, and the bogland that lay on either side, all so peaceful and quiet.

Close to the small town of Millstreet a man with a rifle stepped from the shadow of a thorn-tree and asked had I a pass for the road. He examined my pass and said, " Listen here. A battle is laid for the bridge beyond, and 'twouldn't do for yourself to be caught in it. Stay here in the ditch and hide your bicycle, and as soon as ever the fighting's over I'll be back and give you the all clear."

He was most helpful, getting turf and branches to conceal the bicycle. " Wouldn't it be the great temptation for one on the run in a hurry to see it shining before him, while he'd take not a bit of notice of any woman resting herself on the roadside. I'll be back then." And he went off at a loping run.

It seemed fantastic to be sitting in a leafy ditch looking at the setting sun and the empty, placid landscape while I calmly waited for a battle to be over. Soon a few shots rang out, and in under an hour my chivalrous friend came back and told me, " We had them easy beat without a bit of trouble, but there's one dead on the bridge, and I wouldn't have a lady see the like of that, so I'll take you by the stepping-stones. You'll not have a bit of trouble, for the river's low." He carried my bicycle across and left me.

I went up the main street of the little town, which was thirty miles from the Castle, and I knew I could not reach it that night. All doors and windows were closed, and no reply was forthcoming when I knocked at a door, nor was there any response from passers-by whom I asked if there was a room to be had. Everyone seemed unfriendly until, seeing a group of women, I went up to them and said, " Isn't there one who'd speak a word to an Irishwoman, and she one of the family ? "

The change was startling.

" To think of that ! " they cried; " the word went you were an English policewoman."

" I've come from her ladyship to see if the Castle is burnt."

" 'Tis so; the Staters were for turning the Republicans out, so they fired it before they made off, and there's ne'er a bed you'll find in this place, for it's full up with them same boys."

" Would you be willing to come into my place ? You could rest easy in a chair for the night." An old woman led me through a tiny shop to an even smaller sitting-room behind, where there was a peat fire, which she blew upon till the turf began to glow. " Wait till I put the kettle on for a cup of tea," she said; " and I have some soda bread, but before I do that I'll draw the curtains."

She went to a narrow slit of window, about a foot high, which had red flannel, such as they used to make country petticoats of, strung on a string over it.

" 'Tis as well to be cautious," she added, " for these times they'd think no more of slitting our throats than they would a couple of ducks."

I dozed through the night in the chair by the fire, and before dawn made myself another cup of tea; then, leaving a little money under the teapot, I unlocked the shop door and crept out with my bicycle. It was dead quiet, and the mountain I had to cross showed dark against the sky. It was a long, upward climb, with the world around changing every moment, the sky turning from grey to gold and the rising sun striking patches of vivid green on the mountain-side. Walking and riding, and always thinking the top was at hand, I paused after an hour and a half to see another long rise ahead, all gold-bronze colour. It was completely lonely, no living thing was in sight, and I went on again until at last I reached the top and the road led downwards. What a view! Below was the valley framed in trees, and then ridge after ridge of distant hills, rosy on the sunlit side and fading away to violet and faintest blue. The road slipped away under the bicycle, and presently something else showed in the lovely landscape : a tall spiral of smoke, thin and fading at the top. The Castle had always appeared to be solid deep green, from the ivy that clothed it, with great twisted stems as thick as a man's thigh. Now it was rust colour. All the village seemed gathered outside the Castle, where furniture, china, and pictures lay on the lawn or leaned against trees, while policemen prevented the on-lookers from going too near the smoking ruin.

" Is Mrs. McCarthy here ? " I asked.

The policeman shouted, " Mrs. McCarthy wanted," and an elderly woman with a good, honest face appeared.

" Her ladyship sent me," I told her. " She's broken-hearted about the Castle."

The poor woman burst into tears. " I couldn't stop their wickedness," she gulped between sobs. " When I saw them spreading tallow and paraffin everywhere I knew what was in their black hearts." She paused. " Then it was I went in and tried to drive them out of it. ' Thirty years I'm care-taker here and you'll not burn it ', and the answer I got was for one of them to strike a match in my face, which I struck out of his hand and put my foot on the light. ' Carry out the furniture first,' I told them, and that I made them do, and they muttering and cursing and taking God's holy name at the delay, and all that was left was my own bits in my rooms, for by that time they had the top floor blazing. Well, I got her ladyship's things out and Cromwell's cannon balls, for she laid great store by them."

The next twenty-four hours were spent in a turmoil. The furniture had to be put wherever shelter could be found, looting checked as far as possible, transport arranged to Cork, where I hoped to send it by sea, and intermittently poor brave Mrs. McCarthy to be reassured and comforted.

Two memories stand out from that hectic time. The first is getting the policeman to allow me to look in at the great door of the Castle, which was still smouldering, and the immensely massive stone walls were leaning outwards. The dividing floors had fallen in, and inside that great door the mass of the stone staircase, which went up three floors, lay shattered in a vast heap, with the wrought-iron balustrade, twisted and fire-rusted, writhing through it. Little spirals of smoke came from the ends of embedded oak joists, and above all this desolation the blue summer sky was framed in the roofless square tower. My other memory is of a grave tucked away in a dank, shaded corner behind the church; this was where the coffin I had seen rushed jolting through the Castle gates was buried, and the murdered man within was an Australian. It took my mind back to that distant, sunny, carefree land. What cruel madness all this seemed!

The day I was to ride to Cork the weather changed and was overcast. A storm seemed to be coming up over the mountains, but a more sinister human storm burst on that mountain road, for there Michael Collins, hero of the Free State, was shot dead. Panic seized the people; there was wailing and keening in the houses, and many fled and went into hiding. Sick of horrors, I started for my long ride to

Cork. Thunder rumbled in the distance as I wheeled my bicycle on the steep road out of the valley, and, seeing a motor van coming my way, I signalled to the driver and stopped him.

"Indeed yes, 'tis all the way to Cork I'm bound, and I'll take you and welcome."

As I sat on the hard seat beside him, watching the lightning flash, he remarked conversationally, "I have a load of petrol up behind, and if them boys chance to put a shot in us, the two of us will go up in blazes."

During that drive to Cork we passed one place after another that had been burnt, and as we went by the gate of Mrs. Lindsay's place, all that could be seen of her house was one black and ruined wall.

"A terrible thing was done there, to think of her and her old coachman and the little dog being dragged up the mountain-side and all murdered," I said to the driver.

"And for why would the old lady be giving the British warning of the ambush the way she did?" he answered.

"She did it to save young lives and because she was a brave woman."

"'Tis best to keep your mouth shut these times."

That was the attitude I found in Cork, where there was a sense of great nervous tension and horror at the death of Michael Collins and fear of violent reprisals, whispers of which were already heard. There was also a rumour that De Valera had been seen escaping from the district dressed as a nun—probably an untrue story, but it was believed, as was every other wild statement.

At the furniture remover's the foreman thought I might get a coastal vessel to take his vans up to Dublin, and he advised me where to apply. He was to collect and pack the furniture as soon as the roads were thought safe, for, "There's not a packer I could persuade to go now," he told me.

" Do you think I could hire a car to-day to take me to
Mallow ? " I asked.

" You could not.   There may be all manner of fighting
and ambushing, for there's many hiding in the woods and
the mountains since the killing of Michael Collins.   You'd
best stay here for a week or two, and then maybe the trains
will be running again."

" I can't do that," I answered, thinking of the frenzy of
anxiety my cousin would have worked herself into over such
a prolonged absence, during which there was no means of
communicating with her.

In the end, after having done my business, I started off on
my bicycle, and with the help of occasional lifts reached
Mallow, to find that the last train for Dublin had gone, but
that I could send a telegram.   Mallow was full and seething
with excitement, and I spent a horrible night with nightmare
dreams on a horrible bed, and was called at six for the early
train and asked, "Would you take a chop to your breakfast?"

" No, I wouldn't."

After interminable hours in a crawling train I reached
Kingsbridge Station, my mission accomplished and the doom
of Macroom Castle verified.

Chapter Twenty

OLIVE ARDILAUN

LADY ARDILAUN has been criticized for letting me
take risks on her behalf, but the truth is that in some
ways we were temperamentally alike and both of us were
disinclined to submit to any terrorist tactics and both

disposed to combat them. At this time, fearing she might
be kidnapped for ransom, as some had been, we begged her
never to wander about the large gardens alone.

"If they did take me," she said, "I know it would
kill me, and you could put 'died of rage' on my tomb-
stone."

I took such risks as I did by choice, but, owing to her
great wealth, my cousin had always led a sheltered, guarded
life, and imagination does not take the place of experience.
She had never gone unattended, and to her my ride home at
night was as remote as a polar explorer's efforts would be to
one who had never seen ice or snow.

At this time Ina Jephson, a dear friend to whom I and my
boys were devoted, had brought her furniture over and was
sharing Sibyl Hill with us. There was no central heating,
the house was terribly cold and draughty and even under
ordinary circumstances it would have been no place for
anyone whose health, at the time, was far from good. The
circumstances were by no means ordinary, for we were all
of us labouring under the strain of living through a period
of civil war, and houses were being constantly raided.

Sibyl Hill, for all its bolts and stout shutters, was far from
being even burglar-proof, as was shown by the following
disturbing little episode.

"Bet you we'd be in in two minutes if you shut up everything first," my two boys shouted.

Nothing would stop them, and we had to try. Putting
them outside, we bolted and barred the house, only to hear,
alas! in just about two minutes, the sound of their feet
clattering down the stairs.

"How did you get in?" we asked.

"Oh, quite easily: we climbed on to the water-butt, up
the pipe, and into Ina's room."

I am glad to say that, before this happened, I had persuaded my friend to leave. I was tied by my cousin's needs

and Ina's decision was taken reluctantly and only, I think, because she knew it would relieve my mind.

We had a couple in the house as servants; the wife a dour, excellent worker from the north of Ireland, and William, the husband, from the south. The latter was terribly cast down at the departure of so much furniture.

" Ah then, the house looks destroyed," he complained. " All that ground stuff gone out of it, and the empty rooms naked and bare put a disgrace on us."

" Less to dust," his wife sniffed.

Soon after this the Castle furniture arrived by sea from Cork, and my cousin asked me to house it. William was enchanted when it was carried in.

" Wasn't it well for us to have got rid of them old traps to make place for real quality ? " he exclaimed.

A nightmare Victorian clock of brightest gilt, with a recumbent female spread over the top and an immense glass dome edged with red plush to go over it and preserve its resplendence, had survived all dangers, and it particularly delighted him.

A much more precious article had not survived : a very large antique deep blue, rose, and gold dinner service, which had been packed in two barrels, into each of which the admirable caretaker had inserted one of Cromwell's heavy iron cannon balls. These had worked their way back and forth, crunching the old china as they went till a mere remnant survived, but the rest of the furniture was none the worse for its journey.

No matter how disturbed the country was, one's private life must be lived on a normal level, and I found peace of mind in my garden, where I really enjoyed working. Often when dressed in old clothes, and absorbed in what I was doing, a call would come from St. Anne's for me to come and do something else, and one rainy afternoon, when digging, and having heard no one approaching, a voice announced,

" Her ladyship sent me to say, would you be ready in half an hour to go with her to meet the King of Portugal ? "   It was the last thing I wanted to do, but Olive did so much for me that I owed her some companionship, so I told the footman to say I would be at St. Anne's in time.

Meeting the King of Portugal meant attending a reception where dull speeches were made, and he, poor man, after shaking hands with everyone, went to sleep, for he was ill at the time, and died soon afterwards.

Olive also found her greatest pleasure in her garden, in which she took endless trouble and, from a theoretical standpoint, was quite an expert.

" I should have enjoyed doing some actual work," she once told me, " but it wasn't possible.   Once I pulled up a weed or two, but my dear old Head met me in the very act and looked very pained and hurt, and the next day there were men and boys in every border and by-way hunting stray weeds like sleuth-hounds.

" Another time I said I should like to learn to take cuttings, but when I saw the preparations for my lesson— bags of earth, leaf-mould and sand, pots and crocks and moss, all being carried to the garden tea-room—I felt I was wasting a lot of the men's time.   I was shown exactly how to do them, and thought I had done them perfectly, though there were murmurs about making them ' firrem '.

" When everything had been taken away I went to see where they were to be grown, but retreated quickly when, on my way to the nursery ground, I glimpsed my old friend in the potting-shed, inserting one of them into a pot, while the rest lay on the bench awaiting his expert, firm handling. Still, the fiction was kept up, and those carnations were always called my cuttings."

She had taken over the walled vegetable garden and, with unlimited labour and indifference to cost, had turned it into a setting for flowers, making it a show-place from earliest spring till late autumn. She was a capable and persistent person, and took infinite pains to achieve her results; I learned a great deal from her, and she also learned something from me, for I stressed the importance of the layout and plan—a side she had not sufficiently considered.

" But I don't know what you mean by the architectural side," she exclaimed.

" I mean the setting for your flowers, which are lovely—almost too lavish," I told her. " They just riot and compete with each other everywhere."

" What else should they do ? "

" Make pictures and have some quiet spaces. You have half-a-dozen straight borders : do away with two side ones, keep your centre path, but have some quiet lawn to rest the eye upon, and have some good lead or stone vases or figures from which your walks can radiate. Any group of flowers fitting a picture are better than masses clamouring everywhere for attention."

" I did want to put up a memorial to my old head gardener," she said—" a most devoted friend—but when I went to look at tombstones in Dublin they didn't seem to do for a garden."

" I should think not," I exclaimed.

I found a fine twisted Italian pillar, with a stone basket of carved flowers on top, which became not only the memorial to the gardener but a focal point for part of the new plan, and my cousin was pleased with the effect.

One day, when calling on a friend, we were shown what our hostess called her herb-garden, which contained some interesting plants, but was entirely without design.

" Where could I have a herb-garden ? " said my cousin, who was taken with this.

" It should be a separate garden," I said, " and not just in one untidy corner, such as we saw to-day."

I had always liked the formal Elizabethan gardens, and

thought that such a pattern would fit in with herbs. There was a large circle of ilex-trees in the park, all of them well feathered and clipped, which would make a perfect grey-green background. When I suggested this circle as the site for her herb-garden, my cousin asked me to make it exactly as I liked.

Is there any fun equal to the pleasure of having a free hand to create something one visualizes and believes will be beautiful, holding on to one's vision and overcoming difficulties—even though in the end it is not quite as beautiful as one had dreamed? With an illustrated book on knott gardens, I drew a plan of oval beds, large on the outer circumference, graduating to tiny ones towards the centre, with narrow paths circling them all and twining in and out. This plan, accurately drawn to scale, I gave to the head gardener, and was surprised to find him quite distracted and unable to translate it into fact on the site. I soon got it taped out with pegs and lines, and with a gang of workmen it took shape quickly. We sent for lists of plants from various sources and asked a doctor to name all the medicinal plants he knew.

" Want poisons, too ? " he asked.

" Yes, if you use them and if they can grow in this country."

The gardener was helpful in collecting the herbs together, and by the autumn all were planted. The large beds on the outer circle were filled with rosemary, borage, fennel, rhubarb, and lavender, and the other plants were arranged in graduating sizes. We had wormwood and pennyroyal, balm and poppies, hore-hound and hyssop and basil bush, and endless others which I have forgotten. There are more than twenty different kinds of thyme, and each bed was edged with a different-sized one, the tiny final bed with the inch-high type. The paths winding in and out were of crushed shell, and I had four lead figures of the seasons looking outward from the centre, to suggest healing herbs at all times. My cousin was enchanted, and the following summer decided to give a party for doctors only.

We waited in the herb-garden, which was backed by silvery, grey-green, clipped ilex-trees, which made a fifteen-foot-high hedge; and the many varieties and shapes of the plants, the gentle blue of lavender, the flitting of butterflies, the humming of bees, the aromatic scent, and the formal Elizabethan pattern all gave a breathless, timeless atmosphere.

The doctors, who were to be guided to us across a field, came in droves, very professional-looking in black coats and striped trousers; but the best moment was when we saw a victoria being slowly drawn by a pair of bay horses across the level field, which the others had crossed on foot, and old Sir Lambert Ormsby, a well-known Dublin medical man, sitting in it, his top hat gleaming and his white whiskers floating below. He skipped out as if his eighty-odd years were nothing, and became as absorbed and interested as any of them.

They stooped over specimens; they made notes; they put on spectacles for closer inspection, and one heard such comments as :

" How often I have ordered this ! never realized it looked like this." " The old pharmacopœia had its points." " Never use this now; pity, perhaps."

We found it quite difficult to persuade these learned specialists to come to the flower-garden, but presently the last black coat was ushered out, the little wrought-iron gates closed, and the bees and the butterflies left in peace in the scented air.

After tea, when some of the doctors had gone, those who were not in a hurry wished to go back to the herb-garden, and this time we sat on the circular seats under the great ilex hedge, where they smoked and talked and we listened.

" I should like to write a book tracing the mediaeval use of plants from the earliest day of which records exist."

" That might take you back to the Egyptians—that is, if they knew as much about saving life as they did about preserving the dead."

" Anyhow, I believe there is still much to be learnt about the useful functions of plants; yet, instead of learning, we have forgotten a good deal that was once known. There is probably much still to be discovered."

" Better be careful, or you'll get classed with the herbalist cranks."

" I was reading recently of the remarkable cures some savages achieve, mixed up, no doubt, with faith-healing and totems, or magic or what not; but they seem to have used plants of which we know nothing, both internally and externally. Boiling roots as they did to make compresses for wounds, no doubt they achieved a certain degree of antisepsis. I maintain this sort of thing has great scope for investigation."

" All said and done, we do use a number of drugs of vegetable origin."

" Naturally, but I'm thinking of those we don't use and know nothing about."

So the talk went on till the sun was low and a golden light flowed over one side of the garden and our party broke up, our guests declaring it to have been the most interesting and delightful afternoon they had spent for many a long day.

Once more the wrought-iron gate was closed and all was quiet in that scented enclosure, for the birds, bees, and butterflies had gone to rest.

Some years later, in England, I heard a man say, " The most perfect herb-garden I ever saw was near Dublin." It was that garden, now no doubt a wilderness, with possibly just a strand of feathery fennel, or a star of blue borage and a

ROUGHFIELD

(*Above*) The drawing-room   (*Below*) From across the pond

SAN MARTINO, FLORENCE

tangle of woody-stemmed thyme to recall what it had once been.

As if a curtain had come down on a brightly lighted stage, that chapter of my life came to an end : with no warning, no premonition, Olive Ardilaun died.

Looking at her as she lay dead, more beautiful than she had been in life, two long dark plaits below her fine chiselled features, and folds of the ivory time-toned satin of her wedding dress draping her form, she seemed as remote from the vital person of the day before as one of the mediaeval Florentine tombs she so much resembled.

My personal loss was overshadowed in those first days of mourning by the flow of messages to be answered and interviews to be undergone. Again and again came the summons for me to speak to someone in the hall and, answering one such call, I found a little old lady in black, who took my hand in her trembling ones and, with a great effort at self-control, murmured with difficulty a few French words of sympathy. I took her up to the bedroom, and the tranquillity of that form brought calm to her.

" Thank you," she said. " I shall never forget that I have been allowed to see such noble beauty and such wonderful dignity."

I remembered the story that formed a link with this frail old Frenchwoman. My cousin was interested in French history, and when reading St. Simon and wanting some help over language difficulties, she engaged this old teacher to come and read with her. After one such session she noticed a pair of black silk gloves which seemed mended almost from end to end, and, getting up and walking past them, verified that there was more darn than fabric. Thinking the woman must be very poor to take such infinite trouble mending those silk gloves, she went to her writing-table and made out a cheque for one hundred pounds.

" You have given me so much pleasure and help," she said, folding the cheque and giving it to her. " This is a little present extra to the lessons. Take it to the Ulster Bank and leave what you don't want to use now for them to take care of."

Brushing aside thanks, she took her teacher to the door. The rest of the story was told by the bank manager.

When the old lady presented her cheque she asked to have two pounds, adding, " Will you take care of the remaining eight ? " and the clerk, looking at the cheque, said " Ninety-eight," whereupon she clutched the counter and seemed to be on the verge of collapse. The manager, who was passing, went to her, thinking she must be in trouble, and when told the facts he guided her to his own room, assuring her that in his long career he had seen many people overcome from lack of money but she was the only person he had seen distressed from having too much. Over a glass of sherry she told her story.

" I thought my dear lady had given me ten pounds, and was troubled that I had not shown the gratitude I felt, but when I heard it was one hundred it was too much. I must go straight back and tell her what my heart feels."

The manager dissuaded her, saying, " No, you go home and take a rest, and then write a nice letter—she would prefer that."

Another time some workmen brought flowers, and I recognized them as having been members of a party for repatriated prisoners-of-war, who had been invited to spend an afternoon at St. Anne's to see the house and gardens. Olive took trouble about the tea, sending for Millions, the butler (this, improbable as it sounds, was his name), and telling him to put some prize cups on the sideboard, and to send word to the gardens that she wanted plenty of flowers arranged. The men, about fifty in number, were to have tea with us, she at the head of one table and I at another, and these tables were loaded with wafer-thin bread and butter, butterfly-sized sandwiches and sugar-coated petit-fours cakes.

"Don't you think," I ventured, "they would be happier in the servants' hall with more substantial food?"

"No," she answered, "they are going to have our sort of tea with us, and the servants to pour it out and hand cream and sugar, and the best china is to be used."

How right she was! for as we stood in the portico to say good-bye, an ex-sergeant stepped forward, saying in a loud, ringing voice, "My lady, I speak for all present, for every one of us wants to tell you what you have done for us to-day. You have sat down with us, you have eaten with us, and all your servants have waited on us, and we feel you have wiped out the shame of having been spitted on in the streets of Berlin when we were handcuffed prisoners. My lady, we thank you with all our hearts."

He stepped back, his face quite crimson.

"Weren't they touching?" Olive said when we were alone. "And you need not worry about their not eating much at tea, because I have arranged for them all to have a good, solid dinner directly they get back to Dublin."

An old woman whom she used to visit in a tenement house said simply, "God rest her soul, for she was good. She would sit here without a proud end on her; she was a friend to the sick and poor."

Chapter Twenty-one

ITALY

I WAS unhappy after Olive died, for I had to leave Sibyl Hill in six months' time, as it went with the rest of the property.

Once again I had to start life afresh. My son Henry was at Cambridge, and Tony was at sea, and I had no plans. I decided to go away for a change, and a letter from my old friend and previous employer, Nelly Baring, begging me to join her at Cannes on the French Riviera, decided me to go there. I took an immediate dislike to the place, the garish colouring, the noise and the crowds of visitors; more especially the visitors, who lived such an artificial life, seeking pleasure in ways in which real happiness is not found. I did like my walks alone up into the hills covered with olive-trees that lie behind the great coast road. There one would come on little peasant settlements, where life, humble and poor as it seemed, was lived on a more rational, and possibly on a happier and healthier, basis than in the luxury hotels.

One evening, seeing a half-tipsy girl sitting swaying from side to side on the newel of the stairway, supported by two men while the onlookers shrieked with laughter, I said to Nelly Baring, "I can't stand this place for another day; I should like to go now to Italy." She agreed to come with me.

We went first to Pisa, and from there to Florence.

We stayed in a quiet hotel on the Lung Arno overlooking the river, and I thought Florence the most fascinating town I had ever seen. Every walk taken, every bridge crossed, seemed to take one back in history and into the era of great art; even the modern jewellery they made and the silks they wore were based on the beautiful old designs.

Each afternoon we took a drive to see the surrounding countryside, and wherever we went the scenery was lovely. The by-ways of Italy appeal to me almost as much as the great monuments of architecture or the noted sculpture. You never go into a village without seeing something that delights you : a perfect fountain, or a wrought-iron balcony against a rose-stained wall ; at the end of the street you may glimpse the silvery, gnarled olive-trees, or the upright dark pinnacle of a cyprus, and to complete the picture there may come a cart drawn by heavy, milk-white oxen.

The weather during this visit was perfect, and undoubtedly the Italian scene went to my head.

Nelly Baring returned home, but I stayed on, and wrote to my son Henry, asking him what he thought of the idea of my buying some place in Italy, as life for the English was so very cheap there—a point I had to consider. He answered that if I found something I really liked it might be a good place.

After this my excursions alone outside Florence interested me more than ever. One afternoon I went in an omnibus to the country beyond Michelangelo's *David*, in the Arcetri direction. A small, neat Italian sitting next to me asked if I were American.

" No, *Inglese*," I answered, adding, " *non parlo Italiano*."

" I speak the English," he answered quietly, and began telling me the names of places we were passing. At the bus terminus he helped me out and said he had to walk to the *Pian di Guilari*.

" How far is that ? " I asked.

" A short walk, and very fine views from there."

With nice manners, he bowed, wished me a pleasant afternoon and went off. I sat on a wayside seat for a little while, and when he was well ahead I decided to go the same way. I found when I reached the village that the houses obstructed any view ; but, having come uphill the whole way from

Florence, I felt sure that beyond it there must be a wonderful outlook. I went up a rough road with walls on either side which ended abruptly at a point where over the wall appeared a building like a fortress which had a large locked gate in the wall, but I found a smaller one unlocked, and went in. The fortress house stood back from a dilapidated courtyard in which was a window looking towards Florence and framing the most marvellous view I had ever seen : first a sea of olive-trees, pricked here and there by cypresses, the ground undulating and falling towards the domes and pinnacles of Florence and backed by blue mountains, fading snow-covered towards the sky. There was a massive door in the house, but this, too, was locked.

The place was built of stone, and looked sound till I skirted the outside of the courtyard to reach the south side, where I saw jagged cracks running down the walls. Here the ground fell away steeply, giving the place a more fortress-like look than ever. Struggling through brambles and nettles, I turned the corner on to a rough, sunny terrace, where a monumental-looking peasant woman was standing with a little boy at her side. She had a fine face, and as she stood in her black clothes against a vine and a grey stone wall, she made a picture, as things so readily do in Italy. On seeing me she greeted me with simple dignity. Would I like to see the house ? I understood and nodded, and she opened a door leading into a large, high, cool room, stone-walled and with heavily timbered ceiling. The vine had grown over the windows, which were without glass, and the light filtering through the leaves was greenish, giving an impression of the room being under water. I wondered who the place belonged to, and tried to make her understand my questions; but she was puzzled till I touched her and asked, " *Casa a voi?* " upon which she laughed and talked rapidly, from which I gathered that she only kept the keys, and the owner of the house was the Signora of the

Villa Vittoria.   Meanwhile the little boy kept looking at me with great, dark eyes.

Leaving the main room, we came into the entrance hall, from which a stone staircase went upwards, and looking above me I saw birds—martins and swallows—winging swiftly from point to point.   The woman was explaining something, and I caught the word *cielo*, from which I gathered that somewhere the roof was open to the sky.

I said good-bye, intending to go back to the bus terminus and think no more of this strange, lonely house; but as I thanked her with signs and nods I saw that my stalwart guide clearly had some other intention, for she and the child walked down the road beside me, and when we reached a gate in the wall she held me by the coat and pulled a bell. The door was opened by my friend of the omnibus.

The two talked rapidly in Italian, and then he said in English, " The signora like the Casa San Martino ?   Very ancient building—Savonarola come there often.   It belong to my *padrona*; you will see her, *si* ? "

My guide had gone, and I waited in an uninteresting, dark hall.

" Marta ! " the butler called, and a pretty girl appeared. " My daughter will ask permission," he explained.

I was surprised to see the girl, who was dressed in a short, smart frock, unhook a long black skirt which hung in the hall and slip it over her head.   Wearing this skirt, which reached her feet, she extracted hairpins from a packet and pinned her dark curls into a tight knot, and then kicked off her high-heeled shoes and put on square-toed, low-heeled ones.   While I was watching this performance she caught my eye and gave a gurgle of laughter before knocking at a door.

" *Avanti*," came in answer, and she slipped inside.

This made the whole adventure seem more and more like a fairy tale, but the girl's father explained in the kindest tone,

" Our Signora is old, and cannot like modern fashion, so Marta and her sister Camilla dress her way when they go into her room, so she should not feel disturbed."

I felt exactly as if I might be calling on Queen Victoria when I was admitted to a room where a short woman with prominent eyes sat in an arm-chair, looking exactly like the old Queen. She wore a widow's cap with white crêpe streamers hanging behind, and her dress was of voluminous black, her only ornament being a large, round, glass-fronted brooch which had a willow-tree and a tombstone worked in hair under it. Her feet, in square-toed black-satin slippers, rested on a plush footstool. On one side of her was a tripod table which had a series of balls for legs and was covered with a chenille-fringed plush tablecloth, on which stood limp black-covered books and gold-framed spectacles. A bamboo easel on her other side held a photograph—not of Prince Albert, but of a stout man with mutton-chop whiskers—which was tied to the easel with a bow of black crêpe.

I had only time to take in this much before she said in an intimidating voice :

" May I ask for what purpose you have come to see me ? "

I felt that to explain how I had been practically propelled into her presence was too difficult, so I apologized for troubling her, adding that I was interested in the fine old house which I understood was her property.

" And why were you interested ? "

Why indeed ? I was not sure, so only said, " The situation is unusually beautiful."

" It is."

I stood up, wanting to get away, but ' Queen Victoria ' asked, " Are you considering buying a place here ? "

" I have not decided, but it is just possible."

" I might consider selling San Martino to a suitable buyer."

As she said this she stared at me as if I was most unsuitable.

" I have hardly seen the place," I explained rather breathlessly.

" If you wish to go over it, Antonio, my butler, would get you the key from Dolores Bartolini, who looks after it; in return I let her store things there."

" Thank you; I should like to look over it."

" The place needs restoring, but it is listed as an ancient monument, and you would have to get permission from the town authorities at the Signoria to do the necessary repairs."

I felt it improbable that I should ever do any, and I said good-bye, uncertain whether to hold out my hand, but she kept her own small, white, dimpled hands clasped in her lap and gave a bow, which I returned. Then I escaped, after a last look round the room.

It would have taken an expert stage producer to put together such a complete period setting. Not only was every piece of furniture, the wallpaper, and the carpet all of the taste of 1870 to 1880, but the atmosphere exuded a sense of moral superiority that was above and indifferent to the sheer ugliness and gloom of such surroundings. What a contrast to come out into Italian sunshine and find Antonio in attendance and Marta smiling through her released curls !

" How long has the Signora lived here ? " I asked.

" Oh, a lifetime," he cried, throwing out his hands. " Fifty years or more. They bought this villa and brought everything for it from England, but the Signor has been dead for twenty years. As a boy I came and married, and now I and my wife and my two girls, we do all for the Signora."

I came again, and Antonio fetched the key, and we went over the house, he urging me the while to buy it. The rooms were beautiful, and the situation wonderful. I ascertained the price, and after thinking it over consulted an

English architect, asking him to come over and see it and advise me whether the fissures in the wall were repairable.

" Never heard of the place," he said, " and it may not be worth my while to do anything about it. It sounds as if it had been shaken by an earthquake."

" Will you come and inspect it ? "

After some hesitation he agreed. " Yes, if you care to call for me in a taxi and take me back."

He seemed a somewhat ungracious young man.

" How in the world did you find this astonishing place ? " he exclaimed when we got there. " I've lived and worked in Florence for fifteen years "—he wasn't so young as I had thought—" and I never knew of its existence. It's early— built about 1200—and never been spoilt by restoration. And what a marvellous site ! Those cracks are earthquake shock, as I thought, and that side must be buttressed. It can be done in local stone, and the men will work just as they did when it was built, so that it won't look bad."

" Then if I buy it would you help me so far as to see to the buttressing and the roof-mending ? "

" I'll do up the whole place, but you mustn't interfere," he said.

" If I buy it," I told him, " I should only agree now to your doing the buttresses and the roof, and I would like you to understand that quite clearly. That is, if I should buy it."

" Don't keep saying ' If I buy it ' or ' should I buy it '. Of course you must buy it; you found it, didn't you ?— well, there you are, it was meant for you. Of course this is not the fashionable quarter, but if it had been on the Fiesole side it would have been bought and done up long ago, and would have cost three times as much."

" I shouldn't care for the Fiesole side," I replied.

Despite his autocratic manner, I liked the architect, for I felt sure he was an artist and that his enthusiasm was genuine.

I had to go back to Ireland to see to my furniture, but before leaving Italy I had bought San Martino and had a written agreement with the architect as to what he should do regarding structural repairs to it in my absence. I felt some anxiety as to whether I had done wisely in buying the place. From my first meeting with the butler in the omnibus every-one had seemed determined to make me do so. I also felt a thrill at owning anything so beautiful.

Chapter Twenty-two

RESTORING SAN MARTINO

GOING to Sibyl Hill for the last time, I had to say fare-well to all my friends and to sort out my possessions. Olive Ardilaun had left me the Macroom furniture which I had rescued, and some Muckross pictures; I kept these, and disposed of things I cared for less.

I could, however, forget these depressing activities for some hours every day, for I started a correspondence course to learn Italian, which was divided into three parts, the last for " advanced students ". Alas ! I never became such a student, but I worked as hard as the most conscientious school-girl. At the end of the course I wrote a letter of thanks to the teacher I had never seen in the most polite, I feared fulsomely polite, Italian; but received an answer of such exquisitely phrased compliments that I feared he must really have thought my effort merely boorish. In spite of my teacher's assurance that I was the mistress of the most elegant Italian, when I returned to Italy no one could understand a word I said, nor could I understand their rapid talk, all the words seeming to run into one another. My work at the language, however, was not in vain, for before long I could speak fluently, if not correctly, and understand and be understood.

The first thing I did on arriving in Italy was to rent a small house close to San Martino and start on the restoration it needed. The massive buttresses had been put up, against the earthquake cracks, and looked in keeping with the place, but nothing else had been done. The main room still looked as if it was under water, the glassless windows being obscured by the vine. The birds still flew in and out of holes in the roof.

Antonio, the butler, became a friend and a support, and with his help I engaged local workmen, often a father and one or two sons, all delightful people and quite unreliable. I wrote to the architect and told him that now I should carry on the work alone. He was angry, and came up to see me.

" I shouldn't have touched the place if I had believed you meant to attempt the restoration by yourself," he said. " No doubt you will ruin it."

" But you haven't even done the roof, as you agreed to do three months ago," I reminded him.

" You don't know Italian workmen, but you'll find out how they can let you down."

" All the more reason for my seeing to it and being on the spot to keep them up to it."

" I wash my hands of the whole thing, then. Don't imagine that I want work; I have more than I can do, and it was extremely kind of me to be willing to do it. But that it is rather unique and unspoilt I shouldn't have thought of doing it." And off he went.

Months later, when we had made friends again, he came to see me, and was generous in his approval of all I had done. In a way I was sorry not to have had his help, but I knew I could do the work infinitely cheaper by direct local labour than by putting out contracts, and probably quicker by being there with my own men.

Although always polite and willing, these workmen took a very casual view of hours, coming and going as they pleased, so I called them together and explained that either they must come regularly and keep to the hours agreed, or they would be dismissed and a builder from Florence employed in their stead.

Upon this they broke out into a tremendous chattering, sounding like a flock of excited birds, but the outcome was assurances and promises that they would all be as punctual and regular as the monastery bells.

The restoration was different from anything I had ever previously attempted. The workmen, who were first-rate at their own craft, used the traditional methods unchanged for centuries, and the courtyard was restored to perfection. It was pierced with stone-mullioned, unglazed windows, and they enjoyed carving any piece of stone that was missing, often staying after hours absorbed in what they were doing, and but for lack of weathering you could not tell the new work from the very ancient. They sang and whistled at their work, and it was as pleasant to hear them as to look at them—boys of sixteen or seventeen wearing decorative gay colours, such as canary-coloured trousers and blue shirts. But the fathers aged and grew fat too soon.

Good as these men were in dealing with stone and timber, plumbing seemed to begin a series of trials and pitfalls. The plumber I engaged was supposed to be a master of the mysteries of laying on water and making drains. He was a tall, sardonic-looking man with a small, black-eyed son, and he had the maddening habit of leaving his work in a leaking state and being surprised when water spread and dripped through to the next floor. One morning, finding a cascade coming down the drawing-room wall, I cried anxiously for the plumber, and after his name

" Pinetto " had been shouted from place to place, news was brought and excited talk broke out, for it had been learned that the man had gone to a distant " Festa " and would not be back till nightfall.

But the cascade was serious and refused to be checked by corks or wrappings, and somehow he must be fetched, so, as I had bought a car and the chauffeur knew the way, off we went. As we approached the village by a road that wound upwards to the church we saw numbers of people following a procession which was a mixture of pagan superstition and Christian emblems. A shocking life-sized plaster figure of the dead Christ was carried, followed by priests in birettas and cassocks and short, white, lace-edged surplices, while men wearing masks, some with the heads of animals, capered about, and others played pipes or flew coloured balloons. The priests and some of their followers went into the church, but most of the people were moving about in the open square, which had stalls and booths around it. One woman had a crate of snakes, and drew from it one after another of these reptiles, winding them about her arms and neck while the audience hissed and whistled applause.

How were we to find our plumber in this crowd ? The chauffeur got out and started the search, shouting without self-consciousness, " Mario Pinetto, Mario Pinetto, the signora herself has come for you." This cry was taken up from booth to booth, sounding like some ritual chant, until suddenly there came a triumphant " *Ecco*, he is there," and arms were thrust out towards a scarlet figure capering on a small platform. This figure might have been the model used in an ancient painting of a minion of Satan shovelling the sinful into Hell. He was lean and tall, his tights ended in turned-up points beyond his feet, and every part of him was closely covered in glaring scarlet except his face, and even there his cheeks were painted red and his dark eyes and eyebrows were elongated and turned upwards with black paint.

On his head was a high, pointed scarlet cap, and he was gesticulating and selling toys, which he handed to the buyers in a long pair of tongs, while his small son, in identical garb, handed up the toys from a box under the staging.

No English plumber, elusive as he may be in crises, would behave like that, and I felt helpless, but the chauffeur had no hesitation. He rushed to him, talking and gesticulating, and after a friend had been found to finish the selling, the scarlet figure, with a splendid leap, hurled himself from his stand and ran to the car.

" We come with you," he exclaimed. " We put all right immediately."

" Can't you change your clothes first ? " I asked.

" Only when I get home; there I dress."

We drove back, a large red devil sitting in front and a small one by my side.

Before the plumbing was finished we had a display on the outside wall of the house. Instead of the usual waste-pipe, the water from the bath discharged into a number of earthen-ware pipes, each one of these terminating at one end in a cup into which the straight end of each pipe fell, and when each pipe was finished it was made water-tight with cement. Before cementing the pipes it amused the plumber to try how they would function sitting loose, so he filled the bath to the brim, turned on the taps and raced out to see results. Other workmen gathered round, and were delighted to see a whole series of little fountains leaping from the cups, but as the gutter was choked, the courtyard soon became flooded.

" *Rigolo allegro !* " they cried.

It may have seemed gay, but it was very damping to stone walls.

When my furniture arrived I moved into the house before the repairs were finished. The architect had given his opinion that I could not put my " eighteenth-century sticks " into that place, and I had retorted that I could and would. Never had they looked better than in those fine, dignified rooms, as he agreed when he saw them.

"Strange how good things fit in anywhere," he said as he looked around.

Chapter Twenty-three

LIFE NEAR FLORENCE

ITALIAN servants have something in common with the Irish of the past. Both races showed a devotion to their employers that was almost feudal, and took pride in their surroundings, for they felt they were members of the family. When Dolores, the peasant woman who had first shown me the house, and whom I had employed in the furnished rooms I had rented, suggested that she and her husband and their little boy should live at San Martino and do everything for me, I agreed, though I little knew what treasures I was acquiring. Dolores cooked admirably, on a stove with a series of holes which burnt charcoal and needed continual fanning, and on which I couldn't even boil a kettle. When she was out marketing, Bartolini, her husband, cooked equally well, and was first-rate at helping me to make the garden.

They were both serenely good-tempered, and I only once saw Dolores upset. It was the day she first took her little boy to school, and, asking her what was the matter, she told me.

"They put him in a black shirt, and they have taken down the picture of our Madonna and her Son, and put up one of the Duce, and above him a bundle of whips. Dear signora, don't say anything—a word may be dangerous—but I am afraid, so afraid our country may be scourged with those whips. It is wrong that babies should not love the Divine Mother, and be taught to believe only in force : many bad and cruel things are being done now, but no one dares speak ; it is too dangerous."

The old chauffeur I first engaged was not a success ; finding him drunk, I dismissed him. Immediately he made a most dramatic scene, falling on his knees and saying over and over again, " *Sono orfolorlino*," which was not surprising, seeing he was quite seventy. When I said he must give up his uniform he shrieked, " And would you have me walk away in nothing but a towel ? " while tears streamed down his face. I assured him I shouldn't mind in the least ; but relented so far as to let him keep the trousers, upon which he cheered up at once and was all smiles.

Certainly the spirit of opera comes naturally to Italians.

I remember one day about a year later arriving at Florence at midnight during a bitter cold spell of winter. Tired from the journey, and hoping the taxi I had ordered would be at the station, I climbed down from the carriage, and saw Bartolini before he saw me. He was hung about like a Christmas tree with rugs and hot bottles, and his dark eyes searched up and down the train until he saw me, when his welcome was touching. I was wrapped in rugs and begged to hold a hot-water bottle to my chest, for the cold was incredible and unprecedented.

On the drive up he poured out news of San Martino, interspersed with ejaculations of joy that I was back. The moon was shining and the ground was covered with snow, and as we arrived at the outer gate I saw my house was lit up from end to end. As soon as the courtyard bell clanged the door flew open and the Bartolinis' six-year-old son, dressed in white, ran out and fell on his knees in the snow, kissing my hands and pressing flowers into them.   And this at one o'clock in the morning, while his mother, looking, as she always did, like a benign, stout madonna, stood with outstretched arms to welcome me.   It was a perfect operatic scene : the house gleaming with light from every window, while the moon cast sharp shadows on the snow, my travel-worn figure being alone out of place.   I was led into the dining-room, where my heart failed me, for not only was the heat overpowering, but the table was loaded with food. Dear Dolores must have been cooking for hours, and I am not good at coping with food in the middle of the night.

However, they had done their part, and were happy when I told them how much I valued and cared for them and trusted them, and heard *il picolo* say in his pretty English, " Good night, happy dreams, and God keep you."

During the two years of which I spent the greater part in Italy I came gradually to see that it was not my setting, for, much as I loved the beauty of the country, I felt alien from it.   The spectacular splendour of the panorama from my house was disturbing and made me restless : this sunset must not be missed, that storm effect over the Vallombrosa mountains should be watched.   The climate was bad.   The winters are cold, with rain storms and snow, and icy winds sweep down from the mountains.   The long winter passes and spring comes; its loveliness takes one's very breath away.   How aware the Florentine painters were of these enchanted weeks when the earth bursts into blossom, and the olive-trees show silvery buds.   The domes and spires of Florence float above mists as moisture is drawn from the ground by this sudden warmth.   Alas, the heat increases, the flowers wilt and the summer sun becomes an intolerable burden.

Autumn brings relief with another perfect interlude when grapes are trodden and olives gathered.

Gardening matches the climate in its extremes, so enchanting in early spring, when narcissus, anemones and iris flourish with an exuberance never seen in our English gardens, but the riot is soon over. I sent to a Scottish firm for summer plants—roses, delphiniums, lupins, and others—and sowed annual seeds, but all were disappointing, rushing into blossom only to run to seed with yellow, sun-dried leaves in a few days. Italian gardens have few flowers, but they have terra-cotta pots and oil-jars in which orange- and lemon-trees are grown, and I did the same, driving round the country to collect antique earthenware receptacles. These are slightly irregular, and often larger than those turned out by modern means. Many of my jars, including some stained on one side with bright cerulean blue, I bought from peasants, who were a good type, with kindly, dignified manners. After every deal we drank a glass of their own home-made wine.

I got to know the farmers—if people who cultivate so few acres can be called farmers—who were my nearest neighbours, and they asked me to share their midday meal, which I did, arriving one day unexpectedly. We had vegetable soup, a macaroni-and-tomato dish with excellent thick gravy which I was told was made of pounded pigeon's liver and oil, followed by fruit and cheese, all served in gay pottery plates and dishes on a checked cloth. Almost all we ate was produced on their own small strip of land : their garden gave the fruit, tomatoes, and vegetables, their vines and olive-trees the wine and oil, and their two goats the cheese. I think they never bought meat, but kept chickens, pigeons, and rabbits, which supplied them with all they needed. They worked hard, and I have seen them out at five in the morning, sometimes still being at it by moonlight. I bought an outsize, wreath-rimmed pot from them, which joined the others in my courtyard and terrace, but the lawn, which I had pictured a smooth, restful green, had to be sown anew every year, and even then the summer heat turned it yellow, and it ended looking like a thin and hungry brown carpet.

I had been told that San Martino, standing high up above Florence, would never be very hot, but although it was true that the house, which had thick stone walls, could be kept bearably cool by shutting every window and drawing the curtains in the early morning, by the evening the air felt exhausted, and to go out at any time of the day was overwhelming. I stood the heat badly, but even so I might possibly have adjusted myself to the material side of life in Italy had it not been for the fact that once work on the house and garden was finished I felt useless, and at all times alien to the social life.

I had a great many acquaintances, having come with some introductions, and one link had led to another. My place being three miles from Florence, in the less-known country, it made a good excuse for an outing for callers.

There were many Americans resident in Florence, who kept their villas well heated at great cost and had plenty of highly paid servants. There was also a constant flow of Americans passing through Florence, as part of their grand tour on their way to Paris, which was their Mecca, and where they would spend most of their time before returning home. Some of these travellers would be sure to know one or more of their compatriots, and many of them were brought to see me. My memory of these people is something like the impression that remains in one's mind of a crowd seen in a film. They would have appeared different in their own houses, where one knew they would have been so capable, so kind, and so welcoming, and where they would be individuals one could not fail to remember.

No matter how many came to call, the Bartolinis would be delighted; the mere sound of a car coming up my lane would set them twittering about getting out the *argenteria* and preparing tea in the beautiful dining-room, with its white walls, which curved in lovely lines where it merged into the ceiling. While talking to strangers whom I should never see again, the door would be thrown open, and Dolores would invite us in to enjoy the good things she had prepared, in such a charming manner and with such a look of pride that I could never bring myself to tell her I should really not have been sorry to have cut the visit short.

There was one set made up of both English people and Americans who were completely taken up with playing bridge, and another set of nice, elderly English whose chief occupation was calling on one another and going to the Anglican Church.

No doubt there were interesting people in Florence, but I did not know them, and yet there was a tradition that in the past it had been the meeting-place for brilliant, intellectual writers and poets.

For those who liked dancing at hotels and going to Sunday races there was a gay life, and one day I was asked to have luncheon with a widow who had a pretty daughter. Twelve of us, having had sherry and cocktails, sat down to a meal of course after course of rich, marvellously cooked food, with ices and various wines, followed by coffee and liqueurs. I asked my hostess if she could face a very simple lunch with me, explaining that I should not know how to contrive such a feast as she had given me. When she came she said how badly off she was, but that she was doing all she could for her girl, and I laughed, saying, "Your entertaining doesn't look like that of a poor person."

"It's the economical way of doing things," she told me. "We have only one servant, but every fortnight we give a party such as you came to, and for that we hire Tomasso, who is a wonderful chef, and does the catering and brings the waiters. Then we live for quite a time in the evenings on what is left over, and lunch out practically every day with

someone who has been to us. I do get tired," she sighed,
" but it gives Sheila a wonderful time."

I felt glad that I hadn't a daughter.

One day I was planting shrubs with Bartolini, and a
friend who had been giving me lessons in Italian joined us.
She spoke very good English, and as we were chattering
away over our work she burst out laughing.

" Do you know," she said, " you both keep saying you
are planting ' corsets '."

I turned to Bartolini, exclaiming, " Why didn't you
correct me ? "

He and my teacher broke into rapid Italian, and I gathered
that my devoted servant could not bring himself to criticize
his signora, and that he understood all she said so nicely.

It struck me then that if I lived on in this country I might
ultimately become a sort of fly in amber, cared for and
protected like the old woman from whom I had bought my
house, for Bartolini's using an absurd word rather than put
me right was on a par with Antonio making his daughter
dress up in long skirts to prevent any jar to his mistress'
feelings.

Then one day when returning a call I found a plain,
middle-aged American, who hardly paused for greetings,
continuing her conversation by saying, " You see, I'm in a
proper fix over the hospital. The one nurse who never
fails me—and we always have more than we can do—has
gone sick, and doctor says she must quit for a month, and
I don't know who will take her place. I've been ranging
all the villas, and everywhere I'm offered money which I
don't want. I can't get hired help; I want a pair of hands."
Turning to me, she told me at great length all about this
place, and how she and her sister had started it in war-time
for soldiers when the town hospitals were chock full and
glad to hand over the light cases to anyone who would look
after them, and that the doctors helped and came every day.

They had intended to close down when peace came, but the men brought their wives, children, and parents, and now they had more patients than ever. The big hospitals were still crowded, and they hadn't the heart to turn all these poor creatures away and shut up. "It's just too bad," she ended, " if we have to close because folks are so selfish they won't help."

Of course I was disturbed, and wondered if I ought to help, though it was ten years since I had done any nursing, and I didn't want to begin again.

She must have guessed what was in my mind, for she said, " I don't even rightly know your name, but maybe Providence has made us meet, and say, are you willing to come along ? "

I wasn't at all willing, and the weather was getting hotter, but rather reluctantly I agreed to attend every day for the month that her regular nurse was to be away. Nevertheless, I felt that if Providence had contrived this meeting, it was taking a rather mean advantage of my private discontent at being useless and using it as a lever to make me consent.

I found it a new strange experience, for it was unlike any English institution, being more like a busy and varied outpatients' department. There were no beds other than an emergency couch. Italian doctors or surgeons came every day except on one day a week, when a dentist attended. Only local anæsthetics were used, and at first I thought I should not be able to endure the screams, the heat, the crowd, and the haste with which everything was done. Often it was necessary to hold patients down while operations, generally trivial, but often painful, were carried out with neatness and speed, but it was not until the day when adenoids and tonsils were removed by a good-looking young surgeon, vain of his skill, that I actually did revolt. Parents brought their children, who yelled in the passage while awaiting their turn, and presently I was told to hold a child upright for the operation.

" No," I said, " I'm sorry; I will sterilize your instruments outside, but I won't stay here; I can't bear it."

The surgeon looked hurt and surprised.

" You would enjoy seeing my beautiful and so quick work," he told me.

But I heard no more, for I was out in the passage, being clutched at by mothers with howling children in their arms who wanted to know when their turn would come and what were they to do with Mimi, who had been sick—should they take her home ?   Escaping from them, I boiled instruments and washed blood-stained bowls, which were being continually replenished by breathless nurses.

The last patient had been attended to and I was tidying up when the handsome doctor came in.

" So ! " he said.   " You stay out of the surgery when I tell you to stay in, and I say that for good reason.   I want you to see how much better Italian way is than English way with tonsils and adenoids.   They make much trouble for the patient; they give a child anæsthetic that makes him sick after and hurt him.   I give a local spray.   They lay him down and he swallow much blood; with me they stay upright, leaned forward, and swallow no blood.   I order ices for them, and that freezes their little gullets, and they are well and happy in one half-hour.   Next week you come and see my operations ? " he asked hopefully.

" No; I'm sorry, I'd rather not.   I can't bear all that screaming."

" Then you scream, too; that would make all right, and I should not object."

" I have never done that, and I am too old to learn," I said.

" Ah ! that is what is wrong with you British : you keep all emotion here," and he clasped his breast.   " We Latins, we let it out "—he flung back his arms—" and then we are free. Emotion is like sepsis: it must have a vent. You shut in so much you have to get a psychic analyser to drag out what you bury."

At that statement I broke in, " I have never needed anything of the kind, and I like the English character, and prefer their self-control to Latin excitability."

I feared I had been rude, but I was hot and tired, and irritated by this man's complacent lecture. But instead of resenting what I had said, he replied, " Signora, I salute your spirit," and, bowing and kissing my hand, he departed.

The dental day was hard work, with a queue of people waiting. Extractions were done by a rotund little dentist, and cavities were prepared by the nurses. We became quite expert at cutting away decay, sometimes by hand, sometimes using the treadle, and observing our work in the magnifying reflector to see all was clean before the dentist did the actual filling. The work went on nearly all day, after which we would be left to tidy up.

One evening after the dentist, carrying his bag, had gone, the door burst open and a stout cab-driver in a shiny hat rushed in holding his jaw. We told him the dentist had gone and he must come the following week, upon which he responded with a cataract of despairing speech. His evil tooth must come out, for he could neither sleep nor eat, and he called on the saints to help him.

" I will take out his tooth."

This statement came from a self-effacing mouse of an amateur nurse and, coming from her, it seemed quite incredible.

" Have you ever taken out a tooth ? " we asked.

" No, but people who do must have begun once, and I have seen so many taken out here that I am sure I can do it."

" We haven't the cocaine and the syringe."

" We must do without."

Then she became most professional, gagging his mouth and marking the tooth, after which she selected her forceps, tilted back the chair and stood on a footstool.

"Now, please all hold him and keep his head steady."

Hold him we had to, for at the first twist he gave a bellow and tried to bound from the chair. Unperturbed, the valiant little creature twisted and turned, and then drew out the bleeding, fanged tooth, while great tears rolled down the victim's unshaven, crimson cheeks. He soon recovered, with the buoyancy natural to Italians, and for a moment we thought he was about to engulf the mouse-like nurse in an embrace, but he was only expressing gratitude and admiration, and he went off with his head wound about in a purple muffler.

A very different scene occurred when a young monk in a white habit had to have his poisoned arm operated on. As he lay on the table with his thin, dark face and shaven head resting on the hood of his habit, he looked like a primitive painting of a dead martyr. His arm had to be opened up from wrist to elbow and the bone exposed, but during the whole time he lay still with closed eyes. The operation was a slow one, and when it was done and the arm bandaged, I was told to make him rest on the couch, but he refused, saying gravely, " I will go my way."

Impulsively I asked him, " Tell me, brother, did you suffer terribly ? "

" I suffered nothing," he replied. " Instead I was taken into Heaven."

His face was beautiful as he said this, as if still reflecting a vision from another world.

I struggled through my month at that exhausting hospital while it grew hotter and hotter, and I lost weight and returned to San Martino, glad to rest in the closed and darkened house. But I was sure now in my own mind that I did not want to live in Italy. My eldest son was coming to me for his vacation, and I dreaded telling him of this decision, but when I had explained it all he said he was glad, as he would rather have me in any poky hole in the country in England where he could come for week-ends than have me live so far away. I was so relieved that I nearly wept, and I determined to get out of this roasting Italy and find my poky hole in England.

I took steps to sell San Martino, and almost at once had a chance and lost it. An American came to see me in a large car, accompanied by her chauffeur, her maid, and a secretary. She told me she had only reached Florence that morning. Looking round my room, she said, " The train is still running in my head, but I have a mind to buy this house."

" You must see over the place and think it over," I said, not wanting to rush her; but that chance was gone, for two days later she returned.

" Now, why didn't you fix it up with me ? " she said. " I can tell you, I'm pretty miserable; for I've bought a villa, and this place is way up more what I wanted; but a business woman—an American lady—got hold of me the very day I saw you, and some way persuaded me to buy a place the other side of Florence."

Directly after this Mussolini brought the exchange down from 130 lire to the pound to 90. It was a gesture of pride, and involved many in loss and despair, but the floating American population left for France like migratory birds.

Ultimately I sold the place for what it cost me and, telling my architect friend, I exclaimed with some bitterness, " Isn't it maddening ? All that work and risk, and I have made nothing—absolutely nothing."

" You haven't lost money ? "

" No."

" You have enjoyed doing it, haven't you ? "

" Yes, of course, quite immensely."

" If that is the case, I just cannot see why you should be distressed. You have made a beautiful thing that should last for five hundred years or more and give pleasure to others, and you have enjoyed doing it and gained a new experience. And against all that you worry because you have not made a thousand pounds or so, which in the long view would have no real significance. And don't regret your life here or think it wasted, for all your life you will be the richer. I don't mean in money," he smiled, " but in far better things : in appreciation and in memories."

Now I agree with his values, and I have heard that San Martino has survived the war, and with the kind help of the British Consul I have traced the Bartolinis. Indeed, I have many happy memories. Once Tony, my younger son, came on leave from his ship and enjoyed a carnival in Florence, throwing chocolates and flowers at pretty girls, and carrots, with deadly aim, at men in grotesque masks. Nor can I forget the hours I spent sitting on the loggia in the cool of the evening, watching the fireflies threading across the starlit sky, and often hearing below my boundary, first the twang of a guitar and then Antonio's sweet tenor voice, soon joined by one or both of his pretty daughters, in gay songs or popular airs from operas.

There was a balcony high up on the building which when I came had a pierced seat in it and a shaft that went right down to the foundations. It was not desirable as a method of sanitation, so, despite protests that thus it had been in existence since Savonarola came there, I closed the shaft and fitted a new wide seat which looked over the extensive view. On Sunday morning as I sat there with a friend, hearing the bells come faintly from many near and distant spires, she exclaimed :

" Heaven couldn't be more lovely than this; it is quite perfect, and just the amount of church I really like."

All my visitors were taken to see the Certosa monastery,

which lay below me about a mile away, and consisted of a series of buildings crowning a small hill and surrounded by an immense wall. On entering, we would be met by a benevolent-looking monk dressed in a coarse white habit, who would lead us up a long stone staircase, open a great door at the top, and show us into a sheltered, sunny garden with a lovely well-head in the centre.

" Yes, Michelangelo made that for us," he would remark, as if it had been made yesterday.

Bounding this garden were twelve small stone houses, in each of which lived a member of the priests' Order, who never spoke except to recite the daily Mass and services of the Hours. They cultivated their own small gardens, and their food was prepared by the brothers and passed through a hatch.

A not very intelligent Englishman whom I had once taken to see this place, and who could speak no Italian, was especially bewildered by the inhabitants of those cell-like little houses.

" But what good do they do shut up like that ? " he kept asking.

I put the question to our guide.

" Some in this world do not know the power of prayer," he told me. " Their days are divided into eight hours' work, eight hours' prayer, and eight hours' rest."

When I told my companion this he was more puzzled than ever and exclaimed, " But when they have prayed for themselves, their country, and the King of Italy, I can't think what they do with eight whole hours."

Having had this query translated, the brother looked long at my friend, with kind, dark eyes, and then said, " I think the signor has not yet gone far on the mystic way."

Chapter Twenty-four

JOURNEY TO ENGLAND

HENRY and I left San Martino and decided to see something of France on our way home. We stopped at Avignon, where we stood on the bridge which we had so often sung about when we were children, and also at Dijon. Here we asked a porter at the station if he knew of a quiet hotel, and he responded eagerly, saying that if we did not want a grandiose place, he would come with us and bring our luggage to where French people went, choosing it on account of the cooking, for the proprietor was a chef and knew his business from end to end. He was quite right, and we had excellent meals and service in the unpretentious, cheap little hotel, where humble people drank their wine sitting at iron tables on the pavement outside.

We wandered about the old town and visited antique shops without finding anything of interest, until the evening before we left we saw a restrained empire bureau in a little sweet-shop which, as the door was locked, we could only see by peering through the window. When we asked the man next door if he knew whether his neighbour was likely to come back that evening he did not know, but we explained why we were bothering him, and told him where we were staying, though we felt sure that was the end of the matter. However, just as we had finished dinner the waiter told us there was a lady outside, who turned out to be the owner of the sweet-shop, and, sitting at one of the tables on the pavement, we concluded a bargain. Some weeks later the bureau arrived in Sussex, and proved to be as nice as we had thought it looked when we saw it through a dusty window in the evening light at Dijon.

From there we went on to stay at Annecy, where my

mother had once taken me as a child, and I remembered the place from that visit of so many years ago. It had been a kind of pilgrimage, for my mother had a profound veneration for St. Francis de Sales, whose native country it was, and we were to go and see his house, which was in the neighbourhood. A carriage was hired for the great day, and we were to take a picnic tea with us and have it before we went to see as much as was shown to the public of the rooms where the saint had lived. The drive inland from the lake was through woods, and my mother stopped the carriage and got out by a clearing overlooking the château, saying she would take a walk while we unpacked the basket. We felt sure she wanted to be alone to pray.

While we were spreading a cloth and laying out the things and heating water over a spirit lamp, I saw my sister Winifred looking anxious and peering into the basket. Presently she said in a horrified whisper, " There's no tea; we've forgotten it." A dreadful fear seized us, for we felt the whole outing would be spoilt and we should never be forgiven. Feeling we couldn't bear it, we decided the only thing to do was to go at once to the big house we could see below us and entreat them to give us some tea. Hand in hand we ran down the hill, praying that our mother would not return before us, and breathlessly we told our story to the man-servant who opened the door.

" Wait here and I will tell Mdlle. de Sales," he said.

Almost immediately a figure in a white gown came down the stairs, explaining that she had just had a bath to get cool and asking what we wanted.

My sister told our story perfectly, adding, " You see, my mother has always loved St. Francis, and she has come all the way from Ireland to see as much as possible of his surroundings, but she is ill, and if she has no tea she will be upset."

The lady kindly said of course she would give us some and

when we had had it we were to come to this door and she would show us more than was usually shown to the public. My mother, who always judged by results, was gratified that as a result of our omission we were shown the precious relics and many of the rooms generally kept private. Before we left we watched her kneeling at the saint's " prie-dieu ", her handsome face taking on what we called her wonderful, far-away, church look, seeing which Mdlle. de Sales smiled and whispered, " I am glad you forgot the tea."

We were so near tears with excitement and relief that we could only murmur our thanks.

On this second visit to Annecy with my grown-up son we stayed in a small hotel near the lake, which was filled with French families of humble class, among them being a tall, good-looking woman at whom they all looked askance, never speaking to her. One day as I walked alone in the woods on the hillside I came on a sunlit glade where this girl was lying full length, wearing no clothes except for a filmy scarf, making a picture that Titian might have painted. Seeing I was not shocked, she drew herself up on her elbow, smiling, completely without self-consciousness.

" Madame would rest herself ? " She indicated the mossy ground.

" You are on holiday ? " I asked.

" Yes, I and my friend who has taken the villa on the other side of the lake and placed me here for a change from Paris; I visit him when he sends his auto for me. At this moment *je me trint les reins.*"

I wondered what she was exactly, and as though reading my thoughts, she told me something of her story just as some people will to complete strangers when they are lonely.

" I began my life with nothing—no family, no money, hardly any education, nothing but work and poverty before me. And then I met my first friend. He was good, and I belonged to him for five years."

Broadstone House, the first house I built

At work on the Roughfield roof, 1937, on left is the stout bricklayer who built himself in

(*Above*) The three condemned cottages at Marden which I restored, 1938-39

(*Below*) The living-room at Mumpumps

" You could not have married him ? "

" But no, Madame ; that could not enter at all. He was married, with a family, but he needed the solace I could give him, and he did so much for me, giving me lessons in literature and the art of dress and deportment. He also taught me to save, telling me that of all he gave me I was to put something away. ' Just a little every week,' he would say, ' and it mounts and means safety for you, my child.'

" Then his business took him to South America, and my next friend was different—young and gay, but not serious, wanting too much drinking, dancing, and spending ; and so I left him. Now I am settled seven years with my present friend, and all goes well ; and when we part I have a *dot* if I should choose marriage, or start business in lingerie and hats. For, you see, I am a serious business woman—not like those ' cocottes ', who have no thought for the future."

" What happens to them in the end ? " I asked.

" If they live, the ' Commune ' keeps them and makes them occupy themselves with the care of the public lavatories." She spoke in a tone of contempt, adding, " They pay for not having foresight and discretion."

This odd interview has remained in my mind, partly, I think, because I had never known anyone so frank about her particular profession and so French in her view that her life had been fortunate, well-balanced, and provident.

When we walked back to the hotel together I was amused on meeting a stout couple to notice the man's furtive, admiring glance at my companion in her smart clothes, and the malevolent, angry look in his wife's beady, dark eyes ; nor was I surprised when that afternoon, my sun-bathing friend having been called for in a fine motor-car, this woman sidled up to me and said :

" Madame surely does not know how the person she was walking with occupies herself ? " Her little eyes snapped avid enquiry.

" That is not my affair; I found her so well-mannered and so good-looking," I answered, and left her.

We arrived in England tired of hotel life, hating the crowds and the noisy bands, and started to search for a permanent home. The Sussex country was soothing after our travels, and once the coast was left behind, it seemed more rural than many counties farther from London. We hired a car and, with a list of places to be sold, went to see them, but one after another seemed hopeless until we arrived at a farm with a hundred acres of land. It was luncheon time, so we ate our sandwiches on the edge of a wood where there was a lovely view over distant hills, and massive oaks in the foreground gave the landscape a sense of permanence. No other dwelling was in sight, and it was peaceful and isolated, beyond the radius of daily-bread workers, and it looked as it must have looked for centuries, and there seemed no reason why it should not appear the same for many more. Certainly the land was neglected. We went back to see the house, which had a fine sloping roof of old weathered tiles, though inside it was dirty and almost derelict. Part of it was early and oak-beamed, but it had been cut up with modern partitions, and was dark and damp. There was an early Victorian addition on the north side, consisting of two square rooms with a narrow passage in between.

" Do you think anything could be done with it ? " Henry asked.

I saw that all sorts of things could be done with it; that it could be made into a very charming house, so I answered, " I think we have found your poky hole."

" You wouldn't call it by that silly name ? "

He seemed worried at such an idea, but I reassured him, explaining, " Its own name is quite odd enough—it is called Mumpumps."

Chapter Twenty-five

MUMPUMPS

MUMPUMPS was a most ramshackle, neglected place when we bought it, and while repairs were being done I stayed at the local inn in the village, going to the house every day to see to the work. One rather wet day when, dressed in an old mackintosh and rubber boots, I was making a collection of tins, bottles, and rubbish where a terraced garden was to be, some people came on to my ground and stood looking down at me from the hill above the house. Trespassers, I thought, and the tradition of our early training caused me to resent their presence, for we had been brought up to regard trespassers as an obnoxious kind of vermin. My father's rule, as his predecessors' had been, was that any tourists—and many came to Killarney—who dared to bathe off our shore were to have their clothes collected and taken up to the house by the fishermen who, when not hauling, were usually lying ambushed behind gorse-bushes, and when the offenders emerged from the water they would be told to go up to the house and get them. There was a legend that once a minister of some religious denomination had to take this three-quarters-of-a-mile walk stark naked to collect his garments.

Having grown up with these prejudices, I looked with distaste at the group of people who were watching me, and presently an elderly man came down to where I was poking about in the rubbish.

" I hear this place is sold," he stated.

I assented.

" Do you happen to know who has bought it ? " he asked.

"Yes, I do know," I answered, extracting a half-buried tin.

"Please tell me the name of the buyer," he persisted.

Looking straight at him I said, "It has been bought by someone called Mrs. Everett."

Doubt seemed to dawn on him.

"You are not by chance that lady?" he queried.

"Yes, I am; and I suppose you thought I was the char-woman," I answered tartly, and then we both laughed, and he introduced himself as Sir Frederick Fison and my nearest neighbour.

From him I learned what he believed to be the origin of the name Mumpumps. The place had belonged, in the Middle Ages, to the monks at Battle Abbey, and in old records it is called *Ponds Monasticorum*, and that last mouthful could easily be corrupted into Mum for short, so he thought, and ponds could readily be turned into pumps, if water was so drawn for cattle. In early Victorian times, wishing for a refined name, it was known as Mount Pumps. His own property, so he told me, was called Boarzell, which was a clear corruption from Boarsdell.

One of the first difficulties to be got over was the disreputable state of the place, which was due to neglect on the part of the nearly bankrupt farmer. One day when I was fishing with an elongated rake in the pond, which seemed to have been a magnet for endless rubbish, someone asked, "Do you like doing that?"

I looked up, and saw the elderly village policeman standing above me, his enormous boots giving a pantomime look to his foreshortened figure. I considered his question.

"Yes," I said, "I think I do, because I see white water-lilies where now I fish out old boots and dreadful rabbit skins. These will be buried on the bank you are now standing on, and against it a stone wall will be built, which will become full of rock plants. Besides, I might find treasure left by the monks, and that would be the greatest fun."

" Any treasure found on any premises must be reported to the nearest police station—that's me—and I would inform the proper authorities," he told me.

" I must find it first," I said, amused at his official view. But I never did find any.

The place swarmed with rats, and when I told the agent it ought to be called Rat Hall instead of Mumpumps, he promised he would send me someone who would clear them all out. I had forgotten about this promise when one morning a large, light blue car drew up, and out of it stepped a proportionately large sporting figure, dressed in a pearl-grey bowler hat, a checked coat, riding-breeches, and box-cloth gaiters. I wondered what he could want, and thought it must be something to do with racing or horses; but he came to the point at once, saying he had heard I was infested with rats. Could this magnificent person be a rat-catcher? I had pictured that job being filled by a dirty, tramp-like man in a battered cap, and I murmured, " Are you really a rat-catcher? "

" I don't catch 'em by the tail myself," he said, with a hearty laugh. " I employ a dozen fellows to do the actual work, but I see that it is properly done, and I arrange the contracts."

That last word arrested me, and I asked what it would cost to do my place.

" A hundred a year," he answered. " And it is no good to do it just for a twelvemonth; you have to keep it up."

That was out of the question, and when I told him so he assented at once, and with real kindness said if I would show him round he would help me to get rid of them by myself. He went on to say that he had several contracts of many hundreds a year at dock and grain stores, besides others at the rate he had suggested to me, so no wonder he owned a large blue car! When we came to the garden front he went at once to an old yew-tree which overhung the pond.

" Here's where they live," he said. " They have more than one entry and exit, and their burrows run right along the bank. You should get a little trough made about eighteen inches long—just a couple of boards set at an angle with straight-cut ends—and take it out at dusk, full of a wet mash—anything you like : soaked bread or porridge, and they relish a taste of fat—and put it down near this tree where it will stand steady. The next night feed them again, adding just a little poison, preferably strychnine, but not too much, mind : a very little livens them up and they get used to the smell. On the third night you give them a stiff dose mixed with the mash that will finish a lot of them, then take the trough away and scour it, pick up and burn any of your stuff left about, and leave the rats alone, repeating this system exactly at the end of a fortnight."

I followed his advice with success.

Gradually the place was reformed, the additions and alterations to the house finished, the garden shaped and planted, and a large barn which had been condemned as a cowshed was removed, the foundation stones being used for walls. I was glad to see it go, for it stood between the house and the lovely view, but it had been the home of white owls, who would float silently across the pond at dusk, and I did regret taking it from them. I tried to compensate them by having barrels nailed and lashed to trees, with alighting boards and comfortable beds of hay inside, but the owls' resentment was evidently profound, for they disappeared and were not seen again. Once a grey squirrel came out of a barrel and my cat spent a night in another.

We liked Mumpumps, and I made an interesting garden there.

About this time my younger son Tony came on leave

from his ship and begged me to let him leave the Merchant Service. He had been a difficult child to guide, and he seemed unable to concentrate or to understand figures. I had once asked him, when he was at his preparatory school, why he could not do better, and he answered, " Perhaps I ought to be given private intuition." He was a happy, good-tempered boy and most generous, and, despite his difficulty over lessons, everyone, including his masters, liked him. I was advised to send him to the training ship *Worcester*, and from there he went into the White Star Line running to Australia. Although he was popular on board, no one could get him to work out the position of the ship, and the captain, on hearing of this, said, " I'll show the boy if you'll send him up to me."

In response to this unprecedented, if alarming offer, Tony presented himself at the great man's cabin, and was given a patient lesson, after which he was told to work out the problem by himself, but when the captain saw the result he gave a roar of laughter, for Tony had put the ship in the middle of South America.

The prospects in the Merchant Service at that time were not good, and I felt sure that he ought not to be forced to stay at sea, even if he could manage to master the necessary mathematics, so another opening was found for him, and he was promised an appointment in the Sudan Cotton Corporation if he went to Wye College and did well there. I felt that with his limited educational background this would be too hard for him, but Tony was determined to succeed, and did well and got his nomination. He went off to the Sudan in wild spirits, equipped with his new outfit, and his letters were full of how much he liked the life and the work, but the 1929 depression came, and with it orders from the London office that the staff must be reduced. The axe fell on the recently appointed, and Tony came home in a desperate state, quite broken by this blow, and it was some time before his naturally happy temperament reasserted itself. He liked a hot climate, and felt keenly the cold of an English winter, and after some months at Mumpumps he went to Kenya, where he has made his home, keeping himself entirely by managing farms, except during the war years, when he served in the Kenya R.N.V.R.

When I think of Tony and his early struggles I wonder if it was I who lacked " private intuition ", for he had a good brain in certain directions. I think that sending him to sea was a mistake.

Mumpumps was very near the road and the farm, which we felt to be its one drawback, and soon after Tony left us this disadvantage was emphasized by a decision to widen the road, for which sixty feet of our land was taken, putting us that amount nearer. Besides this, the wood which screened us from the traffic was to be cut down, and though we tried to fight this order, the authorities had compulsory powers. People view such things differently, and the official in control, whom I had asked to come and see the situation, after hearing my impassioned plea to leave us our privacy, only remarked, " Can't see as it would hurt you; for my own part I likes a bit of life "—meaning the streams of buses and cars on the London to Hastings main road. An appeal to the engineer was equally useless, for when I asked him why he could not take the level land on the other side, which would cause no distress and be far less costly than making a great embankment over our falling ground, he explained that the way he had drawn it, it looked straighter on the map.

My elder son, Henry, who was a barrister living in London but coming home for week-ends and vacations, felt as I did, that if we could sell the place with its charming garden we could build our permanent home on one of the many lovely sites which we owned away from all disturbance. We employed a London house agent, and were encouraged by the enthusiasm expressed by their representative sent to inspect the property.

"Sell it! Of course we can, and quickly, too," he exclaimed. "We always succeed when a place has individuality and charm. Clients who fancy it won't be able to find anything else to match it; you just leave it to us."

A week later a large party arrived with an order to view, among them a number of gaily dressed girls, one of whom asked, "May we go over it all by ourselves?"

"Of course, go anywhere—anywhere you like," I answered.

There was an elderly man with them who decided to sit down while the others explored, and we chatted and found we had mutual links in Ireland. Through the window we saw figures flitting about the garden, and later heard them running through the bedrooms and up and down the stairs, and after half an hour they all rushed in to where we were waiting.

One of them, rather older than the others, and who looked like Romney's Lady Hamilton, announced, "I am going to buy this place; it's adorable."

"Made up your mind already?" I said, thinking she was half joking.

"Yes," she said. "I've quite decided, and you'll hear from my solicitor to-night if I can get at him, or to-morrow for certain. I've been looking for something I really liked for ages, and now that I've found it I'm going to have it."

That was how it came about that Lady Tredegar bought Mumpumps.

Throughout my life I had never had a house which gave me a real assurance of permanency; on the other hand, our hundred acres of woods and fields gave us the feeling that we belonged to this particular part of the earth. We were conscious of this the very first day we saw it, when we lunched beneath a hedge and looked at the serene and lovely distance flanked by oak-trees.

The panorama seen from my Italian house was far more spectacular, and much as I admired the splendour of the outlook, I always had a certain sense of being alien to it.

The site we now chose on Mumpumps lands looked towards distant hills, with a woodland foreground, which changed with every varying light, but always suggested a picture by an eighteenth-century English landscape-painter. It was distant from all disturbing elements, and silent but for the sounds of wild Nature, and at all seasons we should see the flushed sky of sunset. There we built our house, and there I hope my son and my grandson will always look upon it as their permanent home.

Chapter Twenty-six

BUILDING AND RESTORING

I BUILT my first three houses before the 1914 war. In 1916 I was in Ireland, and had to repair the house Lady Ardilaun lent me, which led to my doing work for her and others, always employing my own men. In Italy I restored the ruined and very ancient house I had bought, and on my return to England I built new houses and restored old ones until the last war put a final end to such efforts.

I have sometimes been asked whether I have had trouble in controlling a gang of men. I never have. I have always liked my men, and have had loyalty and help from them, as I think is generally the case with small country builders who know their workers individually and are on friendly terms with them. I found, too, that by being employed by a woman they have a sense of co-partnership, possibly more than they would have under a man. They had never known or heard of a woman who acted as architect and builder and supervised everything, and I think they enjoyed working in these unusual circumstances.

Once a local contractor had said he was sure that the lady would make a muddle of the houses she was building, and the phrase became a catchword; when a job went particularly well the men would refer to it as " a nice piece of muddle ".

I have had good service and loyalty from those I employed. Once I sent my carpenters to take down an army hut I had bought. They came back surprisingly quickly, and when I remarked on this they announced with pride that there were a lot of fellows clearing them, " but we got done the first of the gang, for we weren't going to have our Missus beaten."

Once in Ireland I gave an hour's money to a bricklayer who had been drinking and told him to clear out. Upon this he became abusive, saying he'd go straight to his trade union and I'd never get another man, and so on. That night two of my men came to see me. They had gone four miles into Dublin, and over a glass of beer they told me : " We just came to tell you that after work we went to see the secretary of the trade union and told him you was quite right, so you'll have no more trouble from that one. We were in dread you wouldn't see he had drink taken and were afeared he'd pitch off the scaffold, so when he turned nasty we were minded to put it straight and came here so you wouldn't be fretting over-night."

I found the men less trouble than some of the people for whom I worked. When I built a house, employing a builder to carry out my plans, I sometimes found the greatest difficulty in making a client realize that the plans must not be changed once the building is begun and the contract signed. One woman changed her mind so often over the plans that when at last she was satisfied I made her repeat words usually connected with the marriage service : " Speak now or for ever hold your peace."

But far from holding her peace, she was always demanding changes and additions, and when I was firm and stern with her, she would slip round to the builder and arrange to have these alterations made, which of course I found out almost at once, and told her she would have a very heavy bill, beyond her contract.

" I am sure you are wrong," she told me. " I get on so well with the builder—in fact he's much easier to deal with than you are, and never minds my little extra fancies."

When these extra fancies came to a formidable sum she was outraged and extremely angry, and blamed everyone but herself.

An old lady once asked me to come and plan a house for her; while doing the job, I was to stay at her son's house, which was situated in the central bogland of Ireland. On my arrival I found it was a typical Irish country mansion, large and imposing, with immense servants' quarters and plenty of servants. We had tea in the spacious drawing-room, where I joined the old lady, her son and his wife, and one unmarried daughter, and directly after tea my would-be client said, " Now I want to tell you all about it. Twenty years before he died my dear husband called me into his office—that is where he did all the estate accounts and saw his tenants, but of course that time we were alone—and this is what he told me : ' Should I die, you have a jointure.' I couldn't bear to think of it, and of course when I married I was very young and didn't know anything about business, but my dear husband said to me—I mean that time in the office—I had got to attend and understand, so of course I did; I always did try to do what he wished."

The old lady was so absorbed in her somewhat rambling saga that I thought it best to let her tell me the kind of house she wanted in her own time and way.

"Well, as I was saying, he told me I had a jointure secured on the estate, but that there was no suitable dower house. You know then I had three daughters with me, but now two of them are married to such dear good fellows."

"Yes, you were telling me about the dower house," I prompted.

"You see, it makes it easier for bedrooms." She paused, and I saw the connection, but she wiped out the saving in bedrooms by murmuring, "Grandchildren, such dear grandchildren."

"Yes, tell me about the dower house."

"You see, there wasn't one, so my dear husband, always so kind and considerate, told me he was leaving me three thousand pounds out of trust to build just what I liked."

We had reached a milestone, but as the dressing gong had sounded, it was suggested I might like to go to my room.

"We'll go into it all after dinner," I suggested, "if it wouldn't tire you."

"Yes, indeed; I want to so much. I have so much to tell you and to show you, and it is so kind of you to help."

After dinner my old lady asked me to sit on a sofa at her side, close to a table which had on it three albums.

"Now I want to explain to you," she began. "Ever since that talk with my dear husband in his office, houses have interested me so much, and wherever I have been abroad, and even on visits in Ireland or England, I have collected pictures of things I have been struck with and have put them in these books." She opened one of the albums. "May I show you?"

She had been struck with a great many things: there were photographs of marble staircases and oak staircases, panelling in plain linen-fold or elaborate in the Grinling

Gibbons manner, marble mantelpieces, vast Gothic stone mantelpieces and Georgian mantelpieces with inset pictures. There were external views of buildings from the Versailles type to the Elizabethan with twisted chimneys, and as we went on and on through these books I saw vistas of show-rooms in historic places and one surprising photograph of a picturesque cottage.

" It looked so pretty and peaceful," she explained, passing quickly to more grandeur.

" Now you must tell me what is in your mind to build," I said.

" I realize," she answered, closing the last book, " that I cannot have a large house, and I shouldn't wish for that; but all my life I have lived in good-sized rooms, so I shouldn't like poky ones."

" I am sure you wouldn't; but what would you require on the ground floor ? "

" I should like an inner hall beyond the main one for hats and coats and things—you would agree to that, wouldn't you ? "

" I quite see its convenience."

" Then we must have the drawing-room and the dining-room and my daughter's sitting-room; a breakfast-room is useful for meals when we have no visitors, and I should like a small sitting-room besides the drawing-room for when we have visitors, as it might be so awkward if the district nurse wanted to see me and I had nowhere to interview her."

" I see.   Is that everything except the service part ? "

" There must, of course, be a sewing-room, but that could be upstairs, and you would arrange the usual offices."

" I should like to know your views about the offices."

" Only the usual thing—a kitchen and scullery, larder and store-room, pantry and servants' hall.   And there is just one thing I should like—a flower-room which could be off the inner hall, with water and a sink.   It is so convenient in the

country." Possibly sensing a lack of response, she added,
" You see, if I had a flower-room I wouldn't ask for a stillroom."

Having agreed to see the selected site in the morning, I
went to bed, wondering how I should detach my old lady
from the attempt to fulfil her dear husband's plan, and the
next day we went together to see the chosen place. The car
stopped at the bottom of a steep, rounded hill.

" I have had a path cleared through the brambles and
gorse, and there is nothing growing on the top where I
thought the house should be." She went slowly up the hill,
helped by an ebony stick. " There, isn't it a wonderful
view ? " she added.

Certainly there was a wonderful expanse of sky and the
beauty that can be seen in all wide spaces, but there was
something desolate in that flat bogland that stretched away
in all directions except for the rounded tops of trees below us
in the Park which we had just left. The ground was
covered with short grass, except where outcrops of limestone rock showed on the surface, and when I borrowed her
stick and moved a thin spit of earth I saw there was scarcely
three inches of soil above the rock.

" Very difficult to cut foundations in," I remarked.

" But you would have to put cellars under the house,
wouldn't you ? " she countered, as if that simplified
foundations.

I was to go by an afternoon train, and in the drawing-
room after luncheon, as we were having coffee, I went and
sat near my old lady, to whom I had become quite attached.

" I am afraid I may distress you," I said, " but you would
want my honest opinion ? "

" Indeed I would, and value it."

" To start with, the house you are thinking of would cost
at least twenty thousand pounds, and then it couldn't con-
tain the lovely things you have admired."

" Would it really cost so much ? "

" Yes, indeed; and in addition, on that hill you could never have a garden or get a tree to grow, and you would have to endure every gale that blew. In the present state of Ireland I think it would be a mistake to attempt it, and then perhaps have it burnt down."

" Yes, I see those difficulties."

" I am so sorry to have to discourage you, but you have had your dream and the very real interest of observing beautiful things, and enjoyed building a wonderful house in your mind. You would only shatter that dream if you tried to realize it. If I might advise you, rent a house in the lovely country round Dublin and see how you like it."

" I wanted to do what my dear husband proposed, but if you really think——"

" Yes, I am quite, quite sure that you cannot do it, and that your husband would agree if he were here."

Did I see a flicker of relief ?

As I was packing my things in my bedroom the daughter-in-law knocked and came in.

" I just want to thank you so very much," she said. " We all feared you would urge my mother-in-law to start building, and we are so relieved."

Soon after there was another knock at the door. This time it was the daughter, and her words sounded like an echo.

" I just want to thank you so very much. I want to live near Dublin, and all you said was just what I felt; it was like thought-reading, and I am so relieved."

A friend who came to me on another occasion acted very differently.

" I have saved enough to build a cottage," she explained. " You said you would do it for me, so will you get the land and settle everything ? I am going abroad to-morrow."

" Surely you want to tell me just what you want ? "

" No, only that it must be warm and easy to look after ;
I shall leave it all to you."

That was eight years ago. She got her cottage—the
sort of place so many people want now, and at a quarter of
present-day costs.

When restoring old houses, built before the Georgian
period, one is always faced with the same problems : chimneys that smoke and damp everywhere ; faults that cause
great discomfort and which must be put right. At Mumpumps I had these difficulties to deal with. The farmer who
had owned it, and who was on the edge of bankruptcy, and
grateful to me for having saved him from this disaster, gave
me a friendly warning on no account to open up the fireplace
or we should be smoked out, and in his opinion it could not
be cured. As soon as he had gone I called my men and told
them to clear the whole thing out, taking away first the two
blood-red cupboards which flanked a grate not much
bigger than a large sugar-basin, and when this was done
and everything cleared away, a noble opening was exposed,
eight feet wide and with a massive oak beam as mantel-
shelf. When we lighted some paper on the hearth to test the
draught, the smoke came straight into the room, not a wisp
going up the flue. Having had experience of open fireplaces, I knew each one must be treated individually by trial
and error. One of the men went up the chimney and found
two flues leading into it, one to a boiler exposed to the open
and no doubt used for cooking pigs' food, and the other to
the old kitchen. These would cause a large pocket of cold
air, turning the smoke back, so the two flues were immediately sealed up from inside the great chimney and the
result tested again with paper. This time most of the smoke
disappeared satisfactorily, though some hung at the sides of
the wide opening and then seeped back into the room. I
was acquainted with the theory of leading air from outside to

below the fire, but have found that in old houses where these large open fireplaces occur ample natural draughts exist, and an additional one is usually of no help, so the next move was to exclude the corners on the upper sides of the opening where smoke was wandering and falling back. For this we got some thick brown paper, such as is put under carpets, and, standing in the fireplace, I cut it into shape and tacked it up, testing every one of the many fittings. One side had to be different from the other, but ultimately we guided that smoke till it flew straight up the chimney, and then the slightly charred paper was extracted and used as a pattern for sheet iron, which was fixed in its place. To make doubly sure, the hearth was raised. For looks we put in a very fine iron fireback, which we had bought in Amiens in a speculative spirit and to save it from being shipped to America. The smoke from that fireplace has behaved perfectly ever since.

Sometimes this problem is evaded by hanging a copper canopy over the fire or by lowering the opening with a sheet of plate-glass below the mantelpiece, but these expedients are generally avoidable.

The next work was to cure the damp in the old part of the house. To do this we opened up the foundations from the outside and found, as I had expected, that the oak framing rested on large stones, the intervals being merely packed earth. It is useless tinkering with this sort of thing or trying to cure it with cement and pudlo; it has to be dealt with yard by yard, a proper excavation made and a concrete-and-brick wall built with a slate damp-course for the old walls to rest on. When this was done the stone floors were taken up, earth and clay removed and replaced with a concrete float and joists and floorboards. I have restored other old houses dating from the seventeenth century, and have had to deal with the foundations in just the same way.

I think restoring and saving old houses when they are of architectural interest is a duty one owes to the past, and it is a satisfaction to feel that one is collaborating with the builders of centuries ago and preserving their work, possibly for centuries to come.   About ten years ago I went to see three cottages near Marden in Kent which were reputed to be very early and had been condemned for demolition.   They were oak-framed with plaster panels and, though they had evidently been divided in recent times into three sections, they were really one house, and had a massive central chimney and steep-pitched tile roof. Though they were neglected and looked almost derelict, I thought the structure could and should be saved, so I bought the place, and, in spite of many difficulties, was helped by getting an excellent set of men who worked with enthusiasm and interest.   There was the usual underpinning and making of new foundations, but the main walls were so far out of the perpendicular that with the utmost care we drew the framing a little nearer to being upright.

At the time the house was condemned one portion had been occupied by a family of gypsies who, when they were turned out, were reputed to have left a curse on all who came into the place.   I had heard this from the men, who whenever anything turned out particularly troublesome to do would say, " That (something) curse is working against us," as if they almost believed in it, so I suggested that the kindly old Roman Catholic priest should be asked to come from Goudhurst with bell, book, and candle to exorcize the evil thing.   They were horrified.   " Don't do no such thing," they pleaded, evidently thinking priestly magic worse than any curse.   Just after this talk my foreman drew me aside and said he wished to tell me something.

" More consequences of the curse ? " I asked.

" Oh no, that's all done with," he said; " but the trouble

is we are being eaten alive by fleas : my wife caught nine on my pillow last night, and it did put her about."

" No wonder," I said.   " I'll write to the county council pest officer and have it seen to at once."

This official duly arrived with his car full of elaborate gear, but when I told him we were troubled with numbers of fleas, his face fell.

" No bugs or lice ? " he asked in a disappointed voice, clearly feeling as a keen shot might on being told there were only rabbits when asked for a day's sport and more exciting game had been expected.   However, the house was cleansed from end to end, for whether the gypsies had left a curse or not, they certainly had left their fleas.

When repairing the base of the great chimney I found it was built of two-inch sun-dried bricks which were laid in the old English bond; that is, one course wholly of " stretchers " and the next all of " headers ", which dated this brickwork as long before the first quarter of the seventeenth century, for after that time the Flemish bond was used of alternative " headers " and " stretchers ".   One of the early sun-dried bricks had the clear imprint of a cat's paw, indicating that a cat must have walked on it more than three hundred years before we extracted it.   The modern name of this very old house was " Cornwall ", and a kind archæological expert, after research through Hasted's *History of Kent*, suggested that this name may have been a corruption from Combwell, as in the valor of that monastery's possessions in 1535, the date of the dissolution, they name " one acre of meadow at Marden ".   I was glad to feel I had saved the place from demolition, though the site on which it stood was low, and not a spot which I should choose for building.

When building a new house the choice of site lies in one's own hands and is of the first importance.   Some houses seem to have been put down in a haphazard spirit, whereas every house should, in its type and position, fit the land upon which it stands, and should be visualized by the designer from the first. I once took a friend to see a very beautiful place which had a distance like an old master landscape, and below it on either side majestic oaks over-hanging a deep, dark pool, with other oak-trees behind.

" To build here," I said, " you must have a house of dignity, severe and balanced, which would have massive stone vases on the flights of wide, low stone steps taking you to the lower level. You couldn't have a trivial garden; it is all too splendid."

" It doesn't sound a bit cosy."

" Of course it doesn't, but you must fit your setting, and you can have what you call ' cosy ' in the little valley site we saw. There you could have wandering paths and an irregular, low house which would have its own charm."

Another time I was taken to an unusual place where a building was to be erected—a piece of high land jutting over an immense view which stretched far below. Here I visualized a light, airy house, with something of the quality of a ship in full sail, colour-washed primrose or faint rose, and having a circular, glass-sided loggia supported on light, delicate pillars. When a year later I went to see what had been put there I saw a squat, heavy, dark building, askew with the panorama it overlooked.

If possible it is best to choose a site for building which has some old timber and to preserve what is there, for a garden grows up quickly, and with the addition of one or two fine trees the place will give an impression of perman-ence, instead of that unfortunate just-finished, raw look.

Many years ago I was seeing to a house near Reading, and on my way passed a new housing estate on land that had evidently once been a park, for near the entrance was a fine cedar, and farther in several great oak-trees, all notched for felling. I took down the name of the contractor, and wrote at once urging him to reconsider the removal of those fine trees, suggesting it would mean very little adjustment of plans to keep them and that, left standing, they would improve the whole aspect and be a boon to the tenants. I asked him to submit my letter to his employers before doing away with the trees, but when I passed that way again three months later they were gone and no growing thing was left there. Only dreary, arid rows of semi-detached houses in process of erection were to be seen, where for hundreds of years those majestic trees had stood.

Chapter Twenty-seven

GARDENING

THROUGHOUT my life gardening has been for me the happiest and most soothing of occupations. For success a good plan is essential, and as important for the setting of flowers as a good design for a house. Indeed, I feel building and garden planning are closely allied.

This feeling for what is mutually suitable can be observed in various periods. The grandeur of Versailles suggested the ignoring of flowers, but provided fountains and a series of balustraded steps, garnished with vases and statuary, as a setting for so splendid a palace. The tidy architecture of Holland evoked the Dutch garden, which rightly came to England together with their style of building; and how suitable were the round, oval, or serpentine beds, gaudy with salvias, lobelias, and " love-lies-bleeding " in the gardens of Victorian villas. How wise, too, was the reaction led by Mr. William Robinson of eschewing symmetry and allowing flowers to riot in abundance around the pseudo-antique homes that succeeded the villas and the era of bedding-out. Through lack of education in the fine arts, certain unfortunate examples both of homes and gardens have been mistakenly accepted as patterns to follow.

Some vagrant minds seem incapable of considering any plan; the homes they build appear to have been dropped inadvertently and without thought, and their gardens suggest the efforts of an enterprising hen scratching where its fancy leads.

A certain degree of formality adds to the charm of a riot of flowers. Italian gardens, which are so beautifully laid out, are usually helped by fine sculptured ornaments, stone well-heads, vases, and ornamental water, but they have few flowers; English gardens usually lack these things, but have an abundance of bloom. There should be a combination of the two, for we can learn much from the past.

We might allow a few vases to adorn our scheme, and fill them with the erstwhile condemned geraniums beloved by Victorians, but we need not encircle them with the girdle of calceolarias they chose to set them in.

Dare we venture on a little statuary as a terminal to some glowing vista? I confess I have not been able to place any figure or vase, wrought at a later date than the eighteenth century, in a garden of my making.

There are those who can afford to give large sums for Italian carvings; others must do the best they can. One of my bricklayers brought a London friend to see my garden. We sat in view of a leaden Georgian vase, and feeling, I suppose, that we shared a taste, my visitor told me of his own effort.

" My bit of ground," he explained, " is scarce ten feet square, but I've made the most of it. I saved coke clinkers, and with them and some empty tins I built a fair-sized mound. On the top I placed a plaster head of Shakespeare;

the base was broken, so I didn't have to pay a lot for it. At the same shop I found a kind of a Swiss goat called a shamey, with only one leg missing, and that I've got at the bottom, looking up. Sort of makes you think in a manner of speaking, and at the same time it fills the eye."

I was touched at this pathetic effort to achieve decoration and symbolism, though I could not wish to fill my eye with either a bust of William Shakespeare or a three-legged chamois.

He was a nice man, and I felt more in sympathy with him than with those gardeners, who ought to know better, who place cement rabbits and other whimsies in their grounds. They deserve to have living rabbits let loose in their gardens to gnaw their azaleas and eat their carnations; but it would perhaps be unduly vindictive to suggest such a punishment, however suitable.

With such a variety of taste clamouring for satisfaction, present-day sculptors might with advantage to themselves consider this potential market for their works. I would, however, suggest that a creature with eléphantine limbs, or any object executed from the memory of a nightmare vision, would not harmonize with the flowers that bloom in the spring, or indeed at any other season.

On the other hand, it is just possible that modern sculpture executed in broad planes, with no bias towards naturalism, executed by a trained artist who could express rhythmic beauty, might look superb in a garden large enough for a massive conception to be viewed from a distance. Having accepted such modern decoration, a horrid vision takes shape in my imagination, and I see lumps of stone hacked about by someone who had never learnt to draw or model, which might be called " Fecundity " or some such name, and might be described by a quite meaningless and absurd phrase as being " subconsciously fundamentally functional ".

Let us have done with so thorny a problem, and enjoy

thinking of actual work in the garden; for to the true gardener this is rest and refreshment. Wars may rage and be forgotten; time itself ceases to count, for hours or minutes pass equally unrecorded. Work can be endlessly varied; if you need ease, then sow seeds, prick out seedlings, take cuttings, put lily-bulb scales in rows in boxes full of peat; or, having done all these things, deal tenderly with them, and encourage their growth. If, on the other hand, you feel you want to work off your energy or your irritation with life, take your spade or fork and dig. The happiest time I have found for this is the early morning before breakfast; you won't have any irritation to work off then, nor will the telephone ring or any household disruption disturb you, and you will assimilate something of the fresh serenity of Nature and absorb the peace and beauty peculiar to early morning, which will strengthen you for the coming day. A garden, too, reflects the gardener's individuality and taste. Some people like minutiæ, and they can cultivate the whole range of tiny exquisite flowers and rejoice in them. I like effects in the pictorial sense, and am indifferent as to the rarity of any plant if it helps my picture. Some people take little interest in general effect, but have a passion for what is most difficult to grow; they can surround their precious treasure with a zinc collar and put a sheet of glass on three legs to protect it, and gaze with pride at its shy puce blossom. The grower of the rare and difficult can have his fun, too; he can contrive to have underground water in summer and turn it off in winter, and at a pinch he can even achieve underground heat. There is the gardener who only cares for one species—lilies, roses, or what you will—and others who love a plant for itself and its own special beauty. Of all types, the commonest is the gardener who grows anything anywhere with exuberant energy and little thought, but with satisfaction to himself. In whichever direction your taste may lie, to get full enjoyment out of your garden one thing only is essential, and that is to work in it yourself.

Your work, however, in any kind of garden will reward you far more richly if the layout is good. Proportions out of doors should always be on an ample scale. Steps should be wide, and eighteen inches on the flat with low risers. I was asked to come and see a sunk garden newly made by a local builder; it was too well built and quite dreadful. When the owner asked me if I liked it, I did not feel able to say that the mean, steep, cement-laid steps suggested the entrance to an underground public lavatory in a town, and that the sharp-edged, hard red-brick walls looked like a prison for the unhappy plants they enclosed.

During the war I had of necessity to grow vegetables. The average countryman thinks that growing cabbages is really worth while, and looking after flowers a time-wasting nuisance. I have no enthusiasm for cabbages, but I did get some satisfaction from producing a great deal of useful food. When, owing to neglected fences, a whole herd of cows broke into my kitchen garden, ate all that was in it, and left the ground a trampled quagmire, I was at first outraged, but later I felt almost relieved. Now, with no qualms of conscience I could return to my somewhat neglected flowers. I could even be amused at seeing the stampede of the cows across the field after their devastating damage had been done, the bull leading with bits of the strawberry net flying from his horns as he curveted and kicked up his heels, followed by his seventeen wives. I was the more justified in giving up the kitchen garden because at that time I had no man to work there. Before the war I employed a labourer who would do as he was told, and I found that the single-handed gardener, who, knowing very little, thinks he knows everything, is a nuisance and a menace. Recently just such a man came to see me when his employer was ill and said, " For the first time for ten years the tulips have been planted out proper, for I weren't interfered with. I got a line and a six-inch stick and I had a row of white and a row of red, and another of yellow, just the right distance apart, and when the time comes they'll show up a treat."

Although I miss the help a man might give, I like being alone in my garden, letting worries and anxieties fall away as the hours slip by, and occasionally conscious of the unity of the earth, the trees, the flowers, the birds, the butterflies, and myself; realizing, if only for a moment, that we are all a part of the same pulsing life, deriving from the same source, and attaining ultimately the same end.

Chapter Twenty-eight

ROUGHFIELD AND AN ECHO OF AURELIA

WITH my foreman I put in the pegs for the foundations of our permanent home in April 1934. The house was finished by the following January. During the previous winter a road was made to reach the ground we had chosen, first passing through fields and then dipping down into a wood and rising again to where the house was to stand.

Every day I arrived early at the site, and stayed till the men had gone, and after I had finished going round each department, noting what materials were wanted, and seeing to the work on hand, I could rest under an oak-tree and feel an inner peace, as intimacy with the beauty of the distance grew upon me. All that summer the weather was perfect, the men were good-tempered and worked willingly, taking a pride in what they were doing.

Some years later my old scaffolder told me, " We was all in the pub one night talking over the different places we had worked in, and we agreed that the happiest job we had ever been on was yours at ' Roughfield '." This was the rather harsh-sounding name we had given our house because that was what the land upon which it stood had been called for the past two hundred years.

Is it fanciful to believe that some special grace is given to a structure when such good feeling has gone to the making of it ?

One could hear whistling and snatches of song as the building advanced, and a real sign of good fellowship was the many jokes that were bandied about.

Once, through misdirected energy, an elderly bricklayer had failed to study the plan and had forgotten the opening of a small lavatory, and had by mistake built himself in.

" Here, Joe," he called to the foreman, " I've made a fool of myself and built up the doorway so I can't get out. Send a couple of fellows to help take it down again."

" Oh no, I won't," was the reply. " You stay there till the lady sees you, and then we'll get you out with a pulley."

The poor man's plight was watched with gales and shouts of laughter, and even I felt weak as I looked at his indignant face peering out of his self-made prison.

Such simple jests amused us all. From the moment we settled in at Roughfield we felt we had at last found our permanent home. The place had a remote, wild, and peaceful atmosphere. At night one heard the barking of foxes and the songs of nightingales, and at dusk the crowing of roosting pheasants. Yet in those easier times friends could drive down from London for a day's outing. The garden gave endless scope, and I had visions of extending it to a near-by wood, where lay a dark, mysterious pool, shadowed by oaks—a perfect setting for a wild garden. That idea has remained a dream, for the war ended all such hopes.

Among the friends who came to stay with us was the maid who subsequently became the life-long friend and companion to Mrs. Berens (the dear aunt with whom I had gone to America), who used to refer to her as " My blessed Virgin Mary ".

Mary told me, in her slow, gentle way of speaking, that she was now managing affairs for Aurelia, who had to be kept by her family.

" Mary," I exclaimed, " to hear about Aurelia is like stepping back into another life, recalling those many and difficult years when I was responsible for her. What is she like now ? She must be very old."

" She is nearly eighty, but still active and, in a way, just the same as she always was. As she has no income of her own, I manage the money that is subscribed for her. I do my best, but it is rather difficult ; for, you see, she gives away anything she gets, so I pay directly for all I can, like the rent and the coal, and I tried paying a restaurant for a good meal every day, but she would send poor people to have it, saying they needed it more than she did. As she is a vegetarian, it had to be a vegetarian restaurant."

" What ? " I exclaimed, startled by such a surprising statement. " She's a vegetarian, who used to eat such quantities of meat ? Why, I remember once when she was with us in Paris we took her to a bourgeois restaurant where large helpings were provided and she ate two underdone steaks, one after another. Even the waiter was taken aback."

" Yes, we were very surprised ; but she told us she had had a dream of a dying goat which she was sure had been sent to her as a message that she ought to eat nothing that had been killed. At first we thought that such a sudden change might upset her health, but she denied the very idea, saying that she was always well."

" What does she do with herself ? "

" She seems to know a great many poor people, and she does a lot of collecting."

" Collecting ! How ? " I asked with a pang of early memory.

" She has a peerage list, an army list, and a clergy list—Crockford's I think it is called—and she has three different typewritten letters, and sends the suitable one to every name listed in these books, asking for help for herself, for of course she has connections with the peerage and with the army through her brother, General Sir Herbert Stewart, and with the Church, and I am afraid she pretends to be in great want. We can't stop her. Whether she gets a great deal of money we don't know, but we think she must, for sometimes she has so much to spend and so much to give away. My dear lady used to say of Mrs. Aurelia, ' She may be a saint in the next world but she is very trying in this one.' "

We sat quiet, looking into the fire for a time, and then Mary went on slowly, " She gave a party not long ago, and asked me to come and help her, which meant she wanted me to come and dress her for the evening, for though she has all Mrs. Berens' clothes for her own use, I take care of them and don't let her keep them. If I did she would only pawn them or give them away. I took down a grey chiffon dress which she looks so well in, and went to her cellar—she will still live in a basement—where I found her with half a dozen loaves. She asked me to get some butter and anything I thought would make nice sandwiches, and to cut them while she went to get the inside of the piano, which a man was mending and which she said she must have for the party because Madame Volpi had promised to sing. Off she went, and while I was cutting the sandwiches the guests began to arrive."

Mary paused and then resumed, " It really was rather unpleasant, for I didn't know any of them, and they seemed vexed at Mrs. Aurelia not being there. They were such different sorts of people : a good many foreigners and Jews, some quite well-to-do-looking people in evening dress, and other humble ones. But it was all right directly she got back and came in, bursting the door open. You know her way, so delighted to see everyone, and she insisted that the little man who came behind her carrying the inside of the piano must also stay and enjoy himself. Then she called out, ' The party can't begin till I am dressed, so all hide your faces for the transformation scene. Come on, Mary.' I had everything ready, and in about two minutes she was in the grey chiffon, with a wreath of gold leaves in her hair, and she can still look handsome. It all went quite wonderfully; she told stories and there was music, comic acting, an acrobatic dancer, and singing by Madame Volpi, and I almost thought the ceiling would come down. Some of them sat on the floor, and they all ate and laughed and talked, and Mrs. Aurelia enjoyed it so much herself."

" That is why she could always make things go well for any gathering," I said.

" I must tell you what happened in the end. Mrs. Aurelia stood up and said, ' You all know I am very poor, and so I am going to ask someone to hold this plate at the door, and anyone who can spare something can put it on it —pennies or pounds,' she ended, laughing. A dark, quite smart-looking young man took the green plate, a lot of money was put into it, and then I don't know how it happened, but the man was just gone and the plate left empty on the floor. All Mrs. Aurelia said was, ' Well, I must give another party.' "

So she was just as imperturbable and sweet-tempered as ever. How persistent character is ! With that immense capacity for enjoyment which she still retained, she was not only unaware of class distinctions, but completely un-conscious of their existence, and could make the casual work-man who brought the piano share the evening's entertainment with rich Jews in a way that would make it seem right and natural.

After a gap of thirty years, as I sat in my quiet room remote from all the anxieties and incredible happenings associated with Aurelia, she came to life again in Mary's picture of her party, and once more I felt the old exasperated affection for her. But I was thankful to have escaped from everything to do with that phase of my life, and thinking over the many years I had lived, I recalled other scenes and other people.

Chapter Twenty-nine

ARTISTS AND OTHERS I HAVE KNOWN

I WAS quite young when I stayed with the Rosses in London. Robbie Ross, Oscar Wilde's faithful friend, had been at school abroad with my brother, and through my brother Robbie had for years exercised an influence on me that he was quite unaware of. His youth in the early 'nineties was lived in a sceptical circle. He was small for his age, and at fifteen looked about twelve, but he was precocious and intelligent. At school in France he studied the Bible, finding contradictions and what he thought were absurdities, and making notes of his discoveries and of all he had heard derided at home. He turned these efforts into an impish form of amusement. In his spare time he would go out with his Bible and his notebook and sit on a public seat awaiting an audience. If an old lady joined him he would bend over his books, apparently absorbed in de-

MYSELF

AURELIA IN SERIOUS MOOD

BEDROOM AT SAN MARTINO

votional study, and when the old lady, inevitably impressed, said, "I like to see a child so interested in the Bible," Robbie would lift large, soulful eyes and respond, "It is the most wonderful book in the world." He would then go on to expand all the contradictions and fallacies he could think of, making special play with St. Joseph's descent from David and the Immaculate Conception, and murmuring that either the one had nothing to do with the case or the other was a much later invention. The interview would end with the old lady retiring in horror and telling him he was a very wicked boy. My brother repeated as an accepted fact all that Robbie said, and at the time I was convinced that the whole Bible story was false. I met his sister Elise in Dorset; she picked up this link, and we became friends. She was some years older than I, and to my inexperienced mind seemed the most sophisticated person I had ever known. When asked what plays I had seen, I was ashamed to have to confess that I had never been to a theatre, whereupon she arranged a visit, saying she would enjoy taking me to my first play.

The two brothers, Aleck and Robbie, and their sister, opened up a wonderland for me. They were amused to hear I had never seen anything in London except Euston station, and between them determined to show me a great deal, taking me to private views, to museums and galleries, to painters' studios, and to several theatres. Both the brothers teased me in a kindly way, more especially because I had said I wanted to have a career and be independent and that I thought women should have the same education as men.

One night Oscar Wilde came to dinner and, introducing me, Robbie said, "Young as she is, she's a feminist, and I'm afraid harbours germs of the reformer."

Oscar fixed his fine eyes with their heavy lids upon me and said, "But this is serious : do you realize reformers do infinite harm? Think of Luther and the Puritans, and temperance advocates."

All that evening he talked of the importance of beauty and enjoyment. I was puzzled at his paradoxical way of putting things, but he was vital and eager, with a great power of expression, and so gay and happy that it was a delightful evening. In his youth his looks must have been unusual and arresting and, listening to his brilliant conversation, one forgot his appearance of self-indulgence. The Ross trio were clever, but Oscar Wilde dominated us all completely, though in a very kindly way.

After he had gone Robbie said, " We think him quite outstanding, and certain to have a place in literature."

Many years after that meeting his name came up while I was talking to my cousin, Lady Ardilaun, in Ireland.

" Poor, poor Oscar ! " she said. " His people lived just outside our place in Galway, and I knew him and his brother Willy from the time they were children. His parents were strange people, not fit to bring up boys. I never knew his father well, but he hadn't a good reputation, and his mother, who was a poetess, was pretentious and absurd. If you went to see her she expected a formal notice of your coming, and would then send back a letter saying she would ' receive ' at such and such an hour and day. I remember once going to their small, square, untidy house after this formality had been gone through, and while standing at the open door I heard Lady Wilde's voice saying in a carrying whisper, ' Oscar, will you shoo out the ducks before presenting the visitor ? '

" After some scuffling at the back door, Oscar, then a rather uncouth-looking boy of perhaps fourteen, with straggling, straight black hair and dark eyes, came to take me to his mother. There, in the afternoon, and in the boglands of the west of Ireland, she was lying on an empire couch, dressed in a low-cut ruby velvet dress. She spoke in the most artificial way, quoting lines of her own poetry.

"The first time I thought of Oscar as being original was when I had asked him to a luncheon-party, and during the afternoon we went to look at the gardens, which were of the elaborate bedding kind and, in that style, very well done. The visitors all admired them, and thinking that Oscar, who was barely eighteen, might feel shy, I turned to him and said :

"'Do you like my garden ? '

"'No,' he said clearly. 'It is very dull.'

"Quite taken aback, I exclaimed, 'What do you mean ? '

"'I mean that it is very dull. Don't you think so ? '

"'Don't you think my initials are nicely done ? '

"'Yes, but I don't care for them done in bedding plants, even if they are your initials.'

"'The gardener wanted to do the family crest, but as it's a pig, I wouldn't let him,' I told him.

"'Oh, you should have; it would have been the perfect culmination of absurdity,' he replied.

"Oscar got quite excited picturing how the pig could be done, suggesting flesh-coloured begonias for the body and a house leek, round and prickly, for the eye, and love-lies-bleeding pegged down in twiddles for the tail.

"When I recalled this conversation afterwards I realized that Oscar was certainly not shy or intimidated, and I thought it remarkable for a boy to express an opinion in opposition to older people, wondering if perhaps he might be right. Certainly up to then I had not been interested in gardening, but now I bought books and papers, and before long had altered all that bedding. So I owe my interest in gardening in the first instance to the jolt poor Oscar gave me so many years ago.

"He often came to see me, and was always good company, never saying an objectionable word, though he was sometimes rather ridiculous. The last time I saw him was when his plays were running and he came to call at our London house in Carlton House Terrace, with his head covered in close, tight curls.

" ' Oscar ! ' I cried, ' what have you done to your hair ? '

" He burst out laughing and said, ' It's the Nero touch, and I have to go to Paris every week to get it done. It's made quite a sensation.'

" ' But it's frightful.'

" He went to a mirror and examined himself in various attitudes.

" ' I think perhaps it is, and when everyone has copied me I shall go quite straight again.'

" I had no suspicions about his character. It was so tragic. His trial was a great shock, and I couldn't bear to read about it. Poor, poor Oscar ! "

My cousin got up and took a book from the bookcase.

" Do you know ' The Ballad of Reading Gaol ' ? " She read it aloud, and after she had finished sat silent for some minutes. " I have always regretted . . ." She paused again, " Oscar wrote to me from France after he was released asking me for a little money and a word of comfort, for he needed both. I told my husband, who only said, ' Leave that man alone,' so I didn't write or help him, and he died soon afterwards. He was so terribly punished," she added after another pause, " and I didn't give him the little comfort I might have done, nor did I send him any money. After his death, when I could send him neither, I was so profoundly sorry; but death is final, and we are left with our regrets."

There was an interval between my meeting Oscar Wilde, whom I never saw again, and my going to the Slade School, where at the same session were several students who later made names for themselves. William Orpen, arriving from Dublin, aged seventeen, holder of a gold medal and other distinctions from the Irish School of Art, was extraordinarily capable, winning, with his picture of Sadler's Wells Theatre, the prize for the best composition of the year. Eileen Monsel, who was very gifted, also came from Ireland, where she had done remarkable drawings of country figures and horses in motion. Other new students were McEvoy, who became a fashionable portrait-painter, and Augustus John and his sister Gwen. John, at that time a shy, beardless youth, was soon recognized as a first-rate draughtsman.

After we had left the Slade and gone to live in Dorset, Augustus John, bringing no luggage and wearing a black shirt, came to stay with us at the Wool manor house. He had developed his interest in gypsies, and was himself a fine and wild-looking figure, with a great beard and a quantity of hair. A cousin, fond of hunting and unacquainted with any artists, was staying with me at the time, and was puzzled and not favourably impressed by John. When he liked he could talk very well, but he also could maintain a most daunting silence, and while with us he was in his silent mood, and uttered no word except to ask if he might take his mattress out to lie on in the sun. Day after day he lay on it, with his wide-brimmed hat tilted over his eyes.

" Does he sleep in that black shirt ? " my cousin asked.

" I expect so—you might ask him."

" He wouldn't answer," she said as she looked at his prostrate figure.

After he had been with us for a week, John announced at lunch, " I'll be going by the afternoon train; may I draw your cat ? " He produced a sketch-book and drew for a few minutes, then for the first time he addressed my cousin and said in his deep voice, " I am going to say you a Romany poem," which he did and with hardly a break added, " Good-bye," and strolled away.

" Well," exclaimed my cousin, " of all the detestable men! You say he is a great artist, yet the only thing he does is to draw the cat just as he's going away, and doesn't even show us what he's done; then, never having spoken to anyone, he stares at me with those eyes and recites a poem I can't understand one word of."

Some years later, when building in Dorset, I received a letter which read, " Please get me a house, John."

As this request seemed too indeterminate to act on, I sent him a list of questions with intervening spaces, which he duly filled in and returned, after which I found an unusually attractive house built by a Frenchman, set in woodland, on the Wimborne property.

Knowing that John and his large family were not conventional tenants, I decided that, before I showed him the house, which I felt sure he would like, I would call and see Lady Wimborne, who was a keen Liberal and a leader of Evangelical religion, to get her approval.

" But we should be pleased to have a clever artist for a tenant," she assured me when I had explained the position. " I am much interested in art, and always encourage it as far as I can, and of course I understand that artists are not cut to pattern or just conventional, ordinary people."

John was really pleased with the place I had found in its lovely woodland setting, and took it at once. It needed some repairs, and while these were being done they camped out and amused themselves by decorating a small empty gardener's cottage, where they had meals, painting the walls black and the furniture scarlet.

One afternoon, having finished this effort, the children decided to get the red and black paint off their persons, so they all undressed and, with turpentine soap and scrubbing brushes, set to work to clean themselves up. It was while they were so occupied that Lady Wimborne paid her first call.

One of the clear pictures which I retain of those unusual people is of John's second wife coming to see me. She was a really beautiful woman, with her own special style in dressing, which, through John's many drawings of her, set a later fashion. I can still visualize the group coming up our pine-shaded, sun-dappled drive. Mrs. John, who was leading a grey donkey with a small boy astride it dressed in brilliant blue and another equally vivid small boy at her side, wore a tight-fitting, hand-sewn, canary-coloured bodice above a dark, gathered, flowing skirt, and her hair, very black and gleaming, emphasized the long silver earrings which were her only adornment. Another memory is of their woods with wild cherry-trees in blossom, and of a model with flying red hair, clad in white, being chased in and out of the trees by nude children; and very lovely they all looked, or so I thought.

I am not sure whether it was on that day or another that I was introduced to a young man wearing owl-like spectacles who, I was told, was the boys' tutor.

" Are you also the baby's nurse ? " I asked, for he was wheeling a perambulator.

" Oh no, but I am going to walk to Turkey, and I am having this pram for my books. I shall take nothing else, but I must have books, and this is a most convenient way of carrying them. To-night I am going across to France in a fishing-boat." He trundled his pram away and I never saw him again.

It was while I was working at the Slade School that, through Irish links, I first met George Moore, who was in every way a contrast to Augustus John, and his setting in Ebury Street was very unlike the woodland scenes in which the John family, often unclothed, played and worked. I was a frequent visitor to George Moore's tidy, comfortable house, where everything looked as clean and orderly as he himself. He had lost his yellow hair, as shown in Manet's portrait of him, and what he had left was white and no longer stood on end, but he had retained his pink cheeks and rather infantile look. He enjoyed talking of his student days in Paris and looking back at the incidents of so many years ago, which were evidently golden days to him, but he was quite frank about his inability to learn to paint, adding, with a rather childish vanity which seemed natural to him, " Although I am not an artist in colour, I am in words."

We were interrupted by tea, and he launched into his favourite subject of sex. When he went off on this line I thought him really tiresome, and said firmly that I wasn't interested in that subject.

" Impossible," he exclaimed. " It is the most absorbing theme, the heart of all good literature, and also conditions all our actions and all we do."

I do not know if he knew anything of Freud's theories, but he certainly would have approved them. He went on to tell me of the strange experiences he had had with women who had fallen in love with his books or his portrait and had written him impassioned letters.

" Now, I will tell you a strange thing that happened to me," he said; " and what was so curious was that the same idea occurred to different people in different parts of the world at about the same time. These delightful women felt that they would like to perpetuate my gifts in future gen-erations, and invited my collaboration; a charming idea, the union of beauty on the one hand and what they were kind enough to believe was brilliant talent on the other, the offspring to be the flower of both gifts."

" Where did these enterprising ladies come from ? " I asked.

" Latin countries, of course—South America and South Europe; you could only expect romance to spring from that strain."

" What wonderful stories you do tell, Mr. Moore ! "

He responded delightedly, not accepting my meaning, or

pretending not to, and exclaimed, " Well, of course I should, as a novelist, be able to express my facts well."

At this time he was writing his " Brook Kerith "—or it may have been at a later date, as we often met—and he started to read me a passage which ended in St. Paul having a scuffle and a bout of fisticuffs on a high road with someone —I think St. Peter, but of this I am not sure—and I exclaimed, " But you can't show St. Paul fighting like that; it sounds like a scene at Donnybrook Fair."

" Ah, that's how it strikes you, is it ? I wasn't sure myself, and I wanted to test what a normal reaction would be. I'll modify it or cut it out."

He was best company for me when talking on art subjects. Once I came to see him when he had just been to an exhibition of modernistic pictures of that date, and he was fuming, for he hated such work.

" I have seen that show," I said, amused at his vehemence. " There is a fashion just now for painting anchovy-coloured farm buildings backed by verdigris-green trees and little men with arms like sausages moving planks and wearing brimless bowler hats that are too small for them."

" Horrible ! " George Moore exclaimed. " And all these ugly buildings were shown quite out of perspective, which I found most offensive, whereas I can look at primitive pictures which are also drawn regardless of the laws of perspective and feel no distaste. After pondering on the reason for this difference in my feelings while walking home, I have discovered the cause, and know I am right. It is all a matter of innocence of vision. If you are expressing beauty and truth as you see it, you convey beauty and truth, and, although the primitives didn't understand perspective, what they did was done as well as they knew how. That's what I mean by innocence of vision. Those fellows who painted the pictures I saw to-day know about perspective and anatomy, and their work is false because they deliberately and perversely distort both. What their object is I cannot say—self-advertisement, I suppose—but anyhow their stuff will perish and go into limbo, and isn't worth getting annoyed about."

He was so pleased with his phrase " innocence of vision " that he dilated on it from every angle, shaking his finger at me to emphasize his contention. No visit to him ever passed without reference to the painter Manet, whom he revered and whom he also associated with his own halcyon days of youth in Paris. He loved showing the picture he owned by that master.

I did not feel that George Moore was in any sense a great man, for his small vanities and rather childish resentment at any fancied or real slight seemed to counter such an idea, but perhaps I am wrong, and his writings may have lasting value.

The sculptor Rodin, whom I met in Paris, appeared to me to have the elements of greatness. He invited me and a friend to come and see him any evening at his studio, and when one winter afternoon we went there at about four o'clock, he waved us to a settee without greeting. It was a vast place in which the light was going and great shapes loomed out, some sheeted and some exposed, while the sculptor was standing quite still a few feet from the figure he was modelling. Presently he walked backwards, and again stood still looking at his work and then, striding up to it, slashed away some clay with a flat, spade-like implement, for the form had hardly emerged from a great mass of this grey stuff. He went on like this for about twenty minutes, and it was fascinating to watch the broad sweep of the recumbent figure emerging from the shapeless heap it had been. Meanwhile the studio was getting darker and darker, until at last he realized that he could see no more, and flinging a wet cloth over his work he turned to us, begging a thousand pardons for his neglect of us and his bad manners, and sitting down to explain that every day the good God sent a precious half-hour or less, which was the time of crepuscule when the little things that lie on the surface and distract us are veiled and we see only the solid forms revealed in great planes. That is the inspiring moment which no doubt happens between night and day, but what will you? He shrugged his shoulders.

"Then," he went on, "I am not alert; I lie in my warm bed. You who are both artists, you understand when I tell you of the distracting superficial things which so many painters and sculptors spend themselves on; but they should disregard lips and eyelids and concentrate on the big shapes on which these incidents occur. Always the great whole must be sought in its simplest essentials. Half light, half dark, is the hour when we see best."

I have often thought of Rodin in his dusky studio, and realized that what he said applies to more than just painting and sculpture. In planning a house one should think of the shape as a whole, undistracted by any excrescents or by windows and doors, which are like the superficial features he urged us to forget. He did not mean that they should not be indicated; for a builder to omit windows and doors would be absurd, but one should remember that the whole mass is the important thing, and no surface trimmings can make bad proportions right. The same rule applies to gardens. Work out the plan and the shape the garden is to take, and do not rely on the flowers that will adorn it, which will play their part wherever they are grown, but whose value as a picture will be infinitely enhanced by being set in a good background.

When I started my first house soon after my visit to Rodin, I was so taken up with the many new problems then confronting me that it did not occur to me to consider applying his teachings to my plan, although I have tried to do so in later work.

It was while I was living in my heather-thatched hut supervising this first effort that a dear friend, Kathleen Mansell Pleydel, came to see me. She appeared to be in a nervous and excited state and looking round asked, " Can anyone hear us ? "

" Only birds and squirrels," I assured her.

Speaking in a whisper she explained, " This is very secret, and I know I can trust you to say nothing about it. I am hiding Mrs. Pankhurst for a rest, and I want your help. She has been let out of prison on that devilish cat-and-mouse act; no one is to know where she is, and I want you to take my place on guard when I have to go out."

I found Mrs. Pankhurst a gentle, frail-looking woman whom no one would imagine connected with criminal affairs or capable of enduring forcible feeding in prison. She was physically exhausted, but as she grew stronger it became clear why she had become a leader. The question of women's suffrage which possessed her was a mania— almost a phobia—and she talked and thought of nothing else, believing that the gaining of votes for women would change their status and alter the outlook of everyone in the country. Such sincere, intense conviction drew followers, and when addressing a meeting she could carry her audience to the emotional heights she herself felt. I could not make her understand why I would not join her crusade.

" Don't you want women to have votes ? " she asked.

" No," I replied. " For certain reasons, I don't."

She shot upright from the cushions on which she was resting as if she had been stung, just as one might expect an ardent missionary to do on hearing that one was indifferent to whether anyone was a Christian or not.

" What can you mean ? " she cried, wringing her hands in exasperation. " You, who are doing a man's work."

" I think too many ill-informed people have the vote now

and we are overweighted with them.   Power is in the hands
of a class particularly susceptible to propaganda and ready to
accept bribes, which is bad for the politicians who are
tempted to do this bribing.   I don't want to double that
ill-informed power by giving women the vote."

"But women would raise the whole tone of the
electorate."

"I don't think so," I said.   "I should think that as a
whole women are more ignorant than men, and they are
unlikely to vote with any solidarity as women.   You can't
judge the masses by the standards of your band of en-
thusiasts."

"But surely you want justice for women, which should
be reason enough to make you join us."

"I couldn't join your society because I hate violence and
think that a government should resist it whatever the cause,
just or unjust."

The idea that her violent tactics should be resisted
chilled our intercourse, though not the spate of argument,
but I liked Mrs. Pankhurst, and admired her brave and
ardent spirit, despite the fact that I could not agree with
her.

Another well-known personality I met at that time was
Mrs. Beatrice Webb, who was absorbed in an aim very
different from that of Mrs. Pankhurst, though she shared her
singleness of purpose in her desire to help other people.
But Mrs. Webb was calm without the suffrage leader's
passionate outlook, and her mind was fixed only on one goal.
I helped her in a very small way with her minority report on
the Poor Law by following up cases for her and writing some
stories for magazines as a supplement to her statistical
researches.

Both these women recalled to me Oscar Wilde's extravagant talk of the evil that reformers do when he explained that the fact of their meaning well could not save

them from doing harm, since life itself is a paradox, and even to die we have to be born. Certainly Mrs. Pankhurst meant well, but I still wish that ignorant women—and ignorant men—had not the means of endangering England's safety and altering her laws.

Chapter Thirty

WAR YEARS

ON the lovely morning when Chamberlain told us that war was declared, I felt stunned as I looked at the peaceful, rural scene before my eyes, and my mind ran riot with memories of the last war and with emotional feelings and regrets that I would be thought too old to help in any way. This last idea was shattered by a telephone call from the vicar, who was the billeting officer, telling me in most cheerful tones that he was sending me nine East End boys, whom he was sure I would enjoy putting up. I was equally sure I would not. Some rumour of this must have reached the couple whom I employed, for when I told them what was to happen they promptly responded that they would be going the moment such evacuees arrived.

Mercifully I was saved from this plight by Lady Goschen, my kind neighbour, who suggested filling all my rooms with an overflow of employees from the bank whose officials they were taking in. My servants were quite content with this plan, and we prepared for the coming of my unknown guests.

They were considerate people and gave no trouble, but the country bored them, for we had no films or whist drives or any of the social life of their suburb, to which they returned after a few months.

At this time I lost the couple I employed, and at that crisis, like manna from heaven, I acquired an evacuee; I met her when she was exhausted and covered with brick-dust, having been bombed out of her flat. I took her to my house for a rest, and the next day her husband came to see me and begged me to keep her for the time being, explaining that he himself had to be in London for his work. "You see," he said, "I am the manager of a firm of tombstone makers, and business never was so brisk," and, pausing while looking at me with an air of frustration, added, "and no Carrara marble to be got." He evidently felt the irony of such a situation bitterly. His wife stayed with me for six years, and was my mainstay and unfailing help; while doing her work so capably she would exclaim, "If only people would behave, how happy the world would be!" The innocence and simplicity of this remark does not do away with its basic truth.

Except for the growing of vegetables, my own war activities felt futile. I was the salvage officer, and after urging the importance of saving paper and bones in our village and of taking them to the storage place, I sometimes found the bulk had been burnt because no lorry had come to collect them. No one could blame the authorities, who were distracted and over-driven.

I had been a member of the parish council for many years, and this sense of futility was not missing at our first meeting after the outbreak of war. We started by our chairman, who was not a good reader, stumbling through the list of official directions for Public Bodies on Air-Raid Precautions, which consisted of many columns of small print.

After this reading had gone on for a long time we took it item by item, the first being the warning for air raids and the all-clear signal.

" Any suggestions ? " the chairman enquired.

" I propose the laundry hooter," came in response.

The laundry hooter was discussed from every aspect, and finally unanimously agreed to as the perfect warning : three blasts for the coming raid and one for the all clear. When we had paused for the clerk to write down this decision a timid voice said, " They haven't any steam to sound the hooter at week-ends. Would that matter ? "

The chairman, much annoyed, ordered the clerk to delete the hooter decision.

" Then we must have the church bells," he announced.

" It's only got one," the vicar countered.

" In that case it must be rung very fast for a warning and slowly for the all clear."

" Won't that sound like tolling for the dead ? " someone remarked, an idea which was not commented on.

The next item was shelters.

" There are only two good cellars in the village, and one of them is yours," the chairman said, turning to the owner of a drapery shop.

" It's very damp and full of cardboard boxes which can't be sat upon," he murmured despondently.

" There's the cellar at the ' Stag and Crown '."

" It's full of spirit casks and beer barrels, which might be more dangerous than hat boxes."

" In case of gas are cellars the best place ? " I asked.

Again looking up the directions given, the chairman slowly read out, " Gas usually, being heavy, sinks to the lowest level, therefore cellars should not be occupied during a gas attack."

As this made decision too difficult the question was deferred.

Decontamination came next.

" Where's the nearest station ? "

" Eight miles from here."

" Then we must nominate volunteers to collect victims and transport them."

" Don't all their clothes have to be removed first ? " someone said. " It might be very cold."

" And take them eight miles naked ? " another asked.

" Most unseemly," the vicar murmured.

Yes, that was the order we found when the book of words was consulted, and as this seemed too difficult, it, too, was deferred. In those early days the authorities were much concerned over protection from poison gases.

" We shall now appoint personnel for various posts," said the chairman, wishing to achieve something. " We must have a demolition squad, a Red Cross and First-Aid detachment, stretcher-bearers and transport people, and some of the demolition squad could act as first-aid and repair workers." Then, turning to the clerk, " You have the list of volunteers ? "

Before he could answer an elderly person who had not spoken before said in a plaintive voice, " If you appoint all those people there will be no one left for casualties."

This seemingly silly remark was in a way prophetic, for we had immense material damage, but very little loss of life.

We were on the direct route to London, and of course many bombs fell on our lands.

When almost in sight of victory we had to endure the coming of V.1's ; my friends in the Air Force had explained that when its engine stopped the thing was bound to come down ; it might do so almost at once, or sail on for three or four miles.   Hearing one of the robots coming towards one, and then gun-fire followed by silence, one felt as a rabbit must when hiding in a ditch awaiting the approach of beaters—would the thing fall and explode on our roof or go sailing on and come down harmlessly in the woods beyond us ?

I was a manager of the village school, and one day, hearing it had been hit in the night, I went to see the damage. From there I went to the vicarage close by, and saw one of these little dagger-like shapes coming towards me, then a Spitfire swooped upon it firing its guns, and immediately swung away out of sight. Now all was silence, and I waited, looking up at the house behind me. Then the sky was darkened, and an enormous object came on very slowly, just clearing the chimneys; then from slow motion this monster started lurching like a top at the end of its spin, and I felt sure it was coming down on top of me, yet felt indifferent and as if I were outside my physical self, but the black mass staggered on, brushed the hedge and fell with an explosion that rocked the earth and drove the breath out of my body.

I shall write no more of war. We have all been wearied by tales of other people's bombs, and I have only said something of my own near escape because it brought me a certain comfort and reassurance. I had read that in the face of immediate death fear leaves one; terror and fear may be suffered in anticipation, but not at the final moment, and I now knew by experience that this was true.

Chapter Thirty-one

VISIONS OR HALLUCINATIONS?

EVERYONE has at times had some experience they could not explain. I like being alone in my garden, where one may for a time forget the wars and suffering of this troubled world, and dismiss the small matters that disturb one's daily life.

At such times identity is lost, and for a passing moment we seem to be at one with the life of growing things—an experience perhaps akin to another aspect of being. Call it subliminal self or any other name, some power that is beyond our usual capacities comes into action on these occasions. It does not seem possible to produce proof on demand of these flashes of insight; they are illusive, and efforts to make them manifest fail, but I have experienced them.

When we were wandering about considering sites on which to build the house in which we now live, we had looked at various parts of the farm lands and at the place where it now stands. A tall, neglected hedge ran diagonally across it, and a deep depression lay below, overgrown with brambles, scrub, and reeds. Trees screened the lovely distance. One day I went there alone, with no idea of planning anything and with my thinking mind in abeyance. Then, quite quietly, a picture swam before my eyes of what would be there in the future. I saw it all: the house standing on level ground which now was sloping; the wide central steps flanked by stone vases in place of that bramble-covered, irregular clay bank; the massive old trees freed from surrounding thickets; steps, flower-clad, on the opposite slope of the depression—and in place of this dry, untidy pit I saw water reflecting the clouds.

I felt such pleasure in the garden I had just seen so plainly, for it gave me all the opportunities I liked. On the one hand the formality of a flat terrace and flights of steps leading down to the lower levels, with dry walls for rock plants, which is where I like to grow them, and on the other the free and irregular growth of moisture-loving plants fringing the pond.

When such a vision comes the picture remains clear, things falling into their place so obviously that the carrying out of it is simplified. I had just such a pre-vision over my Italian house and of a cottage I built, and on each occasion before a sod had yet been turned. Often I get no such help, and no attempt on my part, either active or trying to be passive, has any result, and then I must use my normal intelligence and do the best I can. It is only on matters which I have studied with great interest that I have had such supernormal help, and this seems to suggest some watchful, subconscious sight-giving guidance which comes into play on rare occasions.

This faculty has sometimes functioned over pictures and antiques for me; again matters in which I have been interested for the greater part of my life. I remember once when I had been shopping in Dublin I passed one of those auction-rooms, of which there are several on the quays of the north side of the river and in which all sorts of household junk is sold, but where little of interest or value is found. The pavement was littered with iron bedsteads and battered pots and pans. Suddenly I received an impulse to go in and buy, but I was tired and had four miles to ride home on my bicycle, and so I hesitated, for to go into that crowded, sordid, rather smelly place was something I should not normally have done. The suggestion came again most emphatically: "Go in and buy." I leant my bicycle against a bedstead and went in and stood at the back of the crowd. A man was holding up a black portfolio of the kind that was constantly being sold and which always contained a collection of rubbish—newspaper cuttings, Christmas cards, and an occasional photograph. Feeling I must buy it, I called out, " Five shillings." The hammer came down promptly, for the usual bid, if any, was one shilling. Kindly people produced bits of string, and the awkward parcel was tied on behind my saddle.

After tea and a rest I fetched a paper basket, opened the portfolio, and found the usual discoloured newspaper cuttings and rubbish. When the paper basket was overflowing I drew out a drawing, faintly coloured, of pure Renaissance feeling, which I felt sure from the quality of the paper and the work itself was early Italian. I took it to James Stephens at the Dublin National Gallery, who looked through an illustrated book of the period to which it belonged and identified it as a sketch for a fresco in Rome by Pietro da Cortona and asked, " Are you going to give it to the Gallery ? "

" No, I am sorry, but I am not going to," I said.

" We can't afford much—I can only offer you fifteen pounds—but I am sure the Gallery would be willing to give that."

" It is not for sale," I answered, " as I want to keep it; but I am most grateful for your help in naming it."

Sir Hugh Lane told us that once when living in Dublin he had been driving in a side-car through an Irish village, and was half asleep, when he got what he called a " warning " that there were Spanish paintings in a little shop he was passing. He went in and asked if they had any pictures, and they replied that they had just a couple of old black ones. They were indeed quite black and encrusted with smoke-soot, but he bought them, and when they were cleaned they turned out to be interesting early Spanish works. Sir Hugh said he had had several such " warnings " about pictures, and this bears out my idea of the watchful sub-conscious.

Sometimes this gift takes protective action. For instance, when we went to live at Arfleet, near Corfe Castle, we rented that little house furnished for the first few months from a painter. She had made the rooms charming, but I disliked her own works, which were oil-paintings of women, mostly done in lilac under harsh green trees and throwing purple shadows over mauve-pink figures. I couldn't venture to take them down, but, having some remnants of brocade and silk, I pinned these over the paintings just inside their frames. One day I was playing the piano, which stood in a corner of the room, when suddenly a scene flashed up as vividly as if by normal sight. I saw a train curving towards Corfe Castle, which could not be seen at all from the house, and at an open window my artist landlady, with a white scarf round her neck, was looking out at the field path which led to Arfleet. I called my maid, Martha, saying, " Come, quickly, and help me to take off the veils."

Standing on a chair, I soon had the pins out and the pictures on view, and just as I had the room tidy there came a knock at the door, and there stood my landlady with a white scarf round her neck, and before long she said, " I looked out of the train window to see if any of you were coming or going."

How could I have explained those silks covering all her own pictures ? My flash of second sight saved me from this embarrassing predicament.

There are some strange dreams which leave a lasting impression and do not fade away like the usual muddled kind, and so seem to be less subjective. On one occasion when I was returning from Italy I had a " couchette " for the long night journey. The carriage was hot and the double windows were impossible to open and, lying there feeling the atmosphere oppressive, I suppose I fell asleep.

A momentary pang of pain went through my head and my heart beat heavily; then I seemed to float clear of my body and, still in the railway carriage, I looked down on it huddled under a checked rug and thought what a poor, miserable thing it appeared. The carriage fell away and I found myself, with no effort, moving swiftly in a star-filled sky, and presently I realized that I had a companion—that someone of a higher order than anything I had ever known was with me.

Words are limited and often inadequate to express an exact sense or to make a deep impression, but my guide conveyed meaning without the use of words and apprehended by response in a more lucid and incisive way than any spoken words could have done. I understood that this experience had been given me to help me to do better with my life. I was confused and wished to explain this, but again I knew that every thought in my mind was clear to my companion. Then I was told in this wordless way that every soul sent to earth was given good gifts, but few used them or developed them as they were meant to do, making no effort, and often repressing their best impulses, which then atrophied. Two gifts had been given to me: the love of beauty and the sense of pity. It flashed through my mind that I had not let my love of beauty wither, for I had tried to express it in many ways, but this passing thought was taken up and corrected with the criticism that I looked at everything from the material standpoint and had not seen that the loveliness of the world was of divine origin and its source infinitely more perfect than mortal eyes could grasp. Then I saw the night of stars set in a vault of a wonderful depth of darkness and below them wisps of cloud lit by an invisible moon, shifting and changing with lovely patterns. I saw it with heightening insight, which was at once understood by my strange companion, and the message reached me, " Already you see more fully."

[279]

Did that mean that I was no longer tied to that poor body which I had left huddled in the train? No, that hope was dashed. "No, not yet," came the order. "You must go back and use both the gifts which were granted to you."

The scene changed; it was daylight, and I was looking down at woodland and meadows where I could see cattle and sheep, rabbits and birds and butterflies with extraordinary clarity, but I saw also flashes of dull red momentarily surrounding a bird in flight or one of the other creatures, and I was told, "It is fear." Then part of the sunlit land became filmed over with dead grey. "This is where life has been taken from the earth by wrong and covetous treatment, and now you must return."

Once again I was in the railway carriage, looking at my body under the checked rug, and with intensity I put out the petition, imploring that I should not have to go back into it, but as from a far distance I heard the words, " You must." Then I found myself struggling to sit up, my head pierced with pain and my heart pounding in my throat. I staggered into the passage and looked out into the murky night, so different from the night of my vision, and a sad longing to be back in that other world overwhelmed me, that world where I had been for so short a time, where movement needed no effort, where thoughts were conveyed so perfectly without speech and where perception was heightened.

My heart steadied, and then my naturally sceptical mind reasserted itself. Had it all been a mere dream, and that idea of leaving my body caused by some faintness from the bad air? Could the messages I thought I had received have come from the promptings of conscience, and had some of the ideas been suggested by the writings of Rudolf Steiner or by other books I had read? Nevertheless, the memory of this experience has remained vivid. After returning to the carriage I fell into a dreamless sleep, waking in early

daylight to find the friend with whom I was travelling—
Baronne Favoret de Kerbrech, the widow of a French
general and quite sixty-five years of age—dancing nimbly in
white silk stockings up and down the confined space of the
compartment. Her quick movements and twinkling feet
dispelled the shadow left from my emotional vision.

" I dance every morning," she told me, " to keep me
young and supple."

" And you succeed," I answered.

When we reached Paris I parted with the little dancing
baronne and went on to Ireland.

Just before the break-up of my marriage, which was to
lead to an unhappy and anxious period of my life, I had one
of these strange vision-dreams, which remained clear and
rather haunting. I saw myself in trouble, seemingly
surrounded with an aura of fear and distress, and, looking
down on my own figure, I felt quite indifferent and undisturbed as I watched my distraught condition, and I was
puzzled that I could accept it so calmly. I was told, again
not in words but by an illumination clearer than any speech,
that I had been given this moment of separation from my
human body in order that I should know that only a part of
the whole person functions on the earth, and that the trials
and frustrations of life are not of very great importance.
Living in the world is experienced as a discipline in time and
not a permanent abiding place for anyone.

Was it only a dream ? I do not know.

Chapter Thirty-two

CONCLUSION

TOWARDS the end of their days the old seem to disparage the times in which they live and to look back nostalgically to the period of their youth. I had meant to avoid this outlook and to be an acquiescent, approving old woman, yet my mind cannot but reflect something of the turmoil of the world as it is to-day. In 1512 Sardus Aquinus wrote, "For every man there lurkith hys wilde beast." War and its aftermath lets loose this "wilde beast", and even those who took no part in the fighting feel the repercussion.

It is the fashion to believe democratic government to be the perfect system, and almost sacrilege to think, as I do, that it is a bad one. In countries with a small population and where a high standard of education has been achieved it may succeed. France has lived under it longer than any other country, and has suffered financial corruption and defeat, and her politicians are regarded by most Frenchmen with contemptuous hatred. How can there be a good government when every party has to outbid its opponents with bribes in angling for the vote, and sometimes to secure it by disregarding the needs of the country or its safety? Fifty years ago John Morley, speaking of some project he wished carried, said, "It must be well larded with personal and other attractions so that it may slip easily down the public gullet." Ever since then the bidding has had to be progressively higher. Some of the promises do not materialize and are conveniently forgotten once they have secured votes, others occasionally recoil on those whom they are supposed to benefit, like the Rent Restriction Act, held out as a great advantage to tenants, but actually resulting in the cessation of building by landlords and the falling into decay of cottages where upkeep was not covered by the return they brought, thus adding to the pitiful lack of homes to-day.

The alternative need not be dictatorship—the most dangerous of all systems. Some way might be devised so that those who ruled us were chosen for their integrity of character and ability, and so that they would act impartially for the welfare of all sections of the people. Is such an idea a wild Utopian dream? Most of our High Court judges are selected for just such qualities. Another matter which disturbs me is the industrial life such numbers of men and women have to lead; the present difficulties facing us seem to make this inevitable, but may one hope that the future holds something better for our people? The creative instinct which is in all of us should be expressed in our work; and is necessary for happiness and development of character. There is a look of real satisfaction in the eyes of a carpenter or a bricklayer surveying what he has made, just as there is in a farm-hand laying a hedge, thatching a rick, or ploughing a field, and this real satisfaction is felt by men doing any kind of work where they can see the result of their own efforts. It could be achieved in a small community making parts which those who made them would finally see assembled. No sense of achievement can be felt by men and women spending their working hours tending a machine or making a mechanical movement, hardly knowing what it is for.

For a balanced life we all need contact with the earth and awareness and enjoyment of the changing seasons. The instinctive opposition to schemes which would add twenty thousand industrial workers to small country towns is a right and natural reaction. The inhabitants of every threatened area know that by such an addition to their numbers the character of their little town would be changed and they would lose their contact with the countryside. I can see no way of a better life for everyone in England unless we can reduce the population, settling perhaps half our people in the Colonies and dividing the remainder between town and country, thus achieving a balance so that we could feed ourselves and export enough to supply our needs.

We are trying to meet our immediate difficulties by exports, and to do so we must put more people into factories, sell more to buy yet more food for the increasing numbers, and use more agricultural land for buildings. We give family allowances with the hope of providing more lives for the production grind, but if this results in larger families they will be produced by the feckless and least self-respecting parents, although we pretend there are no such people, so much do we hate facing unpleasant facts and so much do we like to forget about them as soon as possible. We have already put from our minds some of the evacuee children and their mothers and the depths of squalor they had reached, not always from poverty or bad housing, but often from temperament; just such people had large families in order to get more from the dole when unemployed. To increase our population from the lowest physical and mental strata is biologically wrong; decent working people are not going to have more children than they themselves desire for any small money bribe, and the great mass of English working people are decent. But the promise of State insurance from the cradle to the grave will not foster self-reliance, which, together with good craftsmanship, are the native characteristics of the Englishman.

I trust the future may be better for English men and women than living and working in a crowd, hemmed in by buildings from birth to death. Blake's vision of " Dark Satanic Mills " is still with us; electric glare and chromium plate cannot remove the essential darkness.

Many years have passed since W. H. Hudson wrote of

factory workers, " All that they value and seek and strain after all their lives long, their works and sports and pleasures, are the merest baubles and childish things; and their ideals are all false, and nothing but by-products, or growths of the artificial life—little funguses cultivated in heated cellars." We give them films for their false ideals, watching others play football for their sport, and betting for their pleasure; but deprive them of the fundamental needs of human beings.

I have lived for seventy-six years, and writing these scraps and bits of memories has helped me to turn my thoughts to the past, and to put the things of the present from my mind—the things I cannot amend. I have much to be thankful for, living as I do in a beautiful setting, seeing the sunset all the year round, my garden at hand claiming care and bringing peace and contentment.

Henry, my elder son, has given me companionship and affection all his life, and I can stand aside and see him happy with his wife and children. Tony has settled in Kenya Colony and is managing a farm, which is the right life for him.

Nevertheless, I would not say " O, call back yesterday; bid time return." For me there can be no future but the approaching ultimate end that awaits us all. Is it approaching? Olive Ardilaun used to say, " I shall die when I am seventy," which she did, and then would add, " You, I think, will live for a long time—as long perhaps as the old Countess of Desmond did," of whom it was said :

> She lived to the age of a hundred and ten,
> And died of the fall from a cherry tree then.

What a terrible thought—to see all my friends go, to remain like a monument of the past in a changed world, to keep such wits as I have got, and to feel my very bones grow brittle and bent, craving to be done with bearing their burden. No, I should have to take to climbing trees long before I reached my century. Doctrinal religion does not help me, for I lost my faith in it almost at the dawn of my life, although I may accept the basis that unites all religions. I have little assurance as to what awaits that which may survive the worn-out body; yet I have been granted a momentary lifting of the veil to catch a glimpse of the eternal through beauty, whether from a phrase of music, from the splendour of earth and sky, or the miniature loveliness of a flower.

These flashes make my spirit soar with hope beyond reason, for they seem in some mysterious way to be a link with things immortal, and make me able to say with Ronsard :

"*Je te salue, heureuse et profitable mort.*"